THE REFERENCE LIBRARIAN'S

POLICIES, FORMS, GUIDELINES, *and* PROCEDURES HANDBOOK

with CD-ROM

Rebecca Brumley

Neal-Schuman Publishers, Inc.

New York   London

Published by Neal-Schuman Publishers, Inc.
100 William St., Suite 2004
New York, NY 10038

Printed and bound in the United States of America.

The paper used in this publication meets the minimum requirements of American National Standard for Information Sciences – Permanence of Paper for Printed Library Materials, ANSI Z39.48-1992.

ISBN 1-55570-569-3

Dedication

To all who know that
we are not there yet:

So come back Woody Guthrie
Come back to us now
Tear your eyes from Paradise
And rise again somehow
If you run into Jesus
Maybe he can help you out
Come back Woody Guthrie to us now

—Steve Earle,
"Christmas in Washington"

TABLE OF CONTENTS

PREFACE

In every area of service—staffing, collection development, access, privacy, and beyond—reference professionals and managers face "big-picture" challenges that require a constant search for new solutions. The Internet, e-mail, electronic resources, and other technologies have forced us to invent new methods and standards of service. Even relatively more minor concerns—like those inevitably difficult questions about genealogy, health, government, and so on—often call for innovative responses. *The Reference Librarian's Policies, Forms, Guidelines, and Procedures Handbook with CD-ROM* takes on the problems faced in day-to-day service and provides effective, proven responses developed by our colleagues in response to their institutions' own needs.

This guide places the work and wisdom of over 180 libraries at your fingertips. Culling a healthy mix from both public and academic libraries, it contains more than 475 of the best real-world policies and forms in use today. Implicit in this international blend is recognition of the fact that good service possesses similarities and differences between institutions. Helpful reference ideas are everywhere, and it can be a great learning experience to "see how the other half lives."

Reviewing a variety of solutions can save you time without sacrificing your own institution's unique situation. The information assembled here is designed to eliminate the need to start from scratch when it comes time to create, revise, or update policies or forms. All of the materials are ready-to-use. Each topic features multiple examples offering the chance to select the policy best suited for your own context. Coverage extends from academic to public libraries, but these policies and forms can also be used in medical, special, and even school libraries. Each policy is reproduced on the companion CD-ROM in MS Word format, making it easy to download, modify, reproduce and utilize.

HOW TO USE THIS BOOK

The Reference Librarian's Policies, Forms, Guidelines, and Procedures Handbook with CD-ROM is divided into eight parts that cover the full range of reference services in libraries.

Part I, "The Reference Department: Mission and Management," highlights materials that demonstrate the importance of creating clear objectives and definitions of services.

Part II, "The Reference Department: Personnel," is all about the human element because people are an essential ingredient of your reference service. From development to training, ethics, privacy, and confidentiality, these model documents will help shape a successful staff.

Note: These first two parts, which focus on the reference department, are divided into two sections — one for the academic library and one for the public library. This separation reflects their inherent structural and organizational differences.

Part III, "Reference Collections: Selection and Evaluation," recognizes that both print and electronic resources play an important role in today's library. The examples will help with the weeding of old titles, the selection of new electronic journals, and the incorporation of Internet links into your reference transactions. There are also general guidelines for selecting both the print and electronic titles for your library.

Part IV, "Reference Services: Circulation and Interlibrary Loan (ILL) of Materials," will help you develop guidelines for the way materials are used in your institution. Among the options discussed are the loaning and borrowing of materials; protocols for holds, reserves, and recalls; standards for fines and fees; and rules for the replacement of lost or damaged material. Because opening collections to the community creates new concerns, there are also guidelines for use of copyrighted material and considerations of privacy issues for circulation and usage records. Interlibrary loan personnel will likewise find sample forms for requesting materials, policies for refusing requests, patron-eligibility standards, guidelines for fines and fees, and much more.

Part V, "Reference Services: Query Categories, Resources, and Assistance Offered," provides exemplary policies for providing homework help; satisfying medical, legal, and financial queries; answering history and genealogy questions; responding requests for referrals; and dealing with many other subject-specific requests. This section also provides guidance for utilizing various materials—maps, photo files, microfilm, and electronic collections. Finally, you will find materials for managing user feedback, handling problem patrons, gathering statistics, offering equipment assistance, and more.

Part VI, "Reference Services: In-Person Patron Assistance," focuses on personal interactions at the reference desk. This portion of the book will help your desk attendant establish patron priorities, set time limits, respond to extensive research questions, handle instructional requests, and address idiosyncratic users.

Part VII, "Reference Services: Virtual Reference," covers both online chat and e-mail reference. These sections also provide suggestions for establishing eligibility guidelines, providing schedules for assistance, utilizing scripted messages, and more.

Part VIII, "Reference Services: Children," explores how the reference department can meet the needs of minors. You will find guidance for selecting materials appropriate to children, assisting teachers, and circulating materials to minors.

Throughout *The Reference Librarian's Policies, Forms, Guidelines, and Procedures Handbook with CD-ROM* you will find cross-references to help connect related topics and create consistent, appropriate policies and guidelines.

As you use this resource, please remember that its range is a testament to librarians and our willingness to share. You may notice policies in these pages similar to those already in place at your own institution. Libraries are at their best when they are willing to learn from one another, and we are all better off for having a sense of cooperative development. In my first book, *Public Library Manager's Forms, Policies, and Procedures Handbook with CD-ROM,* I felt compelled to share the words of Shirley Vonderhaar. She eloquently stated of her library's contribution, "Like many policies in many libraries, it is the distillation of the wisdom of our peers; if you see your hand in our policy, thank you for your help." Know that if you see your policy or one like it in these pages, everyone thanks you.

My hope is that *The Reference Librarian's Policies, Forms, Guidelines, and Procedures Handbook with CD-ROM* will help your library's reference department run more smoothly, freeing you to do the valuable work our users need and appreciate. You now have access to policy language and forms that have proved useful in academic and public libraries across the United States. I trust that there is material here that will work for you.

ACKNOWLEDGEMENTS

I would like to thank everyone at Neal-Schuman Publishers. Special thanks go to Charles Harmon, the Director of Publishing, and to Michael Kelley, my fabulous editor.

Thanks also to my brother, Paul Brumley, whose love and support are in constant supply.

I am extremely grateful to all the libraries and librarians willing to share their knowledge, hard work, wisdom, and most importantly what works. Without them there would not be a book.

Alverno College
   Alverno College Library
   Milwaukee, Wisconsin

Ames Public Library
   Ames, Iowa

Apache Junction Public Library
   Apache Junction, Arizona

Athens Regional Library System
   Athens, Georgia
   www.clarke.public.lib.ga.us/

Athens Limestone Public Library
   Susan Todd
   Athens, Alabama

Aurora Public Library
   Eva Luckinbill
   Aurora, Illinois

Austin College
   John West
   Abell Library Center
   Sherman, Texas

Avalon Public Library
   Susan McClellan
   Pittsburgh, Pennsylvania

Ball State University
   Alexander M. Brackey Library
   Muncie, Indiana

Benedictine University
   Jack Fritts
   Benedictine Library
   Lisle, Illinois

Bethel Public Library
   Lynn Rosato
   Bethel, Connecticut

Boerne Public Library
   Boerne, Texas

Boise Public Library
   Adult Services
   Boise, Idaho

Boston College
   Boston College Libraries
   Chestnut Hill, Massachusetts

Boston Public Library
Boston, Massachusetts

Boston University School of Law
Pappas Law Library
Boston, Massachusetts

Brampton Library
Adele Kostiak
Brampton, Ontario, Canada

Brandeis University
Lisa Wiecki
Goldfarb Library
Waltham, Massachusetts

Braswell Memorial Public Library
Susan D. Reese
Rocky Mount, North Carolina

Bridgewater Public Library
Bridgewater, Massachusetts

Brownwood Public Library Association
Jane Rmeili (Board President)
and Mat McConnell (Director)
Brownwood, Texas

Bucknell University
Courtesy of the Ellen Clarke Bertrand
Library, Bucknell University
Nancy Dagle
Bertrand Library
Lewisburg, Pennsylvania

California State Polytechnic University
University Library
Pomona, California

California State University, Bakersfield
Rodney M. Hersberger
Walter W. Stern Library
Bakersfield, California

California State University Northridge
Karin Durań, Interim Dean
Northridge, California

Carbondale Public Library
Connie Steudel
Carbondale, Illinois

Chelmsford Public Library
Becky Herrman, Director
Chelmsford, Massachusetts

Clemson University
Clemson University Libraries
Clemson, South Carolina

Colgate University
Everett Needham Case and George R.
Cooley Science Libraries
http://exlibris.colgate.edu/services/ill.html
Hamilton, New York

Colorado State University—Pueblo
University Library
Rhonda Gonzales
Pueblo, Colorado

Columbia University
University Libraries
New York, New York

Comsewogue Public Library
Port Jefferson Station, New York

Cornell University
Cornell University Library
Ithaca, New York

Culver-Union Township Public Library
Culver, Indiana

Dartmouth College
Dartmouth College Library
Hanover, New Hampshire

Denver Public Library
Denver, Colorado

Dominican University of California
Alan Schut, Director,
Collections and Cataloging
Archbishop Alemany Library
San Rafael, California

Dorchester County Public Library
Enoch Pratt Free Library
Baltimore, Maryland
Jean S. Del Sordo, Director
Cambridge, Maryland

Eastern Washington University
Patricia Kelley
Eastern Washington University Libraries
Cheney, Washington

Emory University
Nancy Reinhold
Woodruff Library
Atlanta, Georgia

Falmouth Public Library
Falmouth, Massachusetts

Fitchburg State College
Robert Foley
Amelia V. Gallucci-Cirio Library
Fitchburg, Massachusetts

Florida International University
Antonie B. Downs
Green Library
Miami, Florida

Fresno County Public Library
Karen Bosch Cobb
Fresno, California

Gleason Public Library
Carlisle, Massachusetts

Glen Ellyn Public Library
Nancy Zander
Glen Ellyn, Illinois

Glen Cove Public Library
Mrs. Maija Sperauskas
Glen Cove, New York

Glenview Public Library
Jane D. Berry
Glenview, Illinois

Grinnell College Libraries
Grinnell, Iowa

Hamilton College
Randall L. Ericson
Burke Library
Clinton, New York

Hartford Public Library
Hartford, Connecticut

Hershey Public Library
Hershey, Pennsylvania

Horsham Township Library
Laurie Tynan, Library Director
Horsham, Pennsylvania

Houston Public Library
Dr. Rhea Brown Lawson
Houston, Texas

Humboldt State University
University Library
Robert Sathrum
Arcata, California

Huntington Public Library
Huntington Station, New York

Huntsville Public Library
Huntsville, Ontario, Canada

Indiana University–Kokomo
John C. Stachacz
Kokomo, Indiana

Indiana University–Purdue University Fort Wayne
Helmke Library
Fort Wayne, Indiana

Jacksonville State University
Houston Cole Library
Jacksonville, Alabama

Jefferson-Madison Regional Library
John Halliday
Charlottesville, Virginia

Keene State College
Judith Hildebrandt
Mason Library
Keene, New Hampshire

Kennebunk Free Library
Janet D. Cate
Kennebunk, Maine

Kent State University
Reference and Instructional Services
Libraries and Media Services
Kent, Ohio

Las Positas College
　Las Positas College Library
　Livermore, California

Lawrence Public Library
　Bruce Flanders
　Lawrence, Kansas

Lincoln Public Library
　Lincoln, New Hampshire

Logan Library
　Logan, Utah

Long Beach City College
　Nenita B. Buenaventura
　Long Beach City College Library
　Long Beach, California

Louisiana State University and A & M College
　Jennifer Cargill
　Louisiana State University Libraries
　Baton Rouge, Louisiana

Louisville Public Library
　Louisville, Colorado

Manhattan Public Library
　Manhattan, Kansas

Mansfield Public Library
　Margaret M. Frank
　Mansfield, Connecticut

Massachusetts Regional Library Systems
Policy Collection
　Reference Service Policies:
　www.wmrls.org/policies/6regions/
　reference.html

Memorial Hall Library
　Town of Andover
　James E. Sutton
　Andover, Massachusetts

Merrimack College
　McQuade Library
　Public Services Department
　Much appreciation to the McQuade Library at
　Merrimack College in North Andover, Massachusetts,
　for sharing their expertise
　North Andover, Massachusetts

Mill Valley Public Library
　Anne Montgomery
　Mill Valley, California

Milwaukee Public Library
　Kathleen M. Huston
　Milwaukee, Wisconsin

Missoula Public Library
　Missoula, Montana

Mohawk Valley Community College
　Mohawk Valley Community College
　Libraries
　Stephen Frisbee
　Utica, New York

Monona Public Library
　John Seery
　Monona, Wisconsin

Monroe County Library System
　Jeff Baker
　Rochester, New York

Monroe Township Public Library
　Library Board of Trustees, Policy
　　Committee
　Monroe Township, New Jersey

Morton Grove Public Library
　Morton Grove, Illinois

Muskego Public Library
　Muskego, Wisconsib

Nashville Public Library
　Courtesy of the Nashville Public Library
　　Safety Policy
　Nashville, Tennessee

New College of Florida
　Joan M. Pelland
　Jane Bancroft Cook Library
　Sarasota, Florida

New Haven Free Public Library
　Cathleen DeNigris
　New Haven, Connecticut

New York Public Library
　New York, New York

The Newark Public Library
Newark, New Jersey

Norfolk Public Library
Norm Maas
Norfolk, Virginia

North Florida Community College
NFCC Library Staff
Marshall Hamilton Library
Madison, Florida

North Harris College
Maryann Readal
North Harris College Library
Houston, Texas

North Seattle Community College
Phil Roché
Library
Seattle, Washington

North Smithfield Public Library
Carol H. Brouwer
Slatersville, Rhode Island

Northeast Iowa Library Service Area
Waterloo, Iowa

Northern Michigan University
Joanna Mitchell
Lydia M. Olson Library
Marquette, Michigan

Oakland University
Kresge Library
Rochester, Michigan

Omaha Public Library
Omaha, Nebraska

Palm Beach County Library System
West Palm Beach, Florida

Palo Alto Public Library
Palo Alto, California

Pennsylvania State University
University Park, Pennsylvania

Peoria Public Library
Robert E. Black
Peoria, Illinois

Philadelphia University
Steven Bell
Paul J. Gutman Library
Philadelphia, Pennsylvania

Pierce County Library System
Neel Parikh, Director
Tacoma, Washington

Public Library of Enid and Garfield County
Enid, Oklahoma

Queens Library
Carol L. Sheffer
Jamaica, New York

Rice University
Sara Lowman
Fondren Library
Houston, Texas

Richmond Public Library
Richmond, Virginia

Riverside Regional Library
Jackson, Missouri

Rockford Public Library
Rockford, Illinois

Roselle Public Library District
Kenneth L. Gross
Roselle, Illinois

Rutgers University
Jeanne E. Boyle
Rutgers University Libraries
New Brunswick, New Jersey

Ryerson University
Ryerson University Library
Cathy Matthews
Toronto, Ontario, Canada

Saint Charles Community College
Ying Li
Theresa Flett
Erin Lanham
College Library
St. Peters, Missouri

Saint Joseph County Public Library
Donald J. Napoli
South Bend, Indiana

Saint Paul Public Library
    John Larson
    Saint Paul, Minnesota

San Jose State University
    Jo Bell Whitlatch
    Dr. Martin Luther King Jr. Library
    San Jose, California

Santa Monica Public Library
    Santa Monica, California

Sarasota County Library System
    Sarasota, Florida

Schiller Park Public Library
    Tina J. Setzer
    Schiller Park, Illinois

Shiawassee District Library
    Kenneth R. Uptigrove
    Owosso, Michigan

Sonoma State
    Richard Robison
    University Library
    Rohnert Park, California

Southern Connecticut State University
    Edward Harris
    Buley Library
    New Haven, Connecticut

Southern Ontario Library Service
    Toronto, Ontario, Canada

Spokane Public Library
    Spokane, Washington

Stetson University
    Reference Department
    duPont-Ball Library
    Deland, Florida

Stillwell Public Library
    Lynda Reynolds
    Stillwater, Oklahoma

Tazewell County Public Library
    Adam Webb
    Tazewell, Virginia

Tempe Public Library
    Tempe, Arizona

Tulane University
    Lance Query
    Howard-Tilton Memorial Library
    New Orleans, Louisiana

University of Alabama
    Dr. Louis A. Pitschmann, Dean of
      Libraries
    University Libraries
    Tuscaloosa, Alabama

University of Albany
    Gregg Sapp
    Science Library
    Albany, New York

University of Alberta
    University of Alberta Libraries
    Edmonton, Canada

University of California Berkeley
    Thomas C. Leonard
    Library, University of California Berkeley
    Berkeley, California

University of California Davis
    George E. Bynon
    General Library
    Davis, California

University of California Irvine
    All policies reprinted with permission of
    University of California Irvine
    Irvine, California

University of Central Florida
    Penny Beile, Carole Hinshaw,
    Athena Hoeppner, Natasha Hellerich
    Marcus Kilman
    University of Central Florida Libraries
    Orlando, Florida

University College London
    London, United Kingdom

University of Illinois at Urbana-Champaign
    University Library
    Robert Burger, AUL for Services

University of Kentucky
University of Kentucky Libraries
Lexington, Kentucky

University of Louisville
Glenda Neely and Sarah Jent
Ekstrom, Library
Louisville, Kentucky

University of Louisville
Neal D. Nixon
Kornhauser Health Sciences Library
Louisville, Kentucky

University of Maine at Fort Kent
Sofia L. Birden
Blake Library
Fort Kent, Maine

University of Maryland
University Libraries
College Park, Maryland

University of Michigan
Brenda L. Johnson
University Library
Ann Arbor, Michigan

University of Montana
Erling Oelz
Mansfield Library
Missoula, Montana

University of Nevada–Reno
Millie Syring
University Libraries
Reno, Nevada

University of New England
University of New England University
Library
Evelyn Woodberry
Armidale, NSW Australia

University of Oregon
Faye Chadwell
University of Oregon Libraries
Eugene, Oregon

University of Pittsburgh
University Library System
Pittsburgh, Pennsylvania

University of Rhode Island
University of Rhode Island Library
Kingston, Rhode Island

University of Scranton
Bonnie Strohl, Associate Director
Weinberg Memorial Library
Scranton, Pennsylvania

University of South Carolina
Thomas Cooper Library
Columbia, South Carolina

University of South Florida
Tampa Library
Phyllis Ruscella
Tampa, Florida

University of Tennessee Knoxville
Used with the permission of the
University of Tennessee Libraries
Knoxville, Tennessee

University of Texas at Arlington
Gerald D. Saxon
University of Texas at Arlington Libraries
Arlington, Texas

The University of Texas at Austin
Used by the permission of the
University of Texas Libraries The
University of Texas at Austin
University of Texas Libraries
Austin, Texas

University of Texas at El Paso
Carol Kelley
Antonio Rodarte
University Library
El Paso, Texas

University of Texas–Pan American
University Library
Edinburg, Texas

University of Wisconsin Madison
Sharon Mulvey
Chemistry Library
Madison, Wisconsin

University of Wisconsin–Platteville
John A. Krogman

Elton S. Karrmann Library
Platteville, Wisconsin

University of Wisconsin–River Falls
Chalmer Davee Library
River Falls, Wisconsin

University of West Georgia
Reprinted with permission of Ingram
Library, University of West Georgia
Ingram Library
Carrollton, Georgia

University of Wyoming
University Libraries
Laramie, Wyoming

Washington County Public Library
Abingdon, Virginia

Washington Research Library Consortium
Upper Marlboro, Maryland

Washington State University
Reference Policy Manual
Owen Science and Engineering Library
Pullman, Washington

Washington University in Saint Louis
Olin Library
Saint Louis, Missouri

Weber State University
Joan Hubbard
Stewart Library
Ogden, Utah

Western Kentucky University
Helm-Cravens Library
Bowling Green, Kentucky

*Western Massachusetts Regional
Library's System*
South Deerfield, Massachusetts

Wheelock College
Albie Johnson
Wheelock College Library
Boston, Massachusetts

Whistler Public Library
Whistler, British Columbia, Canada

Whitman County Rural Library District
Kristie Kirkpatrick
Colfax, Washington

Wichita Falls Public Library
Linda Hughes
Wichita Falls, Texas

Wilmington Public Library District
Wilmington, Illinois

Part I
The Reference Department: Mission and Management

Chapter 1

ACADEMIC LIBRARY POLICIES

ACADEMIC LIBRARY GUIDELINES

1.1 Service Philosophy

Ryerson University, Ryerson University Library
Toronto, Ontario, Canada

The mission of the Ryerson Library states,

The Library is the primary academic information resource for the University. It promotes learning, supports teaching, and enhances scholarly, research and creative activities by building collections and providing expert services and innovative access to information.

Reference service at the Library is one of the most vital and visible expressions of the Library's purpose and mission and is key to the Library's service roles: to serve as a centre for information, formal education, research and independent learning. In addition, since more users are accessing the Library from home or office, which the Library has encouraged, it is imperative that reference services address this new trend. The Library's building shall not be a boundary to its information services. By emphasizing real-time reference service, the library's goal is to offer service to information seekers at the place where they are when they have a question.

University Of Tennessee, John C. Hodges Library
Knoxville, Tennessee

The University of Tennessee Libraries will provide the highest quality service to all patrons, and will offer instruction and equitable access to information in print and electronic resources.

Library users may expect:
- Courteous and timely service.
- Respect for all questions and the best available answers.
- Knowledgeable, attentive and non-judgmental fulfillment of information requests.
- Confidentiality.
- Proactive approaches and creative solutions to problems and service requests.
- Collaborative responses from trained and skilled staff.

Clemson University, Clemson University Libraries
Clemson, South Carolina

Clemson University is an institution of learning, and the Libraries are a vital part of that process. We are here to help. All questions are welcome, and there are no walls between us and our patrons.

We, the Clemson University Libraries staff, will:

Be approachable.

Treat each patron with courtesy and respect.

Remember that some patrons may become frustrated with the system; thus we will use our knowledge and skills to guide them through the process.

Listen to requests carefully and ask questions directed at finding what the person truly wants.

Be understanding and flexible.

Use library policies as guidelines, not roadblocks. If there is something in the policy that unnecessarily interferes with providing the best service, we will inform our supervisors, and follow up on the matter to ensure that the issue has been addressed.

Find someone who can help if we are unable to do so.

Inform the patron promptly if the request will take some time to complete; we will estimate a completion date and respond back to the patron at that time.

Inform the patron when a task cannot be accomplished, and suggest alternative approaches if at all possible.

Indiana University Kokomo
Indiana University Libraries Kokomo
Kokomo, Indiana

INDIANA UNIVERSITY KOKOMO LIBRARY PHILOSOPHY

The volume of information resources in all formats is increasing at an exponential rate along with an annual increase in cost. With the library's diminishing ability to acquire even a small percentage of the world's information, the economics of access has become a crucial issue for libraries. Integrating access as a part of the collection development paradigm is a modern necessity for libraries to continue to be an information provider. The developments in electronic information systems have made it possible for Indiana University Kokomo Library to provide the access to a vast amount of information. While the library cannot purchase all the material relevant to its users for its collection, it can provide avenues of access to unowned information sources. The Indiana University Kokomo Library's goal is to move toward a logical combination of traditional collections that are owned and providing access to materials that, for whatever reason, cannot be acquired.

The Library is committed to building a collection that supports the basic educational needs of its undergraduate and graduate students, and providing access services consisting of the timely retrieval of bibliographic information and materials from other institutions and organizations to support the needs of students and faculty.

1.2 Mission Statement

Grinnell College
Grinnell College Libraries
Grinnell, Iowa

The Grinnell College Libraries—Burling Library, the Curriculum Library, and the Windsor Science Library—serve the instructional, research, and general information needs of the campus community. The libraries fulfill their mission through on-site provision of books, periodicals, microforms, sound recordings, electronic resources, and other library materials; mediated access to off-campus information sources; and active programs of information literacy: teaching the concepts needed to navigate the profusion of available sources and to evaluate critically the information, texts, and images discovered therein.

As depositories for federal and state government publications, the libraries make such documents available to residents of Iowa and promote the use of these government-supplied resources. The libraries serve as the archives for the official and unofficial records of Grinnell College; through the Department of Special Collections and Archives they seek to collect, preserve, and make available for research sources that document the history of Grinnell College, its cultural and natural surroundings in Iowa, including the prairie setting of which it is a part.

Stetson University
duPont-Ball Library
DeLand, Florida

REFERENCE SERVICES MISSION STATEMENT

The mission of Reference Services is to support the curricular, research, and professional needs of the Stetson Community by locating needed information and teaching and assisting users to access, retrieve, and critically evaluate both physical and electronic information resources.

Further, Reference Services support the mission of the Government Documents Department by assisting both the Stetson Community and the general public in locating needed government information and by teaching and helping users to access and retrieve such information in all formats.

Indiana University–Kokomo
Indiana University Libraries Kokomo
Kokomo, Indiana

To provide the collections, services, and environments to support and strengthen the teaching, learning, and research mission of Indiana University Kokomo.

1.3 Assistance Objectives

Santa Fe Community College
Lawrence W. Tyree Library
Gainesville, Florida

I. Objectives of Service

Lawrence W. Tyree Library strives to develop and implement, through continuous evaluation and adaptation, a program of reference services which effectively meets the informational, educational, recreational and cultural needs of the total college community. Essential to achieving this purpose is a broadly developed collection and a means of providing for its effective interpretation and use.

II. Specific Objectives:

A. To provide accurate, timely, up-to-date reference services whether questions are asked in person, over the telephone, or through the Internet.

B. To select and acquire suitable and timely resources which meet the ongoing needs of patrons. To arrange and maintain these resources in a readily accessible manner.

C. To provide approachable, knowledgeable staff to assist patrons. To encourage staff development in the areas of library reference services, materials, equipment and other related areas to provide consistent, high quality service.

D. To instruct patrons in the use of library materials, equipment and facilities, either through individual instruction, non-credit bibliographic instruction or credit instruction.

E. To cooperate with other departments of Santa Fe Community College in their efforts to better serve the college.

F. To promote an increasing awareness of library services and materials.

G. To periodically evaluate patron satisfaction and reference services by various methods. To periodically evaluate policies and procedures to strive for the best possible reference services.

1.4 Assistance Provided

University of Wisconsin—River Falls
Chalmer Davee Library
River Falls, Wisconsin

TYPES OF REFERENCE SERVICE

A. Reference Interview. Reference staff always determine the needs of the patron, using a reference interview when necessary, to clarify the patron's request.

B. Directional questions. Reference staff provide directional assistance and answer general questions about the library and its services. Questions of a mechanical nature about photocopiers and microform copiers are referred to the Circulation Desk.

C. Ready Reference. Staff provides reference information to the patron on a person-to-person basis, and by telephone, letter, fax, or electronic mail.

D. Reference. When assisting patrons one-on-one with reference requests that require the in-depth use of one or more reference sources, staff instruct them on the use of information resources in order to teach them to obtain information themselves.

E. Instructional Materials. Reference staff prepare and provide instructional materials to help patrons locate library material and use information resources.

F. Interlibrary Loan. Reference staff offer interlibrary loan as an option to University-affiliated patrons to obtain materials not available in the Chalmer Davee Library. Staff review requests for accuracy and to determine that the requested material is not available in the library or in a licensed electronic database prior to forwarding the request to the Interlibrary Loan Office. (See Interlibrary Loan Policy for details).

G. Online Search Service. Reference staff recommend staff-mediated online searches, when the situation warrants, to locate information for University-affiliated patrons.

(See Online Search Service Policy for details).

H. Library Instruction. Library instruction staff schedule formal library instruction classes when a library assignment is a component of a class. Faculty must schedule sessions directly with the librarian who will meet with the class. Generally, classes will be scheduled with a one week minimum lead time. Instructors must be present during a library instruction session. A master schedule of sessions is maintained at the Reference Desk.

The library endorses the Information Literacy Competencies and Criteria for Academic Libraries in Wisconsin (Adopted by the Wisconsin Association of Academic Librarians October 9, 1998). Librarians design instructional sessions with faculty in order to integrate these criteria into the University's curriculum.

Reference staff work with staff from Student Services to orient new freshmen to the library at the start of each new academic year.

High school groups and other groups not affiliated with the University are welcome to schedule a formal instruction session if need dictates.

I. Electronic Reference Service. UW-RF faculty, students, and staff and the non-UWRF community at large can send reference questions to the Reference Desk email account from the library's homepage. Email questions do not take priority over walk-ins or phone questions, but are answered as time permits.

Ready reference questions are answered directly. For more involved reference questions, the patron is provided suggestions for library resources they should consult.

Questions from non-UWRF affiliated users are accepted if the subject is clearly something that the UWRF library is better equipped to handle than other libraries in the area. Questions related to local and campus history or genealogy are referred to the University Archives and Area Research Center. For general questions, the non-affiliated patron is referred to their local public library.

J. Telephone Reference Service. Telephone reference calls are accepted, but do not take precedence over patrons waiting for service at the Reference Desk. Assistance provided to telephone callers differs from that given the patron at the Desk. Generally, staff provides answers to directional and factual ready reference questions and help patrons complete or verify bibliographic citations. Callers requiring extensive subject searches or lengthy assistance are asked to come to the library.

An answering machine picks up the phone at the Reference Desk when a staff member is away from the Desk. Callers are directed to phone back within five minutes if they are calling during regular business hours.

O. Materials on Hold. Librarians generally do not retrieve or hold specific materials for users. Some materials may be held for a short amount of time if a user is leaving the library but will return shortly.

Ryerson University
Ryerson University Libraries
Toronto, Ontario, Canada

Types of Reference Service

- Assistance in finding the answer to specific reference questions.
- Assistance in developing research strategies for reports, term papers, theses, and dissertations.
- Instruction in the use of the Library and its resources.
- Verification of Library holdings and referral to institutions which have materials this Library lacks.
- Orientation to the Library through tours, tutorial sessions, subject specific workshops, etc.
- Compilation and production of various instructional aids.
- Online search service.
- In-depth reference appointments for faculty and grad students engaged in research based endeavors.

Fitchburg State College
Amelia V. Gallucci-Cirio Library
Fitchburg, Massachusetts

Types of Services Provided

Answer Specific Questions:

DIRECTIONAL: Explaining to a patron the location of items or rooms in the library.

REFERENCE: Providing an answer with a specific source in hand. For example, a definition, the location of something in another part of campus.

RESEARCH: Providing assistance in which the following criteria are met:

The patron has some project to complete.

The librarian has to explain various methods of locating the desired information.

Collection Development

All professional librarians participate in ordering materials for the maintenance of a general reference collection and a ready-reference collection. The ready-reference collection consists of the most used materials in the reference collection and those items which will provide a quick answer. In addition, the reference staff acquires, maintains and reviews appropriate online and CD-ROM automated indexes, as well as maintaining and reviewing documentation for the on-line public access catalog (OPAC) and for accompanying end-user searching instruments such as First Search. Click here for more information

Finding Aids

These library guides, which provide appropriate reference information on a variety of subjects are created and updated by the Librarians.

The Interlibrary Loan Service.

This Service is provided to all faculty, students and staff who are members of the campus library community. Refer to the Interlibrary Loan Department for more information.

Library Instruction Programs

Library orientation classes are offered for new students, including freshmen and transfer students, as well as new faculty and international students.

Library instruction programs requiring in-depth subject research are taught in upon request of faculty members.

All levels require orientation in the on-line Public Access Catalog and electronic indexes. Click here for more information.

Reference Online Data Search Program

This service, maintained by the Reference Department, consists of funded searching for faculty staff and librarians and fee-based searches for others.

Restrictions on Reference Services:

No searching is done for puzzles, quizzes, etc. Assistance will consist of pointing out the material that may have information.

Telephone reference will be limited to answers to direct questions. The patrons are encouraged to come and use all the resources of the library. The reference librarian when exceptionally busy, may encourage a patron to call back to retrieve requested information.

Patrons do their own photocopying.

Patrons compile their own bibliographies.

1.5 Assistance Guidelines

University of Texas at Arlington
University of Texas at Arlington Libraries
Arlington, Texas

Reference Service guidelines

Our primary clientele are UTA students, faculty, and staff, but we do not differentiate among types of service at the Service Desk based on a user's affiliation or status. However, due to licensing contracts, not all databases, indexes, and reference sources, including Internet access, are available to all users. Also, a copy of the Library's Internet Access Policy is on file.

Ready reference assistance for specific factual information needs

Assistance and instruction identifying appropriate sources for research

Assistance with information collection and navigating the library system to find identified sources

Assistance and instruction using print and electronic resources

In-depth, one-on-one research consultations with the Subject Librarians

For some reference questions, we may suggest that you ask a licensed professional

Appropriate referrals to library, campus, or community services

Tours of the facilities

1.6 Definition of Assistance Area

Sonoma State University
Jean and Charles Schulz Information Center
Rohnert Park, California

The community is an important part of our environment at SSU, and there are several ways in which community members in the six-county area served by the university (Lake, Marin, Mendocino, Napa, Solano, & Sonoma) can access library materials.

First. Sonoma State University is an open campus, and many people from the surrounding area come to the campus to use the library directly. Anyone who wishes to do so can use all of the library's print resources within the library building. Photocopiers are available for those patrons who may wish to take a copy of a particular periodical article home with them. Adults who wish to borrow books can do so directly (see below) or through their local public or university libraries' interlibrary loan system. Children must have the participation of their parent or guardian.

If an adult wants to borrow books without intervention on the part of another library, he or she may become a member of the Friends of the Library; or become a Community Borrower. Current students at the other campuses of the California State University or Santa Rosa Junior

College are given free borrowing privileges (but must have a current campus ID card), as are members of the SSU Alumni Association. Teachers in the Cotati/Rohnert Park Unified School District may also receive free library cards.

(Please note: Due to licensing restrictions we are unable to offer open access to our subscription databases; these are limited to current SSU students, faculty and staff)

Rutgers University
Rutgers University Libraries
Newark, New Jersey

Whom We Serve, and Why

The primary community served by the Rutgers University Libraries consists of current faculty, faculty emeritus, students, staff, and administrators of Rutgers University.

The Libraries reference and information services are available to all individuals on site, by telephone, by correspondence, and through the online Ask a Librarian service.

The Libraries may engage in mutually beneficial contractual arrangements. These include referral services for the New Jersey Library Network, METRO libraries, OCLC, and the Research Libraries Group. These reciprocal arrangements provide the needed services for Rutgers users who cannot have their needs met within the Rutgers libraries. The Libraries also provide services to certain university affiliates. See Public Services Policy Memo 6: Cooperative Arrangements, for details.

Reference service provided by a Rutgers library as a professional courtesy to outside users (other librarians, independent researchers, etc.) does not take the place of services provided by their primary library—whether school, public, academic, or special. In many instances, it will be appropriate to ascertain that outside users have already exhausted the resources of those libraries, or to refer such clients to other appropriate libraries, especially when we do not have the specialized resources needed or the professional expertise to handle their queries.

1.7 Rationale for Separate Reference Assistance Policies

Santa Fe Community College
Lawrence W. Tyree Library
Gainesville, Florida

The purpose of Lawrence W. Tyree Library Reference Services is to anticipate and meet the information needs of patrons accurately, efficiently and pleasantly.

The purpose of this policy is to provide guidelines for a uniform standard of service of the highest quality. This policy applies to reference services provided at the Lawrence W. Tyree Library for all library patrons. It serves as a resource for present staff and as a guide for new staff. This policy is public information and is available to anyone requesting it.

1.8 Standards for the Reference Assistance Interview

Washington State University
Washington State University Libraries
Pullman, Washington

Patrons frequently do not ask for what they actually need. A skillful reference interview to verify actual needs is critical in offering the best reference assistance and answer.

Find out as much as possible about the information needed before proceeding with assistance.

It may help to rephrase in your own words, the request and ask the patron if you understood him/her correctly.

Also establish how much information is needed, academic level if pertinent, for what purpose (term paper, talk, etc.) period of time to be covered, sources needed (original research, articles, book reviews, gov. docs., etc.)

If you are at a loss as to where to look for an answer to a question, call on another reference librarian for assistance. Never be reluctant to take a problem or referral to another librarian as their answer may save the patron time and trouble and will assist in improvement of your skills and knowledge. Think twice before giving a negative answer without checking all sources and offering some information or referral.

Be extremely careful not to offer misleading, incorrect, incomplete, or erroneous information.

Directions—In giving directions, explanation should be given, when possible, with reference to appropriate printed aids, (e.g., the stack plan, floor plans, campus maps, etc.) and should be very specific. Do not sit and point when the patron could be shown a location.

Library policies and procedures—If you do not know or are unsure, refer to policy manuals, the appropriate unit (Circ, ILL, or Serial Record), another librarian, or the Head of Science Libraries.

Library holdings—In giving information on library holdings, the reference librarian should never give a negative answer without fully verifying the item requested and checking all appropriate collections or sources. If the patron does not want to wait until this can be done or is satisfied with a less than complete search, be sure to indicate that it is possible a more thorough search would locate the material wanted.

Answers to other questions—Should be based on data in standard reference sources whenever possible. The printed information should be shown to the inquirer, or in the case of a telephone inquiry, the source of the information should be cited. It is not our policy to vouch for the accuracy of a particular answer or source, although we should be prepared to give some indication of its reliability. We will not normally cross-verify answers except in the case of obvious discrepancies.

When time permits, follow up on the question:

Did the patron find the information needed?

If possible, return to patrons assisted earlier to inquire if they need further assistance, as some will be hesitant to return to request additional help.

As a matter of course, all patrons should be encouraged to return for further assistance when you leave them with resources or directions.

Active reference assistance is part of our service and will contribute to a positive attitude toward libraries and library personnel on the part of the patron.

The major emphasis in assistance of patrons is instructional.

Reference librarians must use their own judgment in offering the type of assistance needed by library users.

It may be appropriate in some cases to retrieve information for the patron as well as assist them in the use of research tools and other resources.

North Seattle Community College
North Seattle Community College Library and Media Services
Seattle, Washington

The reference interview is the heart of the reference transaction and is crucial to the success of the process. The librarian must be effective in identifying the patron's information needs and must do so in a manner that keeps the patron at ease. Strong listening and questioning skills are necessary for a positive interaction. As a good communicator, the librarian:

3.1 Uses a tone of voice appropriate to the nature of the transaction.

3.2 Communicates in a receptive, cordial, and encouraging manner.

3.3 Allows the patron to state fully his/her information need in his/her own words before responding.

3.4 Rephrases the patron's question or request and asks for confirmation to ensure that it is understood.

3.5 Uses open-ended questioning techniques to encourage the patron to expand on the request or present additional information. Some examples of such questions include:

> Please tell me more about your topic.

> What additional information can you give me?

> How much information do you need?

3.6 Uses closed and/or clarifying questions to refine the search query. Some examples of clarifying questions are:

> What have you already found?

> What type of information do you need (books, articles, etc.)?

> Do you need current or historical information?

3.7 Seeks to clarify confusing terminology and avoids excessive jargon.

3.8 Uses terminology that is understandable to the patron.

3.9 Maintains objectivity and does not interject value judgments about subject matter or the nature of the question into the transaction.

1.9 Reference Service Evaluation

Benedictine University
Benedictine University Library
Lisle, Illinois

REFERENCE EVALUATION

Evaluation of the Benedictine Library's reference service at the local level will occur in conjunction with the periodic North Central Association site visits. The evaluation is to include the following criteria:

1) review and interpretation of reference statistics,
2) analysis of how well the reference section is serving the public,
3) what has been done and what can be done to improve service, and
4) evaluation of the reference collection as determined by the reference collection management policy.

University of Texas at Austin
University of Texas Libraries
Austin, Texas

MEASUREMENT AND EVALUATION

The measurement and evaluation of reference and information services is the responsibility of reference staff and the library administration.

Statistics

Statistics provide a basis for the quantitative review of reference and information services. Each public service unit keeps statistics on inquiries received. Each reference staff member is responsible for accurately recording all such inquiries.

In library units where both reference and circulation transactions are handled at a single desk, circulation questions (e.g., book renewals, tracing of missing books, fine questions) are excluded from reference statistics.

Informal library use instruction that occurs in the course of a transaction at the reference desk is included in reference statistics. Separate statistics are compiled for formal library use instruction. (See X.A)

Procedure

Each question is counted once, regardless of the number of sources consulted. Separate questions, including follow-up questions and new topics, asked by the same user are counted separately.

Definitions to Be Followed for Recording Statistics

Statistics are collected daily for the following categories:

Directional Questions

Directional questions are concerned with physical locations (library materials, offices, rooms, or campus buildings); information about library policies and procedures; and technical assistance with library equipment. Such questions usually do not require the use of reference materials.

ACADEMIC LIBRARY POLICIES

Time: Less than 10 minutes

General Reference Questions

General reference questions are those answered through the use of or instruction in the use of information resources. Such questions require specialized knowledge and use of information resources.
Time: 15 minutes or less

Extended Reference Questions

An extended reference question involves in-depth assistance in the identification and use of information resources. A staff member may continue to work on such a question after the patron has left and arrange to report the results later.
Time: More than 15 minutes

Correspondence

Electronic mail, UTCAT comments, and letters received through US or campus mail requesting information which are answered by reference staff should be listed as correspondence.

Monthly Summary of Reference Statistics

The subject content of questions in the Extended Reference and Correspondence categories may be recorded and retained in the units.

Monthly Summary sheets are sent to the Assistant for Public Services Operations, PCL 3.200, by the fifth of the following month.

Special Surveys

Special surveys may be conducted periodically to determine the relevance and effectiveness of the reference and information services offered. Proposed surveys are submitted to the Assistant Director for Public Services for approval.

Santa Fe Community College
Lawrence W. Tyree Library
Gainesville, Florida

Evaluation

The library will regularly evaluate its information services to ensure that the service furthers the institution's goals and that the goals reflect the needs and interests of the college. Formal and informal evaluations will be used to determine the optimum allocation of resources to provide quality service.

The library will appraise the performance of individual Reference Department staff members and of the collective performance of that staff at regular intervals, using recognized personnel evaluation techniques and instruments agreed to in advance by those to be evaluated and those performing the evaluation.

Chapter 2

PUBLIC LIBRARY POLICIES

PUBLIC LIBRARY GUIDELINES

2.1 Service Philosophy

Newark Public Library
Newark, New Jersey

Philosophy of Service

Reference service at The Newark Public Library is one of the most vital and visible expressions of the Library's purpose and mission and is key to each of the Library's four primary service roles: to serve as a center for information, formal education, research and independent learning.

Reference service is defined in this document as personal assistance provided to users and potential users of information. Reference service takes a variety of forms including direct personal assistance, directories or signs, exchange of information culled from a reference source, readers' advisory assistance, dissemination of information in anticipation of user needs or interests, and direct end-user access to an information system via telecommunication hardware and software.

The Library, because it possesses, organizes and provides access to its community's single largest concentration of information resources, must develop information services appropriate to its community and in keeping with the ALA's Library Bill of Rights: (Appendix A). These services shall take into account the information-seeking behaviors, the information needs, and the service expectations of the members of the community. Provision of information in the manner most useful to its clients is the ultimate test of all a Library does.

The Library shall actively publicize the scope, nature, and availability of the information services it offers. It shall employ those media most effective in reaching its entire clientele or selected segments of that clientele.

The Library shall survey and assess the information needs of its community and create local information products to fulfill those needs not met by published materials.

The Library shall serve its community by collecting and creating information and referral files to provide access to the services and resources of local, regional, and state organizations.

Based on its clients' known needs and interests, the Library shall provide information even if it has not been explicitly requested.

The Library's building shall not be a boundary to its information services. It shall identify and employ external databases, agencies, and services to help meet the information needs of its community.

The Library shall participate in consortia and networks to obtain access to information sources and services it cannot provide on its own.

When the Library is not able to provide a client with needed information, it shall refer either the client or the client's question to some other agency, an expert, or another library which can provide the needed information.

The Library shall use or provide access to information systems outside the Library when these systems meet information needs more effectively and efficiently than internal resources can.

It is the policy of the Library to consider each individual information query to be of equal merit regardless of the age, gender, ethnicity, disability, sexual preference, English language proficiency or status of the inquirer. The Library's intention is to accord equal attention and effort to each inquiry, although the time spent by staff on a question may vary in response to the perceived needs of the patron, the information resources (both staff and collections) available and the method of receipt of the inquiry.

Monroe Township Library
Monroe Township, New Jersey

PHILOSOPHY OF REFERENCE SERVICE

The basic mission of the Monroe Township Free Public Library is to identify, build awareness of and positively respond to the information, educational and recreational reading, viewing and listening needs of all its users. To help accomplish this mission, the Library provides a Reference Department with the following goals:

1. To provide accurate, efficient and courteous assistance and information required or requested by users, whether in person or by telephone, fax or letter.
2. To facilitate access to and optimum use of the Library's resources.
3. To select, acquire and organize sources of information to meet the current and anticipated needs of Library users and prospective users.
4. To supplement the Library's resources through interlibrary cooperation and utilization of external information systems.

2.2 Mission Statement

City of Louisville Public Library
Louisville, Colorado

MISSION OF REFERENCE SERVICES

The mission of the Reference Department is to support the information resource requirements of the community using professionally trained reference staff. The staff will utilize American Library Association materials, as well as monitor customer requests to forecast user requirements. The staff will follow the "Guidelines for Behavioral Performance of Reference and Information Services Professionals" approved by the Reference and Adult Services Division of the American Library Association in January 1996.

The purpose of reference guidelines is to describe the services which are offered by the department, set standards for service, and to provide guidance for reference staff. Reference staff members serve as the link between resources and patrons. In that role, it is important that staff members be:

Knowledgeable about library materials, electronic services, and reference transactions.

Able to demonstrate a high degree of interest in the reference transaction and commitment to providing the most effective assistance.

Protective of each information user's right to privacy and confidentiality.

Objective and not interject value judgments about subject matter or the nature of a patron's question.

Reference customers are people seeking information whether in person, by telephone, fax, email, or other electronic conveyance. Reference services are nondiscriminatory on the basis of age, race, or disability. The department's highest priority is to provide personal assistance to patrons who are on site. Inquiries received by mail, telephone, fax, or e-mail will be answered as expeditiously as possible. At their discretion librarians may return long distance reference calls when appropriate. Confidentiality of user requests is respected at all times.

If the user is referred to another library, librarian, subject expert, or institution, it is important to facilitate the process by confirming that the other resource can provide the information and will extend its services to the user. The librarian may call ahead or check an online catalog to facilitate the process. The librarian will provide the patron and other information provider with as much information as possible to facilitate the search.

Glen Cove Public Library
Glen Cove, New York

Libraries were established to provide information to all who inquire. Librarians are dedicated to gathering, organizing and disseminating the world's knowledge. No matter the format, be it print, media, microform or electronic, the Glen Cove Public Library supports freedom of access to the broadest spectrum of ideas. For many users, the library is the last line of defense in the search for truth.

The Glen Cove Public Library is guided by the following American Library Association statements of access to information:

- The Library Bill of Rights
- Freedom to Read Statement
- Freedom to View Statement
- Interpretation of the Library Bill of Rights: Free Access to Libraries for Minors and Access to Electronic Information Services and Resources.

2.3 Assistance Objectives

Memorial Hall Library
Andover, Massachusetts

Statement of Objectives

To provide personal assistance without discrimination to library users.

To select, acquire, and organize sources of information, both traditional and electronic, to meet the changing needs of library users.

To identify and promote the information needs of potential users in the community.

To cooperate with other community agencies and organizations in their efforts to serve the community.

To ensure that library users receive a consistently high level of service.

To present programs which teach the use of the library and it's resources.

To identify a patron's specific informational needs through a reference interview and then proceed to fill those needs by using the resources available, including the expertise of colleagues and referral to other organizations.

To identify and meet the needs of member libraries of the Northeast Massachusetts Regional Library System in Memorial Hall's capacity as the back up reference center for the region.

To utilize the expertise of fellow staff librarians.

To utilize agencies contracted by the Northeast Massachusetts Regional Library System for specialized reference service.

To utilize the expertise of other agencies to obtain the best information in order to completely answer a patron's question.

To refer patrons to appropriate agencies that can provide needed information.

Boerne Public Library
Boerne, Texas

I. Objectives of Service

Boerne Public Library strives to develop and implement, through continuous evaluation and adaptation, a program of reference services, which effectively meets the informational, educational, recreational and cultural needs of the total community.

II. Specific Objectives:

A. To provide accurate, timely, up-to-date reference services whether questions are asked in person, over the telephone, by letter, or electronically.

B. To provide approachable, knowledgeable staff to assist patrons. To encourage staff development in the areas of library reference services, materials, equipment and other related areas to provide consistent, high quality service.

C. To instruct patrons in the use of library materials, equipment and facilities.

D. To cooperate with other community agencies, organizations, libraries, the Alamo Area Library System and departments within the Boerne Public Library and the City of Boerne in their efforts to better serve the community.

E. To promote an increasing awareness of library services and materials.

F. To periodically evaluate patron satisfaction and reference services by various methods. To periodically evaluate policies and procedures to strive for the best possible reference services.

2.4 Assistance Provided

Brampton Public Library
Brampton, Ontario, Canada

TYPES OF SERVICE

Brampton Library offers customers a variety of information services as described below:

Quick Reference—These questions can be answered immediately using a variety of resources readily available.

General Reference—These questions require more time and resources to provide a complete answer. Staff will assist customers in locating the information required, and to those interested in learning, offer informal instruction on the use of library resources.

Community Information and Referral—Staff will provide customers with information about and referral to community services and programs as required.

Consultation—Staff will consult with customers in an attempt to assist in defining more in-depth information needs and will employ a variety of methods to reach an answer. Duration and depth of assistance will be determined by the customer's needs, staffing and time constraints.

Location of Material—Staff will check library collections to see if the preferred material is available. Staff will place requests or provide instruction on how to place a request for materials not immediately available. If the Library does not own the material, assistance will be provided in borrowing the item from another library or finding information on where the customer may purchase the item.

Library Instruction, Orientation and Researchers Needs—Staff will familiarize customers with all library services and provide instruction in the use of library materials and equipment. The type and amount of assistance will depend on customer need as well as time, resources and staff available. Where necessary, arrangements for specialized assistance will be made. Staff will perform formal library instruction and orientation to groups or individuals upon request.

Referral—When the request for information is established to be beyond the scope of the Library's resources, staff will refer a customer to sources elsewhere. When circumstances warrant, staff may assist the customer in contacting alternative or outside sources. Every attempt is made to satisfy customer requests in the library before referring to outside sources.

Special Collections Assistance—Brampton Library provides specialized reference services to support local history and genealogy requests, and business inquiries. The level of these services will depend on time, resources, staff availability and expertise.

Telephone Service—Staff will provide their full attention to telephone information requests. If a request cannot be answered immediately, arrangements should be made to return the customer's call within a mutually agreed upon time. Staff will request that the customer come in to the library to participate in their research should the situation warrant extensive research.

Correspondence—Staff will provide their full attention to information requests received by correspondence. Staff will respond to such requests in a timely manner.

Interlibrary Loan Service—Brampton Library is part of an information network within the community, within the Southern Ontario Library System and in cooperation with other library systems across Ontario and Canada.

Staff will offer interlibrary loan service whenever the information cannot be located among Brampton Library's resources and falls within the scope of the regional and national interlibrary loan code. Brampton Library likewise shares its resources while maintaining priority preference for its own customers.

North Smithfield Public Library
Slatersville, Rhode Island

Types and Scope of Services Available

The North Smith Public Library will offer services and materials including but not necessarily limited to the following:

Circulating Collections: General interest collections for all ages, large print books, periodicals & newspapers, audio book/cassette tape kits, videos.

Reference and Readers Advisory Services: Reference collections in print and electronic format; Jackdaws, Ready reference by telephone; Programming Story hours for toddlers, pre-schoolers;

after-school specials for elementary school youngsters; Summer Reading Program for school-age children; occasional family, adult and children's programs; Centennial Park Museum passes; display space for exhibits, collections and art work

Access to Technology: On-line databases and indexes; CD-ROM reference products; Internet/World Wide Web stations; Equipment for word-processing and computer skills practice; Meeting Space for nonprofit organizations, community groups and literacy volunteers

2.5 Assistance Guidelines

Athens Regional Library System
Athens, Georgia

Reference Service Guidelines

Service to the public is the first priority of staff assigned to public service desks. The reference staff member on duty shall be approachable, courteous, patient and professional. Answers to all questions are to be provided as quickly and accurately as possible. Service is to be provided without bias and without imposing value judgments as to the importance of patrons' questions. All questions will be treated in a completely confidential manner. Work performed while on duty at the reference desk should not interfere with service to patrons, and staff should be continually alert to patrons needing assistance. When appropriate, the reference staff member will approach the patron and offer to help. Patrons are to be served in order of appearance. Every effort will be made to leave the patron with a positive feeling regarding the service received.

People who come to the library for information should not be required to learn how to use reference tools, but training and instruction should be offered so patrons can become self-sufficient users of new technology. It is the responsibility of the library staff to utilize professional training in searching for information in answer to user inquiries. If repeated or extended research is necessary, the patrons should be assisted to learn the required skills in order to search independently.

Staff should accompany users to the shelf to locate materials. When this is not possible, staff should encourage users to return to the reference desk if they do not find the materials they need. At the end of each reference transaction, staff should inquire if the patron's question has been satisfactorily answered, or if further assistance is needed.

City of Louisville Public Library
Louisville, Colorado

GENERAL SERVICE GUIDELINES

Staff members can provide information but should not interpret that information. Instruction will be provided in the use of library resources, as time permits, enabling users to pursue information independently and effectively if so desired.

A patron may not know how to locate materials thus requiring a staff member to accompany the user to a service area or computer catalog. Users are encouraged to return to the reference desk if they are unsuccessful in finding what they need.

Care must be taken with telephone, mail, e-mail and fax messages because it is easy to misinterpret phone messages and written communications. Only factual information should be given over the phone, with the source cited. Users may have to be told that the library does have information on a topic, but that they will have to come to the library to use and/or interpret it.

Reference staff should always point out publication dates, and the user may be warned that more current information may be available on the topic.

As time permits, reference staff will help patrons to search the Internet for information, and when possible, staff will assist patrons in determining the reliability and authenticity of Internet sites.

Questions requiring an extended amount of research time may be handled at the discretion of the reference librarian.

Boston Public Library
Boston, Massachusetts

5.0 General Guidelines for Desk Service

5.1 Service to the public receives priority over any other duties.

5.2 Reference questions are treated confidentially.

5.3 Whenever possible or prudent, in-person reference receives priority over telephone queries.

5.4 Reference staff will conduct expert reference interviews to determine the reference/research needs of the library user. Reference staff will exhibit model reference behavior at all times.

5.5 Reference staff will rely upon information obtained from reputable sources in order to give the most accurate and authoritative answers to questions.

5.6 Reference staff will also use professional judgment in determining how best to serve each customer's reference needs.

5.7 Reference staff will always cite the source of the answer.

5.8 Reference staff will refer the client to other appropriate sources or institutions when the query cannot be answered to the satisfaction of the client using BPL resources.

7.0 Specific Desk Service Guidelines

7.1 In-Person Reference

7.1.1 Reference questions may require reference staff to accompany clients to the online catalog/databases to explain its use or to the library stacks to help locate material.

7.1.2 Because no two reference questions are alike, there is no time limit to reference assistance.

7.1.3 If there are a number of library users needing assistance, requests that are directional or brief in nature may be given priority over lengthy or complex questions.

7.2 Telephone Reference

7.2.1 Telephone reference generally falls into the Ready Reference category and should take no more than 5-10 minutes.

7.2.2 Telephone reference questions should be limited to a reasonable number; librarians will use their best professional judgment. Reference questions of a more complex nature should be referred to the library subject specialists.

7.2.3 For long and/or complex questions, reference staff will follow-up with the library user by calling them back or another mutually agreeable means of communication.

7.3 Electronic Reference

7.3.1 E-mail reference questions will be answered in the order in which they are received.

7.3.2 Questions of a complex or subject specific nature received either through e-mail or 24/7; Reference will be forwarded to the library subject departments. The originating department will be copied on the response to the client.

7.3.3 Internet reference questions will be answered at those times that the library is monitoring the 24/7 service.

7.4 Reference Letters

7.4.1 Residents of the Commonwealth of Massachusetts will receive priority in the answering of reference letters.

7.4.2 All other reference letters will be answered in the order in which they are received.

7.5 Regional Reference Questions

7.5.1 Massachusetts libraries sending reference questions will be contacted within 48 hours with a status report.

7.5.2 If the question is of a complex nature and will take longer, the reference staff will contact the inquiring library to determine the deadline.

7.6 Electronic Databases/Internet

7.6.1 Reference staff will instruct and/or orient users to the online resources subscribed to by the library and made accessible through the BPL webpage.

7.6.2 Reference staff will use professional judgment to determine when a fee-based electronic database would be the best means of answering a question.

7.6.3 Reference staff will provide authoritative answers to questions.

7.6.4 Reference staff cannot guarantee the validity or accuracy of information retrieved from the Internet.

2.6 Definition of Assistance Area

Wichita Falls Public Library
Wichita Falls, Texas

Service Area

The Library will provide free access to information in-house to all users, and free circulation privileges to all residents within the City limits, Sheppard Air Force Base housing units, individuals who pay ad valorum taxes to the City, and any family members residing in said households. Proof of residence or payment of taxes shall be required.

Western Massachusetts Regional Library System
South Deerfield, Massachusetts

Access to the Berkshire Athenaeum reference collections and information services are available on an equal basis to users of all ages regardless of place of residence. Service is provided through a variety of means: in person, by telephone, by fax, by e-mail, by the Western Massachusetts Regional Library System (WMRLS) van delivery, using the Regional Reference Support Service (RRSS) through the Springfield City Library, interlibrary loan, and by mail. First priority for service is given to in-library patrons.

Lincoln Public Library
Lincoln, New Hampshire

Within the library building, the use of the collection of the Lincoln Public Library is free to all, regardless of place of residency. The home-use privileges of the library collection are free to all residents of Lincoln and Woodstock.

2. Persons residing outside the geographical area but owning property, attending the Lin-Wood Schools, or persons spending six months or longer in Town shall be considered residents. Personnel at the Lin-Wood School are granted full library privileges.

3. Persons spending less than six months in the area may have full library privileges for a fee of $30.00 (refundable). Contingent upon the return of all library materials. A fee of $2.00 per 1/2 hour is required from non-residents for the use of the library's computers, or a 20 use punch card can be purchased for $20.00.

Avalon Public Library
Avalon, Pennsylvania

A. Service to All

The library will serve all residents of the community and the public library system area. Service will not be denied or abridged because of religious, racial, social, economic, or political status; or because of mental, emotional, or physical condition; age; or sexual orientation.

B. Denial of Service

The use of the library may be denied for due cause. Such cause may be failure to return library materials or to pay penalties, destruction of library property, disturbance of other patrons, or any other illegal, disruptive, or objectionable conduct on library premises.

2.7 Rationale for Separate Reference Assistance Policies

Memorial Hall Public Library
Andover, Massachusetts

Purpose of Reference Policy

26

To describe the services and resources which are offered by the Reference Department.

To set standards and guidelines that ensure excellence in reference service.

To provide a philosophical framework for staff that confirms the library's commitment to excellence in reference service.

Glenview Public Library
Glenview, Illinois

Purpose of a Reference Policy

The Reference Service Policy provides library service guidelines for the staff so that patrons will receive consistently high levels of service. The policy describes library resources available to all library patrons. Each service area will have a copy of this policy at hand for reference as well as a manual covering procedures specific to that service area.

2.8 Standards for the Reference Interview Process

Dorchester County Public Library
Cambridge, Maryland

Reference Interview

The reference interview shall be conducted in accordance with the Model Reference Behaviors Checklist (see attached copy) and in such a manner as to draw out as much information from the patron as is necessary to answer the request accurately and fully. If the patron's question is a broad, general one, the librarian should skillfully question him to learn exactly what the patron is seeking. Conversely, if the question is exceedingly specific, the library staff member may attempt to negotiate to a broader level in order to obtain the necessary information for the patron. During the course of the reference interview the library staff member should paraphrase, summarize, and verify the question to make sure the patron and the library staff member have the same understanding of the question.

Points to be covered in the reference interview include whether there is a deadline and the level of information required (basic or technical).

If instructions are given to the patron they should be simple, explicit and not relayed in library jargon. The library staff member should accompany the patron when searching for sources and not simply direct him to an area.

The source of all answers must be cited by the staff member. When the staff member feels that the question has been answered, he should always ask, "Does this completely answer your question?" if the reply is negative, the library staff member should begin the reference interview again.

Western Massachusetts Regional Library System
South Deerfield, Massachusetts

Reference Interview: Sound reference interview techniques should be practiced in negotiating all users' requests, whether the transaction is between library staff and the public, or between library staff and regional interlibrary loan or Regional Reference Support Service (RRSS) staff.

Such techniques involve asking pertinent, open-ended questions to determine what the patron wants and in what form. This interview process saves time and energy for both staff and user. Some phrases to use are: "Can you tell me a little more about..." "I'm not sure I understand exactly what you want to know about..." "Could you be a little more specific..." "Where did you hear about..." or "How do you need to use this information?" Patrons reluctant to answer these questions should be reassured with the explanation that this information helps assist them with their search.

2.9 Reference Service Evaluation

Wilmington Public Library District
Wilmington, Illinois

Evaluation of Reference Service and Policy

Reference service will be evaluated semi-annually. Guidelines for evaluation can include output measures or suggested procedures from HTLS or the Illinois State Library.

The Reference Policy will be reviewed every three years. The Board of Trustees must approve changes in policy.

Part II
The Reference Department: Personnel

Chapter 3

ACADEMIC LIBRARY POLICIES

ACADEMIC LIBRARY GUIDELINES

3.1 Standards for Reference Staff

University of California at Berkeley
University of California at Berkeley Libraries
Berkeley, California

COLLEGIALITY AND COOPERATION

We work together to build a civil environment. We cooperate and support each other. We appreciate diversity.

We treat co-workers, clientele, subordinates and superiors the way we want to be treated, being mindful to respect cultural differences.

We show respect for each other by communicating in a friendly and courteous manner, listening attentively, encouraging the expression of differing points of view, and staying open to questions and opinions from others.

We work together by taking a library-wide perspective, basing discussions on facts rather than rumor, offering constructive criticism, seeking creative and practical solutions, committing ourselves to follow mutually agreed-upon methods and procedures and meeting agreed-upon deadlines.

EFFECTIVE COMMUNICATION

Regular and ongoing open communication occurs throughout the Library.

We are truthful, open and clear in our communication and respect confidentiality when appropriate.

We promptly report final decisions to those affected.

We respond to oral and written requests promptly, mindful that other's work may depend on our response.

We communicate information that is concise and accurate. Whenever possible, we make it available in time for those affected to have input.

We have a clear statement of the Library's ongoing and annual priorities.

We take responsibility for keeping apprised of what's happening in the Library (through reading committee and council minutes, CU NEWS, etc.).

We provide feedback on those issues that affect us or about which we have particular interest or expertise.

EXCELLENCE/CREATIVITY

We pursue excellence and offer quality service within the context of the Library's stated needs and priorities.

We have clearly stated standards of excellence.

We regularly measure our performance against our standards of excellence.

We set realistic priorities among our tasks to ensure that the most important items can be performed to the Library's standards of excellence.

We develop and implement innovative models and standards in response to changes in our environment, providing leadership to the library and information community.

We recommend ways to improve policies and procedures that affect our work.

FAIRNESS

Everyone is important and every part of the Library has an important function.

Within the Library, we seek to administer as equitably as possible the campus-based merit and bonus programs.

We conduct performance evaluations at least annually for all staff.

We evaluate performance based on clearly written standards.

We allocate resources according to the Library's stated priorities.

We expect the same standards of performance from library staff within the same personnel classification regardless of where they work.

We address behaviors inconsistent with the library standards and values in a respectful, constructive and straightforward way.

We have a clear system of appeal within the Library which an employee can use if s/he feels they have been treated unfairly.

PARTICIPATORY DECISION MAKING

We value the opportunity to make decisions that directly affect our daily work.

As the environment changes (new projects, changes in personnel or workload, new decisions to be made), we actively seek input from those who will be affected in order to both frame the problem and brainstorm potential solutions. Whenever possible, we allow time for give-and-take dialog on how best to proceed throughout the process.

We have a right to ask for the rationale behind decisions.

In making changes to workflow and workloads, we work together to adjust the priority on existing work.

PROFESSIONAL GROWTH AND DEVELOPMENT

We believe a highly skilled staff who are given opportunities and challenges are happier and more productive.

To support staff in being successful in their assigned duties, we provide training to all staff.

We have a professional development program to encourage all staff to obtain education needed to grow in our library careers.

As opportunities for career growth arise, eligible staff who are interested can apply and we supported their application.

RECOGNITION

We value a clear and fair rewards policy and a competitive pay structure. We acknowledge each other's successes.

We wholeheartedly acknowledge jobs well done by individuals who excel in their work, regardless of their place in the hierarchy of the system.

We actively pursue a pay structure competitive with the market for all classifications represented in the Library.

We supplement campus compensation programs with celebrations and other forms of recognition to acknowledge outstanding achievements and longstanding contributions to the Library.

SAFE, COMFORTABLE AND HEALTHY WORK ENVIRONMENT

We provide a safe, comfortable and healthy environment for staff and users.

We have a clearly stated set of guidelines for what constitutes a safe and healthy work environment.

We have a library-wide program to regularly evaluate units and make corrections as needed.

We respond immediately and thoroughly to staff concerns about the work environment, taking action per advice of experts on campus when mitigation is needed.

Stetson University
duPont-Ball Library
DeLand, Florida

In order to provide good reference service, librarians in the duPont-Ball Library will strive to fulfill the following standards:

Standard One: Act in a manner that encourages patrons to ask questions

A. At the Reference Desk or on the phone, greet patrons in a cordial manner

B. Use a pleasant, friendly voice when speaking to patrons in person or on the phone

C. Answer electronic reference requests cordially and promptly

D. Answer Reference Desk telephone voicemail promptly and cordially

E. Avoid bringing work to the desk which requires intense concentration

F. Reassure waiting patrons that they will be helped as soon as possible

G. Allow patron to finish asking a question before commenting

H. Remain calm and polite when dealing with patrons

I. Approach patrons who look as if they need help

J. Offer reassurance to frustrated patrons

K. Look up frequently to see if patrons in the reference area need help

Standard Two: Interview patrons to determine their information needs

A. Use good listening skills to clarify a patron's request by identifying the following:
- The subject area and the kind of information requested
- The depth and amount of information needed
- Recentness of the information needed

B. Restate patron's query to ensure complete understanding of the patron's request

Standard Three: Identify and direct patrons to appropriate resources

A. Select resources most likely to contain the information sought, suggesting more than one source, if needed

B. Consider all possible sources and seek more than one reference source, if appropriate

C. Ask for assistance from colleagues, if necessary

D. Provide instruction for use of resources (regardless of format), if necessary

E. Break down reference assistance into logical modules or steps, as necessary, and encourage patron to return to desk for help with the next step.

F. Educate patron, as appropriate, by suggesting additional sources or services which would help the patron

G. Consider all possible resources before telling the patron the needed information is not available

H. Accompany patron to the designated source(s) unless the location of the source is clear by pointing or by locating on a Library map

I. Provide appropriate referrals, if needed, e.g., other campus departments, other libraries (public library, Volusia County Law Library), subject specialists

J. Initiate contact with referral when appropriate (e.g., call the public library, the law library, or a campus department and explain that a patron needs information from them)

K. Encourage patron to check back at the Reference Desk if unable to find what is needed, has trouble using any of the resources, or needs more in-depth assistance

Standard Four: Demonstrate and develop knowledge of information resources and services.

A. Engage in formal and informal study to further knowledge of information resources and services

B. Attend workshops and/or conferences and share information with colleagues

C. Keep abreast of current literature regarding information sources and services

D. Examine new reference tools and share resources with reference colleagues

Standard Five: Create and disseminate User Help Guides and web links

A. Revise or create in-house publications as needed (both print and electronic)

B. Make user guides available electronically via the Library website

C. Make use of in-house publications (research guides, research aids, brief guides, etc.) and contribute information to them when needed

D. Suggest links to appropriate Web resources to the Web Team

Standard Six: Work as a team at the Reference Desk

A. Help colleagues at the Reference Desk when asked

B. Offer assistance to a colleague who is having a problem answering a reference question without undermining the colleague

C. Ask for assistance from colleagues when necessary

D. Alert colleagues to class assignments and frequently asked questions

E. Alert colleagues to reference materials that may be of particular use for an assignment or to new reference materials

F. Help at Reference Desk, even if not "on duty," if reference demand warrants it

G. Remain flexible about Reference Desk hours

H. Keep Reference Desk area neat

I. Follow up on any materials left for patrons at the Reference Desk to see that they are either delivered to the patron or removed from the Reference Desk in a timely manner

Standard Seven: Participate in collection development

A. Contribute to the development of the Library's collections by recommending items to be purchased (both print and electronic) and links to be made to appropriate Web sites

B. Assist in weeding the Library's collections by recommending items to be weeded

Standard Eight: Understand and apply library and departmental policies

A. Explain to patrons not affiliated with Stetson the Library's "Stetson University Library Associates Program" which governs access and membership

B. Enforce Library policies on food, drink, noise levels, and cell phone policy

C. Enforce the Library's policy on use of the Internet.

D. Enforce the Library's (and Stetson's) policy of no soliciting or passing out of organizational literature in the building. Director's permission is needed for posting signs and event posters or flyers

E. Be familiar with the Library's emergency procedures

Santa Fe Community College
Lawrence W. Tyree Library
Gainesville, Florida

Reference Staff

A. Reference Librarians must meet the Association of College and Research Libraries Standards of College Libraries. They should have a graduate degree from an ALA-accredited program. All library professionals are responsible for and participate in professional activities.

B. The library will strive to provide a reference staff that has the knowledge and preparation appropriate to meet the information needs of the college. Personnel responsible for information technology services will be familiar and competent in using information technology and also possess effective interpersonal communications skills.

Washington State University
Washington State University Libraries
Pullman, Washington

The goal of the Reference Service of Owen Science and Engineering Library is to identify and facilitate the transfer of information from source to user.

Standards/Practices

Provide friendly and courteous service; acknowledge users as they approach the desk or if they are waiting for assistance

Practice roving reference—active rather than passive assistance

Follow-up with users

Always consult the on-call or on-duty librarian for additional assistance or when you are unsure of an answer

Attend to the person in the library before those calling or e-mailing their questions

General Rules

Be on time for scheduled desk duty

Transfer outstanding questions to the person replacing you on the desk

When you trade times with another reference assistant be responsible for changing the schedule

Keep a record of all reference questions received during the public service statistics periods tally questions

When you are first on the desk in the morning observe all opening procedures

Be able to offer assistance in the following areas:

Interpretation of library records

Griffin—be able to assist users looking for resources, both known item and subject. Understand and explain: author, title, keyword, number, and subject searching, finding LC subject headings on a record and search for them, interpret library locations, call numbers, and holdings information; search for journal titles and narrow to journals and other publication types; sort searches, use truncation.

Verify journal titles in serials lists if the title does not appear to be in Griffin by the abbreviation or full title from the patron. If an item cannot be found in Griffin and the user wants to obtain it, provide an ILL form. Though IDA and UWIN are available for searching on public access machines, you may need to help a user verify that an item is owned at one of those institutions for quick access or if they are travelling there.

Card Catalog—know that cards were not filed after 1979 but not all items from the card catalog are in Griffin. Use as many access points possible for known item searches.

Serial Control System—call appropriate Serial record unit when there is a question about serial holdings.

Requests for book or journal orders—provide the form for requesting purchases and pass it on to the Owen Collection Development Coordinator.

Circulation and other forms—provide library users with hold, search, and compact storage request forms when necessary.

Answering directional questions:

The American Library Association definition of directional questions is "an information contact that facilitates the use of the library in which the contact occurs, and its environs, and which may involve the use of sources describing that library, such as schedules, floor plans, handbooks, and policy statements. Examples of directional transactions are:

- directions for locating facilities such as restrooms, carrels, and telephones;
- directions for locating library staff and users;
- directions for locating materials for which the user has a call number;
- supplying materials such as paper and pencils; and
- assisting users with the operation of machines.

In giving directions, explanation should be given, when possible, with reference to appropriate printed aids (e.g., the stack plan, floor plans, campus maps, etc.), and should be very specific.

Answering subject questions

Question the patron to determine purpose, level, general subject area, amount of information needed, and resources already consulted.

Be familiar with the Library of Congress classifications.

Know the titles of basic and frequently requested reference books such as CRC Handbook of Chemistry and Physics, Bergey's Manual, and Thomas Register (see list in training notebook).

Be familiar with the Owen Electronic Resources list:

Know which databases are available and how to access (based on list)

Know how to print, download, e-mail citations

Know how to do basic and advanced searching in FirstSearch and ProQuest (Booleans, limiting, field searching, truncation)

Know what handouts are available and appropriate for questions

Equipment maintenance

Know how to do the following:

Logon and reboot public terminals

Load printer paper, do basic maintenance

Report problems you can't fix

Providing Referrals

For any unanswered question consult the librarian on-call

For status of an interlibrary loan request, contact the Interlibrary Loan office

For copier repair, questions about fines and overdues, and items not on the shelf, contact Circulation.

OWEN STUDENT GUIDELINES FOR REFERENCE ASSISTANCE What to do when the Librarian is away, Students may:

- answer questions related to finding a particular author or title, including determining whether item is in circulation, using Griffin. If the item is not found, the patron should always be advised to check with a reference librarian. Never tell a patron an item is not owned.
- retrieve materials from Science compact storage. Authorization for retrieval from Holland compact storage has to come from a librarian, as per Holland Circulation policy.
- answer directional questions: where a certain call number is, where current journals are, etc.
- give out information flyers and forms.
- direct users to Griffin, the WSU Libraries' catalog.

Students should refer patrons to a Reference Librarian for:

- any item that appears to be not owned.
- any subject questions.
- any question involving use of abstracts, indexes or reference materials.
- instructions in use of databases.
- any question about online searching or OASIS.

If the reference librarian is on the phone or busy with another patron, refer the above matters anyway. If there is no librarian on duty, tell the patron when one will return.

Green questions forms are available for patrons to fill out and leave when a librarian is not available. The next reference librarian to come on duty will handle the question.

3.2 Staff Development

Rutgers University
Rutgers University Libraries
Newark, New Jersey

Development and Training—Professional development is the ongoing responsibility of all librarians to maintain current skills, develop new skills, and to implement the information services needed in a constantly changing environment. To support this development the Rutgers University Libraries will provide in-service training for librarians, encourage and support attendance at other professional programs, and provide the appropriate equipment suitable for service at the highest level.

The Libraries will continue to provide, on a system wide basis, workshops and other formal programs designed to help librarians keep abreast of new technologies and other advances and to maintain traditional skills at a high level. Such programs should include both in-house and external experts.

Individual units will continue to provide local workshops and programs targeted to the needs of local librarians and their immediate constituencies.

All libraries will continue to foster an atmosphere of cordiality and collegiality that encourages colleagues to share their expertise with one another on a formal and informal basis.

Participation in formal and informal educational programs is recognized as a key part of scholarly development.

University of Texas at Austin
University of Texas Libraries
Austin, Texas

Staff Development

Continuing staff development is the shared responsibility of the individual, the supervisor, and the library administration and is encouraged. Staff members should participate in activities which will contribute to their continuing education and improve their job performance. Staff development includes in-house training programs, course work, conferences, lectures, and the reading of professional and subject related literature. Some of these activities may require work released time. Since the needs of the unit must be balanced against requests for released time, authorization for an absence must be obtained. Information on released time is in Guidelines for Travel/Released Time (Policies and Guidelines No. 16). Information on taking or auditing courses is in the Policy on Requests to Take or Audit Courses (Policies and Guidelines No. 3).

3.3 Ethics

Weber State University
Stewart Library
Ogden, Utah

Ethics - Every library employee engaged in public service activities:

- has a responsibility to sustain the principles of the Library Bill of Rights, should learn and faithfully execute the policies of public services, and endeavor to change those policies which conflict with the spirit of the Library Bill of Rights.
- must protect the patron's right to privacy in the seeking and use of acquired information.
- must avoid any possibility of personal financial gain at the expense of the library.
- has an obligation to insure equality of opportunity and fair judgement of competence in actions dealing with appointments, retentions, and promotions.
- is obligated when making appraisals of the qualifications of any individual to report the facts clearly, accurately, and without prejudice.
- is under obligation to always take library user needs seriously and treat these needs with respect. There should never by any discussion of an individual user or group of users or of any transactions between user an library employee outside of a professional context.

No personal opinions should be expressed on a patron's query outside of a professional context.

Fitchburg State College
Amelia V. Gallucci-Cirio Library
Fitchburg, Massachusetts

The conduct of the reference librarian is outlined in the Statement of Professional Ethics issued by the American Library Association. This purpose is accomplished by pursuing the following goals:

To give appropriate reference services to the community.

To provide up-to-date, relevant and readily accessible reference materials and equipment which will meet the needs of the community, including automated indexes, catalogs and emerging technology.

To assist the college's instructional programs, by providing appropriate instructional classes which facilitate the use of library's resources.

To provide access to other sources of information and to other libraries, by maintaining the Interlibrary loan program.

To establish a tradition of good, friendly and direct personal service, by employing skillful yet cordial discourse to assist patrons in their information retrieval process.

3.4 Privacy and Confidentiality Standards

Lawrence W. Tyree Library
Santa Fe Community Library
Gainesville, Florida

Service is made available to all students, faculty, and staff of Santa Fe Community College on an equal basis, regardless of age, gender, race, creed or status. Each request is taken seriously and treated with respect. All reference questions are confidential. The nature of the question asked and the identity of the patron will not be discussed with other patrons. When referring reference questions between staff members, discussion about the nature of the question asked and the identity of the patron will be kept to the minimum required by the referral. The nature of reference questions asked and the identity of the patron shall not be divulged to any agency outside of those to which a patron may agree to be referred without a properly executed order from a court of law.

University of California at Berkeley
Library, University of California at Berkeley
Berkeley, California

UC Berkeley Library's Policy on Protected Personal Information

A new provision was added to the California Information Practices

Act–Civil Code 1798.29, 1798.82. This provision requires any state agency (including the University of California) with computerized data containing protected personal information to disclose any breach of security of a system containing such data to any California resident whose unencrypted personal information was, or is reasonably believed to have been acquired by an unauthorized person.

Protected Personal Information is defined by in the Civil Code as an individual's first and last name in combination with any of the following:

- social security number,
- driver's license number,
- financial account or credit card number in combination with any password that would permit access to the individual's financial account.

It is the UC Berkeley Library's policy not to collect protected data unless it is deemed necessary in support of Library business. Any collection of this data must be authorized in writing by the University Librarian.

An example of a library business need to collect this information would be to identify a person borrowing library materials (assuming there is no better means to establish this identification).

If the protected data is collected, it is vital for it to have a written articulated disposition schedule that is strictly followed. Protected data is never allowed to be stored on any library server, desktop, laptop computer, or PDA that is connected to a computer network. Protected data in paper format must be secured in a locked drawer or file cabinet. Exceptions to the above must be included in the written approval of the University Librarian.

If a breach is suspected on a computing system that contains or has network access to unencrypted protected data, the data owner must immediately:

Remove the computing system from the campus network (e.g., power off the computer, disconnect it from the network jack or wireless network)

Send e-mail to the Director of the Library Systems Office (LSO) and to the LSO Helpdesk to initiate a analysis of the breach.

Send e-mail to the AUL or Director in charge of the unit.

Chapter 4

PUBLIC LIBRARY POLICIES

Public Library Guidelines

4.1 Standards for Librarians

Newark Public Library
Newark, New Jersey

Staff

Reference service staff members shall communicate easily and effectively with the full range of the Library's clientele regardless of a client's age, gender, ethnicity, disability, sexual preference, or English-language proficiency.

Reference services staff shall have knowledge and preparation appropriate to meet the information needs of the clientele the Library serves. Staff responsible for the services shall be thoroughly familiar with and competent in using information sources, retrieval techniques, telecommunication methods, and interpersonal communications skills.

The conduct of all Library staff, including those who provide reference services shall be governed by the American Library Association's Code of Ethics (Appendix C).

Memorial Hall Library
Andover, Massachusetts

Reference Staff

Reference staff members serve as the link between resources and the patron. As such, it is important that staff members be:

- Highly knowledgeable about traditional reference sources and proficient with electronic resources and the technology needed to access those resources.
- Knowledgeable about the town of Andover and its government.
- Open and approachable; friendly but professional.
- Able to communicate effectively with all library users.
- Discreet in the handling of questions that might be confidential or sensitive.
- Impartial in dealing with all patrons.

- Able to exercise good judgment both in the interpretation of policy and in the handling of exceptional situations.
- Able to instruct the public in the use of print and electronic resources.
- Able to evaluate the Internet for authority, accuracy, currency, and content.
- Skilled in the interviewing process in order to help the patron formulate their specific question and make the patron comfortable in the transaction so they will return for further help if their specific need has not been met.
- Take the responsibility to seek continuing education opportunities especially workshops provided by the Merrimack Valley Library Consortium, Northeast Massachusetts Library System, Board of Library Commissioners, and any other workshops and conferences approved by the Library Director.
- New staff members will receive orientation to Memorial Hall Library and to the Northeast Massachusetts Regional Library System. Continual training is necessary in order to provide the highest level of service. Participation in workshops and attendance at meetings on a local, state, and national level is encouraged.

Washington County Public Library System
Abingdon, Virginia

Reference Staff

Reference staff members, whether professional or paraprofessional, serve as the link between library resources and the patron. As such, it is important that the staff member be:

1. Knowledgeable about library materials and services.
2. Open and approachable; friendly but professional.
3. Able to communicate effectively with people.
4. Discreet in the handling of questions which might be confidential or sensitive.
5. Able to exercise good judgment in the interpretation of policy and in handling of exceptional situations.

The role of the reference staff is that of information provider, not interpreter or adviser. They shall provide instruction in the use of resources, enabling users to pursue information independently and effectively.

The reference staff does not evaluate the information. If the patron has trouble understanding the source, an alternative source shall be sought. Staff may advise patrons regarding the relative merits of sources and make recommendations regarding library materials when appropriate. Materials recommended shall be the most comprehensive and the most current available.

Confidentiality of the user requests must be respected at all times. Questions shall not be discussed outside the library, and names shall never be mentioned without permission.

Staff shall use discretion when interviewing users. While it is important to conduct a thorough reference interview, this shall be done in such a way as to minimize discomfort to the user. The staff shall try to identify the issue in question without intruding on the user's privacy. Staff shall be impartial and non-judgmental in handling users' queries.

On-going training is necessary in order to provide the highest level of service. Therefore, participation in library activities ranging from formal classroom instruction to informal groups sharing professional ideas is encouraged as is membership and participation in regional professional organizations, the Virginia Library Association and the American Library Association.

Brooklyn Public Library
Brooklyn, New York

Subject: Reference Service: Competencies and Standards

Application: All Librarians, Librarian Trainees and Library Associates

Policy Statement: The goal of Reference Service at the Brooklyn Public Library is to meet the expressed and anticipated information needs of our borough's diverse community as part of the Library's Mission. All Age Level Specialists are expected to provide with consistency and high standards:

1.) Correct, complete, and timely responses to information queries.
2.) Access to resources, both locally and externally to satisfy those queries.
3.) Support for information literacy among our patrons.

Age Level Specialists are expected to provide reference service, ranging from basic fact-finding through appropriate referral, in a proactive user-friendly environment. Reference service is available to everyone; patrons of all ages, abilities, and skill levels, and to all ethnic, cultural and socioeconomic groups. Each patron can expect to receive attention and time from library staff appropriate to satisfy their needs whether in person, on telephone, or via other electronic communication methods.

Reference Service is managed by the Manager of Reference and Electronic Resources who is responsible for integrating the Library's service principles into service delivery through coordination with the Office of Neighborhood Services. Reference service skills are a professional responsibility and are enhanced through a program of mandated reference training and professional development for all Age Level Specialists.

Competencies and Standards for Reference are defined by the Library Development Office, meeting regional and national standards for reference and under the overarching guidance of the Library's Mission, Vision and Core Values. The Reference and Electronic Resources Manager may establish and communicate unique goals for that service within these parameters.

Procedures or Guidelines:

I. Knowledge of Client Groups

A. Each Age Level Specialist providing reference services should be familiar with the various patron groups served by the agency.

1. Know the age level service competencies and standards within one's own age level specialization area as well as those in the other areas.
2. Know the social, economic, and cultural status of the patron groups served by the agency as described in the summary section of the branch or division profiles.
3. Review the community newspapers, visit local institutions and events, and review and update the local history file regularly.

4. Be familiar with the Library's brochure on "Services, Collections, and Programs for Persons with Disabilities."

II. Materials and Collection Development

A. Knowledge of materials in the various formats which are available at each agency, unique items throughout the BPL system, and of useful collections throughout the region at other agencies is essential.

1. Know and utilize the BPL core reference list materials, the current core list can be found under the Reference Services area on B-Line.
2. Based upon branch and division profile indicators, other useful reference materials beyond the core reference list should be acquired and used appropriately, (including but not limited to the periodicals and local history information files).
3. Be familiar with the unique holdings in the central divisions (including the Brooklyn Collection), Business Library, Multilingual Center, Service to the Aging, and other branches.
4. Know and use BPL reference databases and www links.
5. Be familiar with other resources throughout the borough and city.
6. Know the periodicals and newspaper titles at your branch or division and also at neighboring agencies.
7. Be familiar with Internet-based current events tools.

B. Branch and division staff should collaboratively select appropriate materials and develop reference collections that reflect the information needs of a branch's or division's patrons.

1. Know and effectively implement the current BPL collection development policy including regular implementation of the weeding guidelines.
2. Attend regularly offered BPL reference materials selection forums e.g. Reference Book Look, periodical look and "Best Reference" Services Meeting. Dates for these events can be found in the annual calendar on B-Line and are announced periodically.
3. Regularly review the professional literature reviewing materials to seek current, useful, and diverse potential additions to the branch collections, and
4. Communicate reference needs to the Reference Resources Committee and the various Web Committees as appropriate. Form XXX can be used for requesting new materials to be ordered which don't appear on the Office of Materials Selection's XXX and pick-up lists.
5. Develop and demonstrate a strong commitment to patrons' rights to access to information consistent with the American Library Association's "Library Bill of Rights."

C. The ability to provide patrons with appropriate materials and information requires ongoing development in reference skills and proactive knowledge of information resources in all formats. Know and apply the skills learned from the mandated BPL Reference and Age Level Specialization staff training programs.

1. And apply the skills learned from the BPL core and specific technology staff training programs. (e.g. MS Office products, online reference databases, Searching the WWW, etc.) Look for the monthly calendar of training offerings as offered by the Library Development Office.

2. Regularly review the professional literature reviewing materials to ensure a familiarity with existing, new and emerging information resources. E.g. "Library Journal," "Voices of Youth Advocate," "Booklist," and "Web Feet."

3. Regularly review local publications to ensure a familiarity with current trends and issues which are of interest to the agency patrons.

4. Maintain familiarity with branch or division reference collections in all formats.

5. Utilize proper referral procedures for both internal and external resources.

III. Communication Skills

A. Age Level Specialists are responsible for proactively initiating reference interactions during all service hours.

B. Basic skills for speaking, listening, training, and writing learned in the various staff training programs should be applied to the fullest advantage in providing reference services.

C. Reference assistance and instruction represent a primary communication area of importance to our patrons. Success or failure in this area is a strong measure of BPL accomplishing its mission, vision and core values. The skills that must guide all such transactions should be acquired by:

1. Know and apply the skills learned from the BPL core and specific technology staff training programs, (including but not limited to the Teaching with Technology, Introduction to MS PowerPoint, and Technology Communications)

   a) Offer instruction for using resources, whenever appropriate.

   b) Offer instructional materials to aid in the use of resources, whenever appropriate.

2. Know and apply the skills learned from the mandated BPL Reference staff training programs, (including but not limited to the Ready Reference/Core Skills and Reference Interviewing Skills training programs). Strict attendance to the "Model Reference Behaviors" as learned in the reference training as listed here should be maintained:

   a) Be approachable, (minimize other work activities while at the reference desk).
   1) Smile
   2) Make eye contact
   3) Give friendly verbal greeting
   4) Be on same level as patron

   b) Offer a comfortable environment.
   1) Maintain eye contact
   2) Show relaxed posture
   3) Make attentive comments
   4) Speak in interested helpful tones

   c) Show interest in the transaction.
   1) Give patron full attention (avoid bringing other work to the reference desk)
   2) Be mobile and go with patron

d) Use good negotiation (reference interview) skills.
1) Ask open-ended questions
2) Use basic resources
3) Go beyond immediate resources
4) Summarize and verify queries. Always follow-up!
5) Inquire if the patron's question is completely answered

3. Know and apply the skills learned from the BPL Age Level Specialization training reference component as appropriate for one's own specialization area, and
4. Know and adhere to the BPL Customer Service Values policy. (See Policies on B-Line.)
5. Know and adhere to the BPL TRC Policy. (See Policies on B-Line.)

IV. Programming Skills

A. Administrative activities of reference and research programming exist to ensure orderly and successful programming in standardized formats (refer to and emulate programs on B-Line under "Training," "Public.") throughout the branches and divisions. Planning and cooperation with other departments should play strongly in these activities.

1. Communicate reference programming needs and intentions to appropriate departments on a timely basis, (including but not limited to the Office of Neighborhood Services/Programming and Special Services, the Library Development Office, Marketing and Communications, Information Technology, and Multimedia). E.g. general research programs or research programs for specific subject areas.

B. Agency patron group programming needs and demands should be determined by formal and informal surveying methods.

1. Maintain familiarity with branch and division profile indicators for reference/research needs.
2. Maintain familiarity with the age level programming attributes learned in the Age Level Specialization staff training programs.
3. Attend Reference Service workshops whenever possible, and
4. Seek and acknowledge patron requests for various programming ideas and work with appropriate departments (As listed in IV A above) to launch new programs where current offerings/resources show a gap in service.
5. Try offering innovative reference/research programming as based upon examples seen in the professional literature and at other library systems.

C. Technological requirements of reference research programming demand competencies in reference/research and computing technologies and knowledge of the technology policies and guidelines issued by BPL.

1. Complete training and apply the skills learned from the core and specific technology staff training programs.
2. Maintain and apply the technology skills learned in the Reference staff training programs,
3. Consistently use the public training materials mounted on B-Line.
4. Adhere to the Technology Resources Center Policy on B-Line.
5. Follow the procedures in the BPL Internet use FAQ sheet and TRC Policy.

6. Adhere to and practice the information learned in the Internet Management Training staff training sessions.

V. Professionalism and Professional Development

A. Professionalism and respect, toward patrons and co-workers alike, is essential to maintaining a productive and user-friendly reference service environment.

1. Adhere to and exhibit the behaviors discussed in the Customer Service Values policy posted in the policies manual on B-Line.
2. Complete training and apply the skills learned from the BPL Reference staff training programs, (including but not limited to the Ready Reference/Core Skills and Reference Interviewing Skills training programs).
3. Adhere to the ALA Code of Ethics. (See appendix).
4. Utilize the Customer Service forms whenever appropriate.

B. Professional Development in the areas of research, reference and training techniques are essential in the provision of services to BPL patrons. Age Level Specialists are responsible for their own professional and should work closely with supervisors to support personal advancement in this area.

1. Read professional reference publications on a regular basis. (These can be borrowed from the Reference Manager's professional materials collection).
2. Read lay and professional computing and information publications on a regular basis.
3. Attend and complete the mandated BPL reference services training programs as offered.
4. Review, on a regular basis, new databases and web sites added to the BPL www pages.
5. Participate in local, regional, and national professional association conference and continuing education training activities and online discussion lists related to the provision of reference services and technologies.

VI. Advocacy, Public Relations, and Networking Skills

A. Branch and Divisional advocacy helps bring BPL reference service efforts to the attention of current and potential patrons, elected officials, and other library systems.

1. Publicize the library and its programs to promote an awareness of and support for library reference and technology programs that meet patrons' educational and informational needs.
2. Promote BPL's reference and technology programs at community meetings and other meetings attended for work activities.
3. Actively seek the opinions and requests of patrons in the development and evaluation of library reference services and technology programs.
4. Utilize the homework form #343 to advise teachers about resource issues.

B. Public relations efforts support advocacy by using BPL's internal resources to offer well designed, standardized, powerful statements about reference services for BPL patrons.

1. Cooperate with appropriate BPL departments to utilize effective public relations techniques and media to publicize library reference program activities. (e.g. Office of

Neighborhood Services/ Programs and Special Services, Marketing and Communications, etc.).

C. Networking constitutes the "grass roots" activities for promoting BPL's services and activities.

   1. Ensure that the Brooklyn Public Library Materials Selection Policy is implemented and promoted so that customers of all ages have open and equal access to the library's reference resources and services.
   2. Develop cooperative programs between the public library, academic and cultural institutions and other community agencies.
   3. Extend library services to individuals and groups presently under-served.
   4. Keep abreast of legislation affecting libraries and understand the political process and, when authorized to do so, communicating with elected and appointed officials on behalf of BPL's reference services and programs. Cooperate with the BPL Office of Government Affairs whenever necessary.

VII. Administrative Skills

A. Administrative activities such as telephone interactions, budget-keeping, inter-office communication, and general organizational skills are an integral component in providing good reference service during internal and external transactions

   1. Understand, interpret, implement, and promote the BPL goals, mission, vision, policies and procedures.
   2. Understand and promote quality service to meet the educational, recreational and informational needs of all patrons.
   3. Understand and promote reference services to all patrons.
   4. Understand, interpret, and implement all of the BPL Age Level Service Competencies and Standards.
   5. Complete the training and apply the skills learned from the BPL core technology staff training programs.
   6. Complete the training and apply the skills learned from the BPL managerial skills staff training programs.
   7. Document and evaluate library reference services.
   8. Adhere to the BPL Customer Service Values policy.

4.2 Staff Development and Training

Newark Public Library
Newark, New Jersey

Continuing education of reference service staff is essential to professional growth. It is the responsibility of the individual to seek continuing education and of the employing institution to support its staff's continuing education efforts and, when possible, to provide continuing education programs.

Carroll Public Library
Carroll, Iowa

On the Internet Site for the Northeast Iowa Library Services Area

Personnel Policies

Development and Training of the Library Staff.

It is expected that the Library Director and nonprofessional staff, where deemed appropriate by the Library Director, shall attend professional meetings, workshops, and conferences for the purpose of continuing education.

The Library Director shall be encouraged to attend, with time off, pay, and expenses, any meeting within the State that he feels would be beneficial for him to attend. Any meetings occurring outside the State require specific Board approval.

Non-professional Library staff members shall be encouraged to attend, with time off, pay, and expenses, the district meeting of the Iowa Library Association and any other library related meetings deemed useful by the Library Director.

The Library Director shall be required to earn a minimum of 3 continuing education units annually. Other adult staff members shall be required to earn a minimum of 1 continuing education unit annually.

Travel expense to and from meetings attended by Library staff members shall be paid by the Library at the per mile rate in effect for State employees.

Dues in the Iowa Library Association for the Library Director and adult staff members shall be paid by the Library on an annual basis.

4.3 Ethics

Whistler Public Library
Whistler, British Columbia, Canada

Staff Code of Ethics

As a part of its commitment to the welfare of the staff at Whistler Public Library, the Board of Trustees wishes to define a code of ethics. This code is intended to provide guidance and support to the staff.

1. Conflict of Interest

A conflict of interest arises when an employee's personal interests conflict with his or her duties and responsibilities as an employee of the Whistler Public Library. A conflict of interest can exist whether or not a pecuniary advantage has been or may have been conferred on an employee.

Employees shall not:

1.1 engage in any business transactions or have financial or other personal interests which are inconsistent with the impartial discharge of their duties.

1.2 place themselves in a position where they are under obligation to any person who might benefit from special consideration or favor on their part;

1.3 deal with an application to Whistler Public Library for a loan, grant, award or other benefit involving relatives;

1.4 extend, in the discharge of their official duties, preferential treatment to relatives, friends, organizations or groups in which they have or their relatives or friends have a pecuniary interest.

1.5 gain personal benefit, directly or indirectly, from any agreement or contract with Whistler Public Library about which they can influence decisions or affect the outcome.

1.6 gain personal benefit, or permit others to benefit, from the access to information acquired in their official capacity which is not generally available to the public through ordinary and proper channels.

1.7 Employees shall not engage in work, business or other types of financial enterprises outside Whistler Public Library that:

  i. would interfere with or influence their judgment or the impartial discharge of their duties as Library employees;

  ii. would create or provide an advantage on account of their employment as library employees; and

  iii. would be employment which has or may have business dealings with Whistler Public Library.

Employees shall be bound to inform their supervisors, in writing, of any business interests of a commercial or financial nature where such interests might be construed to provide an advantage or to be in conflict with their library duties.

Employees shall not solicit, accept or condone the solicitation or acceptance of any gift, favor or form of entertainment and/or hospitality from any person or corporation having dealings with Whistler Public Library whereby the acceptance of such could reasonably be construed as being given in anticipation or recognition of special consideration by the Board.

2. Public Relations

Employees shall treat each contact with the public with diplomacy, tact and objectivity, and shall recognize that such contacts affect Whistler Public Library's public image.

Employees shall refer to the Director any contacts from the media which do not deal with information in the public domain, but which request opinions or comments on policy, procedures or other matters.

Press releases must be approved by the Director or designate prior to issue.

3. Property

An employee shall not use Whistler Public Library property, equipment, supplies or services of consequence, including computer software and other intellectual property, for activities not associated with the discharge of official duties.

4. Confidentiality of Information

Onus is placed on the Director to ensure that employees are cognizant of confidential information held in their departments which may not be divulged.

Employees shall not disclose or release, by any means, to any member of the public, either in verbal or written form, any confidential information or material acquired by virtue of their official position as an employee.

Employees shall not permit any person, other than those who are appropriately entitled thereto, to inspect or have access to information, papers or documents which are confidential.

Formal procedures are in place, in accordance with the Freedom of Information and Protection of Privacy Act, which govern situations where a member of the public requests access to information that is regarded as confidential by Whistler Public Library.

Employees shall not, by virtue of their position with Whistler Public Library, use information for personal or private gain or for the gain of friends, relatives or any person or corporation having dealings with Whistler Public Library.

All personnel matters and files of any employee of Whistler Public Library shall be kept in strictest confidence with the Director, and knowledge of their contents shall be available only to those who are appropriately entitled thereto.

Where an employee is unsure of the status of information, he or she shall confer with the Director for a decision.

5. Political Activity

An employee of the library who intends to be a candidate in an election should consult the Director.

During municipal, provincial or federal elections, employees should ensure that any involvement in campaigns shall not adversely affect their duties as employees with Whistler Public Library.

Library resources shall not be used on any election campaign. No campaign related activities shall take place on library property.

6. Compliance

The Director shall, to the best of his/her ability, ensure that the Code of Ethics is followed by all staff.

Where it is determined that an employee is in contravention of any one of the foregoing, disciplinary action shall be taken which may include reprimand, suspension or dismissal.

4.4 Privacy and Confidentiality Standards

Stillwater Public Library
Stillwater, Oklahoma

Patron Confidentiality Policy

The Stillwater Public Library and Oklahoma State Statutes protect the privacy of library users.

Confidentiality extends to information sought or received; circulation records; database search records; reference interviews; interlibrary loan records; registration records; and all other personally identifiable uses of library materials, facilities, programs or services including the frequency or nature of a patron's visit to the library.

Patron records will not be made available to any individual, group, or law enforcement agency without a valid court order, subpoena, or search warrant issued by a court of competent jurisdiction and presented to the Library Director or his/her designee. The Library Director will contact the City Attorney's office whenever a court order, subpoena or search warrant is received.

All employees, board members, and volunteers of the Stillwater Public Library must comply with this policy.

Names of patrons may be disclosed to another library for the purpose of borrowing materials for the patron through interlibrary loan services.

Any patron who wishes to release information to another individual with regards to materials on reserve must complete a "Release of Information Form" (see appendix A).

The Stillwater Public Library fully supports the American Library Association's Library Bill of Rights, Freedom to Read Statement, Freedom to View Statement, Statement on Labeling, and Intellectual Freedom Statement. (See Collection Development Policy to view these statements).

Wichita Falls Public Library
Wichita Falls, Texas

Patron Privacy Policy

The Wichita Falls Public Library supports the American Library Association Freedom to Read statement and the library privacy provisions under the Texas Open Records Act. Library users should be able to pursue informational and recreational reading in the secure knowledge that no third person has access to their library records without proper observance of due process of law. To support this philosophy and legal status the following rules must be observed:

No personal information concerning a cardholder may be given to ANY OTHER PERSON without a subpoena from a duly authorized judge.

No information concerning materials borrowed by a cardholder may be given to any third person without a subpoena from a duly authorized judge. **Exception may be made for guarantor of a juvenile card with proper identification.

Any patron requesting by telephone a list of items checked out on a specific card must use the barcode number. Staff will not give out any specific materials information without the barcode; they may give out the date due and the number of items only.

While the guarantor of record may check on a juvenile record (with proper identification or with borrower's card in hand), spouses, siblings and other relatives may not check on each other's record without that specific borrower's card in hand.

Staff will refer all requests for personal or usage information regarding any cardholder, including subpoenas, to the Library Administrator. In case of an expected extended absence of the Administrator, the request shall be referred to an Assistant Administrator.

All subpoenas shall be photocopied, one copy shall be forwarded to the City Legal Department for comment, one copy shall be forwarded to the Assistant City Manger, and one copy shall be kept on file, marked with date received, note of disposition and date of disposition. At no time shall information be immediately dispensed without first notifying the City Legal Department and receiving instruction as to City preference in procedure.

In the case of uncertainty or seeming conflict of instruction, opinion shall be sought from the Office of the State Attorney General to assure compliance with Texas Privacy Act.

Personal and usage information shall be forwarded as necessary to the City Prosecuting Attorney to support issuance of "unlawfully detained materials" citations as per City Ordinance 11-93.

**Staff may not at any time identify any person as a Library cardholder to any other person.

Part III
Reference Collections:
Selection and Evaluation

Chapter 5

PRINT RESOURCES POLICIES

SELECTION AND EVALUATION

5.1 General Guidelines

University of West Georgia
Irvine Sullivan Ingram Library
Carrollton, Georgia

Selection Criteria for the Reference Collection

Selection of materials for reference is based on the following criteria:

Selection criteria for reference materials shall be consistent with the Library Collection Development Policy regarding subject scope.

Materials will be selected for quick consultation and ease of use.

Materials will be authoritative, based upon evaluation of the subject content and the author's/producer's/publisher's credentials. Preference will be given to items with favorable reviews in reputable sources.

Materials will be current when appropriate.

Access to similar information in several different sources will be kept to a minimum. Within certain subject areas, some redundancy may be necessary. In those instances, selection will be based on the Library Collection Development Policy, the level of demand for the information, and the unique features or access points that the materials offer.

Sources will be selected for use by the University's primary user population.

When appropriate, items will contain good quality illustrations.

Materials will be selected based on the strengths and weaknesses of the existing reference collection.

When both hardbound and paperback editions exist for the same source, preference may be given to the hardbound edition.

The same criteria apply for electronic sources with the addition of hardware and software considerations and licensing agreements.

Bridgewater Public Library
Bridgewater, Massachusetts

Selection of new reference materials is the responsibility of the head of the Reference Department, with input from other members of the department and from libraries in the region.

Reference material is designed to be consulted for items of information rather than read cover to cover. Collection development will follow the identified needs of the Town of Bridgewater and the SEMLS region. The department maintains standing orders for frequently used reference books which have regular editions such as almanacs, directories, government manuals, indexes and yearbooks. Prior years of these regularly updated materials are either placed in the circulating collection or advertised within the region.

Patrons' requests for particular materials are welcome; however, the Library reserves the right to purchase or reject such requests based on reviews, budget constraints and professional assessment of the item's usefulness to the community as a whole.

Monroe Township Public Library
Monroe Township, New Jersey

SELECTION AND RETENTION OF MATERIALS

The Reference Department adheres to the criteria for selection, maintenance and development of the collection set forth in the Library's Collection Development Policy. Reference materials are selected and retained for their utility, currency, quality, affordability and relation to the existing collection.

While the Library Director has primary responsibility for developing and maintaining the reference collection, every reference librarian who staffs the Reference Desk is responsible for making recommendations for updating and expanding the collection. Public recommendation of titles for purchase is encouraged.

CLASSIFICATION OF MATERIALS AS REFERENCE

The primary criterion for classifying any title as reference is utility in meeting the specific and recurrent information needs of users. Books may be purchased for both the reference and circulating collections, as deemed appropriate by the Head of Reference and Library Director.

SIZE AND GROWTH OF COLLECTION

The Library maintains the reference collection at a size deemed most manageable and useful to staff and public. Emphasis is placed on adding materials that expand or update rather than duplicate information already contained in the collection. The collection is continually reviewed to remove superseded, dated or extraneous materials.

Logan Public Library
Logan, Utah

REFERENCE COLLECTION DEVELOPMENT GUIDELINES

The reference collection is comprised of sources for factual and statistical information.

The collection shall include reference tools recommended for public libraries in the following areas: general reference, the humanities, the social sciences, history and the pure and applied sciences.

Selection in most subject areas is made with the non-specialist in mind. Both current and retrospective coverage will be provided. The reference collection provides selective coverage of subjects of local interest and information on local politics, statistics, and organizations.

Any material under consideration for acquisition for the reference collection will first be evaluated in each of the following areas: Physical format, bibliographic form, usefulness, quality of work, demand, currency of the topic, date of the publication, opinions expressed in professional reviews, the price on the material and local interest.

Materials acquired will include indexes, handbooks, guides, dictionaries, directories, bibliographies, almanacs, encyclopedias, atlases, yearbooks and manuals.

The same criteria apply to both acquisition and weeding. The physical condition of the material, age of the material, subject matter, datedness, and demand will be used as criteria for keeping the material in the reference collection.

Southern Connecticut State University
Hilton C. Buley Library
New Haven, Connecticut

Policy for Print Resources:

The Reference Department strives to maintain a quality collection of print reference resources. Reference librarians are responsible for maintaining an authoritative, current, and comprehensive reference collection that serves the university community effectively and adequately. The basic subject areas that are collected are those that serve to support the instructional programs and research needs of the university community. The collection is available to non-affiliated users. The materials vary in scope and depth of coverage, in point of view and complexity to meet the needs of the largest number of library users.

A reference book is one that by virtue of its format, arrangement, or content is consulted for bibliographic or factual information rather than read in its entirety. Almost all of the books in Buley Library's reference section fit this definition. However, some books that do not meet this definition are shelved in this collection because of their usefulness in answering reference questions. The level of collection varies from subject to subject depending on the courses being taught at the institution and the budget allocated for the department. Factors influencing the selection of reference materials are of the material, the usefulness of the material in relation to existing materials in the collection, the targeted audience, the reputation of author or publisher and book reviews.

Print materials in the Reference collection consist of almanacs, bibliographies (standard, general, and subject specific), biographical sources, concordances, dictionaries (English language, foreign language, and subject dictionaries), general encyclopedias, specific subject encyclopedias, geographical sources (atlases, gazetteers, maps), guidebooks, handbooks, loose leaf materials, manuals, newspaper and periodical indexes and abstracts, pamphlets, statistical/table compilations, basic texts with high reference value, and yearbooks. Government documents are included in the Reference collection if their content falls within the criteria of reference materials.

The reference department aims to collect both current and retrospective materials. The emphasis is on current materials but older materials are purchased depending on the information content and the availability of funds. Only one copy of a title is ordered. Exceptions are made to ensure the availability of heavily used materials. Reference books are ordered in hard copy format with the exception of those items that are withdrawn annually when the newer editions are received.

Most reference books are ordered through a vendor. A few are ordered directly from publishers. Some titles are placed on a standing order list. Standing order titles include materials that need to be current to be useful, such as directories, almanacs, yearbooks, etc., as well as materials published on a particular cycle that we choose to order on a particular schedule reflecting information needs and budgetary constraints. Titles on this list will be reviewed annually for additions, deletions, and changes in the frequency of ordering.

Reference materials do not circulate.

Weber State University
Stewart Library
Ogden, Utah

Selection

a. Criteria for Inclusion

Inclusion in Sheehy's Guide to Reference Books

Favorable reviews received from an objective, professional source such as Choice

The degree of content specialization, i.e. highly specialized works may be understood by so few patrons that they would hardly ever see use in a general reference collection.

The reference nature of the book, i.e. written to be consulted for pieces of information rather than to be read throughout.

Organization for quick and easy use, either in an alphabetical or chronological arrangement, or the item is replete with detailed indexes and cross references.

Always items such as indexes and bibliographies which "point" to the location of information

Borderline decisions are resolved by consensus of all faculty librarians in public services on the basis of what is best for the patron and the curriculum.

b. Replacement of Print with Online Versions

Seldom used but expensive print titles should be evaluated and on consensus of the public services faculty librarians, replaced by the online version to be used as an integral part of online reference service.

University of Louisville
Ekstrom Library
Louisville, Kentucky

Types of Materials

Almanacs, Directories, Yearbooks, Annuals: Current editions of sources are kept in Reference, with most earlier editions being housed in the general stacks. Representative encyclopedia yearbooks and some annual review publications are retained to provide a year-by-year historic record as far back as possible. If the title is not to be replaced by any later edition, it should be considered for transfer to the general stacks for historical reference, or withdrawn if not of permanent value.

Bibliographies–Author: Critical bibliographies of major authors will be in Reference. Most bibliographies of author's works will be in the stacks unless curriculum needs or frequent demand makes their retention in Reference preferable.

Bibliographies–Subject: Subject bibliographies in high demand and of special current interest are housed in Reference. All others will be kept in the general stacks.

Biographical Sources: The Reference collection will contain both retrospective and current biographical tools dealing with professional, national and international groups. Specialized dictionaries having relevance to the region and/or curriculum will also be included. Usually only the latest editions of biographical directories will be in reference, the superseded editions being transferred to the general stacks.

Concordances: Concordances housed in reference should be limited to major works and authors such as the Bible and Shakespeare. Others will be in the general stacks.

Dictionaries: English language dictionaries kept in reference will include the standard unabridged works; a selection of the most authoritative current general dictionaries; usage, slang, dialect, and etymological dictionaries; and a representative selection of such specialized aids as rhyming, synonym, and pronunciation dictionaries. Representative English/foreign language dictionaries will be kept in Reference with a selection of the most authoritative for the major languages. The major unilingual dictionaries of the major living and dead foreign languages of the world are in Reference, including slang and dialect dictionaries for those languages taught in the university curriculum.

Encyclopedias: The print reference collection includes the standard adult encyclopedias in English, and usually one new set is ordered annually. There is at least one encyclopedia set in Russian and each of the major European languages.

Geographical sources: The Reference collection contains authoritative atlases and gazetteers sufficient to cover all areas of the world. Thematic, general world, and regional atlases will be the most recent editions, while the historical atlases should be standard. A small current map collection of major cities is maintained for ready-reference use.

Handbooks, Companions: These materials should be included in Reference on the basis of the need for coverage within the subject area. They should be authoritative and up-to-date.

Histories: While monographs and textbooks will be kept to a minimum, there should be a standard history for each major country or region and for Kentucky and Louisville.

Periodical Directories and Union Lists: Bibliographies of periodicals and newspapers are housed in Reference and should include the major international directories, national bibliographies and union lists.

Periodical Indexes and Abstracts: Reference will have as many current and retrospective indexes and abstracts within the humanities, social sciences and life sciences as the budget permits. There will not be an attempt to purchase all indexes to general popular literature which can be found at the Louisville Free Public Library. Print indexes to individual periodicals will usually be shelved with the periodical, but Reference will house those of frequent and broad-based usage.

Plot Summaries: Reference houses standard comprehensive sets of plot summaries, but does not include study guides.

Sacred Books: The reference collection will include English translations of the sacred books of the world's major religions.

Statistical Yearbooks: An effort will be made to purchase as many statistical yearbooks of domestic and international statistical sources as the budget allows, and to update them on a regular basis with outdated issues being transferred to the stacks.

Style Manuals: The reference collection will contain the general standard style manuals and those for specialized areas included in the university curriculum.

Subject Dictionaries and Encyclopedias: Reference will keep all standard authoritative subject encyclopedias except those of specialized area served by the professional school and branch libraries. A selection of the most useful and current dictionaries for each subject, including subjects excluded above, should be included for general reference purposes.

5.2 Weeding Procedure

Southern Connecticut State University
Hilton C. Buley Library
New Haven, Connecticut

Weeding Policy

The Reference collection is weeded periodically for the purpose of maintaining an updated and useful collection. Subject selectors are responsible for weeding the collection in their subject areas and all reference librarians participate in the deselection of the general reference collection.

The following criteria are used to determine if a book should be removed from the collection:

The importance of the publication—its research and historical value.

The scope and depth of the work.

Does the material belong in the reference collection or more appropriately in the circulating collection?

How likely is it that the publication will be used in the future?

Is there a later edition, which supersedes this publication?

Is the information in the work duplicated in other works?

Do duplicate copies exist on the shelf?

If the book is in poor condition, should it be replaced or refurbished?

Is the information obsolete?

Are there gaps in the collection that should be filled?

Weber State University
Stewart Library
Ogden, Utah

Weeding

a. Decision Criteria

- The item has been superseded by a more current edition, and the item is not part of an annual series set.
- The item in no way supports any personal or academic needs of patrons.
- The information in the item is useless or perhaps even dangerous because of age.
- The item is not, by nature or internal arrangement, a reference book.
- The needs and purposes of the WSU primary patron classes are better served by transferring the item from a restricted status to a circulating status or even to an area or department external to the library.
- The item, because of discovered rarity or value, belongs in a closed, controlled environment.

b. Automatic Serial Updating

The Serials Coordinator shall be responsible for maintaining information in the serials files relative to the handling and disposition of serial reference items and for the automatic replacement and disposal of superseded reference serial items as agreed to by the Serials Coordinator and the chair of the Reference Services Committee.

c. Disposition of Weeded Items

The withdrawal of any items from the reference collection should not be finalized without common agreement among all personnel who work at the position of an item withdrawn from the reference collection should likewise be carried out in accordance with the common agreement of all reference desk personnel. Items, upon withdrawal from reference, shall be routed to technical services, each item with a note indicating the desired action to be taken.

University of West Georgia
Irvine Sullivan Ingram Library
Carrollton, Georgia

Weeding

With careful adherence to the Selection Criteria for the Reference Collection, extensive weeding of the reference collection should be unnecessary. However, library liaisons should evaluate their subject areas yearly to ensure the continued usefulness of the reference collection. General reference materials should be evaluated by the reference librarian annually. Materials which are duplicates, out of date, incomplete, superseded, in poor condition, of greater use in the circulating collection, or in subject areas that are not vital to Reference will be considered for weeding and/or relocation to the circulating collection.

5.3 Archiving and Preservation

University College London
London, England

Preservation policy

1. Introduction

UCL Library Services is the guardian of the written and documentary heritage it houses for the use of present and future generations and takes its responsibilities for preservation very seriously, recognising that it has a duty of care out of respect to the past and in anticipation of the future. This statement of preservation policy sets out what it will do to achieve its duty of preservation—its duty to the future—while maintaining and promoting access—its duty to the present.

According to the National Preservation Office

Libraries and archives contain an irreplaceable accumulation of human knowledge and experience. The written and documentary heritage which they house provides the raw material that allows us to try and understand, explain, order and enjoy the visible and invisible world. Access to the past enables us to understand and locate ourselves in the present and gives us the opportunity to inform the future... in preserving our shared past we are preserving the collective memory for future generations.

UCL Library Services maintains its collections in a usable condition to support the teaching and research of UCL, and, as appropriate, to contribute to national preservation efforts. As a member of CURL, the Consortium of University Research Libraries, UCL Library Services has a responsibility to the community of research libraries and their users to identify and preserve its unique materials and collection strengths.

Preservation and conservation are two interwoven functions. It is the considered planning of these two functions which defines this policy.

1.1 Definitions

For the purposes of this policy, UCL Library Services has adopted the following definitions of preservation and conservation:

1.1.1 Definition of preservation

A broader term than conservation. It includes all managerial and financial considerations including storage and accommodation provision, staffing levels, policies, techniques, and methods involved in preserving library and archive materials and the information contained therein.

1.1.2 Definition of conservation

'Conservation' is taken as direct intervention to prevent/make good damage to materials.

1.2 Mission statement of UCL Library Services

Library Services is committed to supporting excellence in learning, teaching and research for all its members. Specifically, Library Services intends:

- To improve yet further its support for learning and teaching through its collecting activities
- To note the research needs of academics and students in UCL and to identify the most appropriate way to meet these needs
- Through its membership of the Education & Information Support Division, to initiate collaborations on new modes of learning and teaching, and to support research
- As a library of national and international standing, to open up access to its collections for research to all with a need to use the material

1.3 Description of the collections

The collections in UCL Library Services date back to the fourth century AD and form one of the principal academic assets of the College. In terms of books, periodicals and manuscripts, Library Services has very strong collections in many areas. UCL is a 'holding' library and forms one of the main collections of academic material in London and the UK. It houses the libraries of a number of national societies, which have been deposited in UCL, and makes its collections available to anyone with a need to use the materials for research from anywhere in the UK and beyond.

In certain areas, UCL's collections are of national and international significance. In archaeology, UCL has one of the finest collections in the country and its collecting activities are of European importance. The same is true of Jewish Studies, where a partnership between UCL's academic department and Library Services has led to the creation of collections of European significance. The collections in Scandinavian Studies and Dutch are undoubtedly of European stature, and Library Services receives monies from the respective national governments to develop the collections and to open up access to these cultural jewels. Another collection of European significance is that of the School of Slavonic and East European Studies (SSEES), now merged with UCL. This library collection is of international importance, particularly in the field of Russian, Slavonic and East European Studies.

Manuscripts, archives and rare book collections in UCL Library date from the medieval period to the present day and cover a wide range of subject areas. Acquired mainly by bequest and donation since the College's foundation in 1826 as the original University of London, UCL's collections reflect both the traditions and changes in its history. Highlights include the C.K. Ogden and Graves Libraries of rare books, incunabula and medieval manuscripts, rich in the fields of science, language and literature; 19th century collections, notably Jeremy Bentham's manuscripts and the papers of Lord Brougham, with strengths in social, political, legal and educational reform, as well as professorial collections with particular strengths in medical and scientific innovation; 20th century literary collections, notably the Orwell Archive and the Little Magazines and Poetry Store collections of underground and private press material.

Full collection level descriptions of the special collections can be found on the Library's web pages at http://www.ucl.ac.uk/Library/.

2. Strategic objectives for the preservation of the collection

UCL Library Services will ensure that the management of its collections, their security, safe housing, documentation and care are sufficient to meet the requirements of the collections and their users according to agreed priorities and responsibilities.

UCL Library Services's obligations towards preservation are as follows:

- To store material in conditions which meet current, professionally approved standards and to maintain those conditions. Account will be taken of the physical nature and condition, intrinsic value and use of the material, and of the binding, boxing and packaging needed
- To do everything possible to minimise damage from use, promoting good practice in handling
- To provide means of access to the originals in ways which minimise the risk from handling
- To provide suitable equipment to protect the originals while in use, e.g. book-rests
- To maintain agreed standards of preservation throughout Library Services
- To train and develop staff appropriately in preservation techniques
- To provide surrogates where current or anticipated high demand, or poor condition, or both, make the originals unsuitable for production
- To undertake conservation work on documents which are deemed to have particular priority (e.g. intrinsic worth, exceptional historic, symbolic or physical value or interest)
- To withdraw documents from public access if they are deemed to be at serious risk: these can then be assessed for inclusion in a prioritised published conservation programme
- To keep technical developments in the preservation and conservation fields under review; to utilise those which are suitable and incorporate them into the strategy to provide added benefits and more cost effective operations
- To promote and encourage good practice in records management
- To improve physical access by refining and making more accurate the means of identifying particular documents
- To promote the use of materials which are suitable for long-term preservation
- To promote best practice amongst staff and readers in seeking to ensure the security of the material which has been selected for permanent preservation

3. Needs assessment

Statistically valid condition surveys will be carried out from time to time to assess the general physical condition of the collections thereby quantifying needs and providing the basis for more precise conservation planning, including cost projections.

4. Retention statement

Library Services recognises that preservation decisions will be determined by the format and the purpose of acquisitions and that retention is directly linked to preservation. The Library has a Collection Development Policy, written in 1991, which is currently being revised. It will be replaced by an integrated Collection Management Policy covering all aspects of acquisition, retention, relegation and preservation across the Library. This document is currently being drawn up by Subject Librarians in collaboration where appropriate with special collections staff.

5. Security statement

Security measures for the prevention of theft and vandalism to the collections are of the highest priority for the Library. All permanent and temporary storage areas must be safe and secure so as to minimise the risk of theft or malicious damage to collections.

Exit alarms are installed on all Library Services sites, and all stock added to the open-shelf collections bears electronic triggers to help deter theft. There is an established policy for dealing with those who try to remove materials which have not been issued to them. Access control systems are already installed on three sites, and access control will be extended in 2002. This ensures that only those who have a right to be in the Library enter the building, and helps to prevent random vandalism. Access to stores and special collections is carefully controlled. Access points are fitted with strong doors and sound locking systems, protected by intruder alarms and CCTV.

The security of special collections materials themselves when away from the storage areas is covered by strict procedures governing their handling and use by staff as well as readers.

6. Premises and storage

A large proportion of material in the open-shelf collections is intended to support current teaching and basic research. The temperature in the reading rooms is geared towards the comfort of readers rather than the long-term preservation of stock, but much of the open-access stock is not intended for permanent preservation.

The storage areas for special collections are air conditioned, with computerised monitoring of relative humidity and temperature levels. The atmosphere in key storage areas is monitored regularly, so that proper records may be kept, and is directly linked to UCL Estates & Facilities Maintenance Section so that remedial action can be taken immediately in case of malfunction or breakdown of the air-conditioning equipment. The relative humidity level is currently set at 52% (+/- 5 %) and the temperature level is set at 16 degrees Celsius. It is aimed to improve this to BS5454:2000 standards in new accommodation. One of the principal strategic decisions outlined in the Library Estates Strategy of October 1999 is to move the Special Collections to more suitable accommodation and improve storage and reading room provision for research collections in Jewish Studies, Dutch and Scandinavian Studies.

Materials which are not rare enough to be incorporated in the special collections but which are not required for current teaching and research will be stored in the Library's off-site store at Wickford, Essex. They will be brought back to the main sites when requested. Increasingly, electronic copies of journal articles will be transmitted back to the main sites, easing the risk of wear and tear on the originals from repeated van journeys to and fro.

7. Handling library materials

Instruction is regularly given to library staff in handling materials. There are detailed guidelines on handling materials for readers of Special Collections.

7.1 Photocopying of library and archive materials

Library Services photocopying policy has been developed using the National Preservation Office's benchmarks

Readers should not photocopy the following material:

- Fragile or damaged items
- Tightly bound volumes
- Manuscripts and archives
- Rare books or photographs
- Books published before 1850
- Oversize items that would have to be excessively manipulated to obtain a complete image

8. Preventative preservation balanced with active conservation

UCL Library Services recognises that preventative preservation of the collection as a whole is the most effective means of conserving its cultural material. Preventative preservation techniques for the collection as a whole will in general be put in place before treatment of individual items.

9. Selection for conservation

- Materials are selected for conservation according to the following priorities:
- The objectives of Library Services
- Library Services retention policy
- The significance/value/rarity of the material
- The amount and kind of usage
- The physical condition of the material

Within the limits of the budget, journals which are not held in electronic format are bound. Microforms of back issues of newspapers required for specialist collections are bought whenever they are commercially available. Newspapers purchased for current awareness are not retained permanently in the general collections, but readers are encouraged to refer to the electronic backfile.

10. Substitution policy

Where appropriate, material will be selected for reformatting as microfilm and/or digitally scanned files to limit unnecessary handling of originals and to facilitate access. Readers are encouraged to use surrogates where the originals are so fragile that using them will cause further damage.

11. Budgeting for preservation

A separate budget heading has been introduced into the Library Services budget from 99/00 onwards for preservation. Additionally, external funding and sponsorship will be sought to support the Library's own efforts to conserve selected library materials.

12. Education and training

Preservation is the concern of all staff and all users of the library: training of both staff and users in how to handle library and archival materials is central to resolving the perceived conflict between preservation and access.

All new library staff are trained in basic book handling techniques as part of their induction programme and preservation training is part of Library Services's rolling training programme.

13. Risk assessment

Risks to the collections can be classified as follows:
- Natural Routine Risks: Relative humidity, temperature, light, pollution, pests
- Natural Extreme Risks: Fire, flood, earthquake
- Man-made Routine Risks: Handling, wear and tear
- Man-made Extreme Risks: War, civil unrest, vandalism

The management of risk takes into account the local context of the library buildings which are in central London, with high levels of air pollution and traffic noise.

14. Pest management

Storage areas and collections are cleaned on a regular basis and checks made for possible infestation by harmful rodents and insects. When infestation is detected, pest control is alerted to eradicate the problem. Materials least attractive to such pests are chosen for furnishings wherever possible.

15. Disaster control

If Library Services is to safeguard its collections adequately, it must have effective procedures in place to prevent, or enable it to react swiftly to, sudden, unexpected events which could have destructive consequences for all or part of its holdings (e.g. floods, fires, bomb attacks, theft). There is currently a disaster plan which is due for revision using the template provided by the M25 Consortium of Higher Education Libraries.

Library Services central sites have a weekend/holidays disaster cover rota. Staff on this rota are trained in basic disaster recovery procedures.

5.4 Forms: Reconsideration/Challenge Requests

Tempe Public Library
Tempe, Arizona

TEMPE PUBLIC LIBRARY
REQUEST FOR RECONSIDERATION OF LIBRARY RESOURCES

Date _____

Name_____

Address_____

City State_____ Zip Code_____

Phone #_____

Library Card Number _____

Do you represent self? _____ Organization? (Please indicate name)_____

_____

1. Resource on which you are commenting:

Book_____Video_____ or DVD___Audiorecording _____Electronic Information_____

Magazine_____ Content of Library Program_____Newspaper_____Other_____

Title_____

Author/Producer_____

2. What brought this resource to your attention?

3. Have you examined the entire resource?

4. What concerns you about the resource? (Use other side or additional page if needed.)

5. Are there resources you suggest to provide additional information and/or viewpoints on this topic?

Lawrence Public Library
Lawrence, Kansas

Request for Reconsideration of Library Materials
Format: ( ) book ( ) periodical ( ) other
Title:
Author: Publisher:
Request Initiated by:
Address: City:
State: Zip Code:
Telephone: Day: Home:

Do you represent: ( ) yourself ( ) organization ( ) other group

1. To what in the work do you object? (please be specific. Cite pages.)

2. Did you complete the entire work? What parts?

3. What do you feel might be the result of exposure to this work?

4. For what age group would you recommend this work?

5. What do you believe is the theme of this work?

6. Are you aware of judgments of this work by reviewers? (Please cite reviews)

7. What would you like the Library to do about this work?

8. Is there anything good about this work?

9. What would you recommend as a replacement for this work?

This form must be signed.

Spokane Public Library
Spokane, Washington

The Board of Trustees of the Spokane Public Library has delegated the responsibility for selection and evaluation of library resources to the Library Director and has established reconsideration procedures to address concerns, from city residents, about these resources. Completion of this form is the first step in these procedures. If you which to request review of a library resource complete this form and return it to the reference desk at your nearest Spokane Public Library or mail to: Spokane Public Library, attention

Customer Name _____ Date _____

Address_____

City _____ State _____ Zip _____ Phone _____

Are you a resident of the City of Spokane? _____Yes ____No

1. Resource on which you are commenting:

___Book
___Videocassette
___Music CD
___Magazine
___DVD
___Audio Book
___Newspaper
___Computer Software
___Other

Title_____

Author/Artist/Producer_____

2. What brought this resource to your attention?

_____

_____

3. Have you examined the entire resource? _____Yes ____No

4. What concerns you about the resource (use other side if necessary)?

_____

_____

_____

5. Are there resources you suggest to provide additional information and/or other viewpoints on this topic?

_____

_____

Signature:_____

Brownwood Public Library
Brownwood, Texas

Request for Reconsideration

Name of complaining party:_____

Name of organization you are representing:_____

If a member of an organization, what is your title?_____

Name/author of work for which reconsideration is requested:

_____

Copyright year and publisher of work at issue_____

Have you read or listened to the entire work? Yes No

If so, when did you read/listen to the work? (date)_____

Please give page numbers of what you feel is offensive (please feel free to append

additional pages as needed):_____

_____

Please give a brief summary entailing all salient characteristics in the work that contravene the Selection Policy, and if there is some way in which the work could be rendered appropriate (Please feel free to append additional pages as necessary):

I, the Undersigned, understand that failure to fill out this form in its entirety, placing "N/A" where a particular line is not applicable, may forfeit reconsideration of this work. Further, I understand that while my concerns are important to the Brownwood Public Library, that this form in no way constitutes an obligation on the part of said Library to implement the changes desired by me, the Undersigned.

_____ /_____

Signature /Date

Chapter 6

ELECTRONIC RESOURCES POLICIES

SELECTION AND EVALUATION

6.1 General Guidelines

University of Louisville
Kornhauser Health Sciences Library
Louisville, Kentucky

C. Selection Criteria

   1. Primary Criteria

      Primary criteria for selection of electronic resources are no different than those for selection of traditional library materials. Relevance, demand, content, scope, organization, quality, currency and timeliness should provide the initial screening criteria. However, electronic materials must also meet standards set in the list of secondary criteria below.

   2. Secondary Criteria

     a. Access/Networking Capabilities

     Resources available to many users simultaneously are to be preferred over single-user systems. Preference will be given to products accessible on any university campus and the computers of authorized users at remote sites.

     Access to remotely loaded resources through vendor or consortium sites must be considered in terms of: performance of the system at peak loads; performance of the Internet in retrieving files, printing documents, and speed at peak times; and, the need to deploy client software on the local desktop computers. Products that require no locally loaded client software are to be preferred.

     b. Systems and Technical Support

     Library systems staff must be able to provide assistance and troubleshoot problems with software. Both user and operational support must be considered. If the Library's systems staff are unable to provide such support, the company providing the software must have a help-line available to answer questions. The quality of the technical support from the vendor and their responsiveness to problems must also be evaluated if possible.

c. Simultaneous Users

The number of simultaneous users supported by the system must be sufficient to meet the of the Medical Center/University community. The cost per simultaneous user should be considered in terms of the value of the content and fees charged for similar databases or resources.

d. Licensing

The licensing agreement or contract must be carefully reviewed to ensure that the Library maintains its rights for "fair use" and the resource is accessible to all University faculty, staff, and students.

The contract should stipulate the University of Louisville and not just Health Sciences Center faculty, staff and students if possible.

Non-contiguous/non-adjacent campus sites should be covered as well as the main campus areas.

The license should permit normal Library functions including providing reference services, interlibrary loans, and internal photocopy services.

Restrictions on access through passwords, IP addresses or other means should be evaluated in terms of: how cumbersome it will be for key clientele to access the service; whether access from public workstations is permitted; the difficulty in complying with or policing the restrictions; and, the amount of staff time required to manage the system for restricting access. Some questions to consider are: Are passwords required for each user? Is access from public terminals allowed? How many IP addresses can be used?

Whenever possible, the Principles For Licensing Electronic Resources established by AALL, ALA, AAHSL, ARL, MLA and SLA should be followed when reviewing licensing agreements. (Available at http://www.arl.org/scomm/licensing/principles.html.)

e. Software Requirements

Preference should be given to resources that require no special software (other than what is currently "standard", i.e. a web browser, Adobe Acrobat, to be loaded on users' computers.) Special software required on each patron's desktop must be evaluated in terms of ease of use, distribution, installation, and maintenance. Consideration must be given to staff time and methods for installing and maintaining the software on each desktop unit.

f. Training and Educational Support

Handouts, manuals and other instructional information should be reviewed. It should be determined if additional materials will need to be created or if special education programs will be required for staff and patrons. An estimate of the amount of time to learn and teach the system should be made.

g. Cost

The price of an electronic resource is considered in relation to the primary criteria but it is not the sole factor for determining the appropriateness of a title for the collection. Equipment requirements and costs, as well as licensing fees must be considered in addition to the purchase price of the product.

Vendor pricing formulas based on the number of users, networks, buildings, etc. must also be considered. The formula should be based on logical criteria, which meet the needs of the institution.

h. Duplication

From 1999 until 2003 the preference of the library will be to retain previously owned printed materials despite the acquisition of an electronic version. This paragraph may be removed from the policy if circumstances dictate.

If cancellation or discard of an existing paper resource in favor of an electronic replacement is being considered the following archival considerations must be taken into account.

i. Guarantees in the license agreement that electronic archival copies will be available to the library in perpetuity or

ii. Guarantees in the license agreement that the library may procure and retain electronic copies of the product.

When number one above is satisfied by the existence of a copy of the resource held in escrow it is imperative that agreements with the provider specify how continued readability, in light of changing technology, will be maintained.

6.2 Internet Resources

Saint Paul Public Library
Saint Paul, Minnesota

Web Site Selection Criteria

When selecting web sites and internet resources for the library's web links, the Saint Paul Public Library considers the source of the information being presented, the content of the information resource, the cost of obtaining the information and the presentation of the information on users' computer screens. These are general considerations; no one criterion should necessarily be used to override an otherwise useful web site or internet resource.

Source

Authorship - Credibility - Authority

In a medium where just about anyone can make information available, it is important to know who are the creators of a web site and what are their motivations for posting the information.

General considerations in this area should include:

Individuals or groups creating or sponsoring the site should be clearly stated or otherwise readily ascertained.

Consider the authority and/or level of expertise of the author(s) of a web site. What are their credentials? Can they be easily verified?

Top-level domains (.com, .gov, .edu, .org, etc.) can indicate the origin and intent of a web site, but sites should be judged on other criteria, too (In other words, not all .edu sites are good and not all .com sites are bad).

Do the creators/managers of the site offer some way of making contact with them for further information?

If a site knowingly violates copyright statues or other laws, it should not be linked.

Content

Accuracy - Bias - Currency

Just as the library considers the accuracy, bias, currency and overall quality of the content of traditional materials (i.e. books) for inclusion in its collection, web sites to be offered as a collection of links offered by the library to its customers should be carefully examined. As with traditional resources, review sources such as the Internet Scout Report or articles from the professional library literature can be helpful. However, the environment of the web is such that we can examine resources on the web first-hand before deciding to direct our customers to the web site. This is a considerable advantage the library does not often have with traditional resources.

Some general considerations regarding web site content include:

The site should be easily read and understandable by its intended audience.

The site should offer enough information to make linking to it worthwhile for the library's customers.

Large web sites should make some sort of search function or site index available for users to find what they are looking for on the site.

Spelling and grammar should be correct.

The information on the site should be accurate (as far as we can tell).

The information on the site should be free of bias.

Some web sites are little more than advertisements for other goods and services.

Before linking to a site, it should be considered whether the site is more of an ad than an informational source. If a site that is mostly an advertisement is the best source of information to which the library would like to link, our annotation should let customers know of the web site's primary purpose.

The information on the web site should be current. The site should be kept current, regularly updated and maintained. Links within and from the site should also be current. Exceptions should be made for archive sites that are specifically designated as such, although links to sites outside of the archive are likely to go out of date.

Cost

The library should not link to any sites that cost money to access or use.

Sites that require free registration to access the majority of their content should be avoided, but linked to if they provided high-quality information. In the annotation we will let customers know that registration may be required.

An understandable exception to this rule is linking to relevant databases to which the Saint Paul Public Library already subscribes. Links to these databases should be annotated like a web site and include a statement that they are available only from within the library and/or via remote access (with a link to the remote access instruction pages, where appropriate).

Presentation

Design – Structure – Stability – Interface

Besides authority and content, the presentation of a web site should be considered, given some of the technical necessities (monitor, Internet connection, processing speed, etc.) in accessing web sites.

The layout and design of pages is also important to consider when evaluating web site presentation.

General points to consider regarding presentation include:

Pages should load in a reasonable amount of time (consider the users who are using dial-up connections).

Pages on the site should be easy to read and to understand, with an appropriate design for its intended audience. Pages should be readable with regard to background colors, images, font styles and sizes, and text colors.

The layout and organization of pages should likewise be in done in a useful manner, easy to read and to understand.

Design elements of a site should enhance the information being offered, and not hinder the use of the site (e.g. long waits for graphics to download).

Plug-ins and other helper applications should be clearly identified, and visitors should be linked to pages where such applications can be downloaded if necessary. If the use of such a helper application is crucial to the site, we should try to state such in our annotation.

Clear navigation tools and/or instructions are desirable features.

Other presentation considerations include the use of standard HTML formatting and codes, and the accessibility of the web site to users of a variety of browsers, including those for the disabled. These are harder points to pin down, but some deviations from standards may be readily apparent. If the pages of a site do not appear to display correctly or cause some sort of web browser malfunction, the site should not be linked.

Milwaukee Public Library
Milwaukee, Wisconsin

The selection of Web sites is to be consistent with the overall goals of providing accurate and timely information to all library customers.

Scope

The Milwaukee Public Library (MPL) supports a Wide Area Network (WAN) connecting its Central Library and 12 neighborhood libraries. Web sites complement the other electronic and print reference resources in MPL's collection.

Selection Process

The selection of Web sites is the responsibility of the Electronic Reference Services Committee. The Committee may consult with the Coordinator of Technical Services and the appropriate Coordinators of the Subject Services or the Children's Coordinator before adding sites. Web sites are reviewed based on the criteria listed below:

> Accuracy
> Appropriateness
> Arrangement
> Authority
> Comparability with existing reference sources
> Completeness
> Content/Reference value
> Cost
> Currency
> Distinction
> Documentation
> Ease-of-use
> Graphics
> Level

Registration requirements
> Reliability
> Representation
> Searchability
> Technical considerations
> Uniqueness

Retention and Weeding

Web site links are checked and updated periodically. Only the current copy of the web page is available.

Children and Young Adult Web Pages

The Milwaukee Public Library Children's web pages are developed for all children in the city of Milwaukee ages 0–14 years old and the adults that care for them to meet their diverse informational and recreational needs.

The Milwaukee Public Library Teen web pages are developed for all children in the city of Milwaukee ages 13–19 years old to meet their informational and recreational needs.

Please note that some of these web links are not produced by the Milwaukee Public Library. The content of all web links is checked periodically, but content can change rapidly. If you see something that's inappropriate, let us know.

University of Oregon
University of Oregon Libraries
Eugene, Oregon

> Purpose
> Scope
> Access and Location
> General Selection Principles
> Copyright
> Provision of Access
> Duplication
> Deselection
> Policy Review

Internet Resources

I. Purpose

The University of Oregon Libraries supports the instructional and research programs of the University. Toward this aim, the Library collects or provides access to materials in multiple formats, including electronic formats. One important electronic resource, the Internet, is readily available to any library users with access to the World Wide Web. However, while the Internet is easily accessible, the Library recognizes that careful selection of Internet resources and availability of these through the Library's catalog will accomplish several objectives: 1) increase awareness and maximize use of significant sites; 2) provide value-added access to Internet resources often absent when using various search engines to locate resources; and 3) enhance and expand the Library's collection of traditional formats.

II. Scope

This policy will guide the selection of Internet resources, primarily those that are monographic in nature. The phrase, "monographic in nature," refers to Internet resources that are specific documents or bibliographic and numeric files rather than entire collections of resources such as Web or gopher servers. While there are several useful search engines for searching the Internet, focusing on individual titles emphasizes the important contributions that subject specialists make to providing access to Internet resources. This policy also does not address either online bibliographic and full-text databases or electronic serials. Collection development policies and procedures for online bibliographic and full-text databases and electronic serials will address the selection, acquisition, and provision of access for these resources.

III. Access and Location

Records for selected resources will show in Janus, ORBIS, and OCLC. In addition to descriptive and subject cataloging, these records will provide the necessary URLs for locating the resources on the Internet. Eventually III's Web interface to ORBIS and Janus will make it possible to click on URLs from the union catalog and gain access to these resources. Though selected Internet resources will be accessible through the catalog like other materials in the Library's collections, given the nature of their format, the Library does not physically house these resources. Inclusion of a resource in the Library's holding does not preclude it from being linked or located via a subject specialist's homepage.

IV. General Selection Principles

Selection Responsibility: Responsibility for selecting these materials falls to individual subject specialists and the head of collection development as these materials fall into their regular selecting responsibility. Other librarians, library users, and other individuals will offer suggestions to appropriate subject specialists or the head of collection development.

Funding: Collection Development will encourage subject specialists to select Internet resources which are free of charge. Selection of free Internet resources will bypass the usual routing of orders through the Acquisitions Department. This situation will foreseeably change as more commercial resources become available via the Internet. At present and in the future, when funding is necessary, the subject content will determine the individual fund. Subject specialists and the head of collection development will determine the appropriate individual funds to use for purchasing Internet resources. As with all other formats, the Library will consider other allocations for those titles deemed major purchases. The Library will also consider trial periods.

Adherence to Other Collection Development Guidelines: The selection of Internet resources should follow present collecting policies, both general and subject specific policies. Specifically their selection should adhere closely to the chronological, geographical, language, and date of publication guidelines set forth in general or subject specific policies. As with other materials subject specialists should also 1) consider present curriculum and research needs, 2) select materials which meet the standards the Library expects of all materials in regard to excellence, comprehensiveness, and authoritativeness, and 3) weigh the selection of a particular fee-based title against other possible acquisitions from material budgets.

Specific Format Criteria: In addition to content, subject specialists should closely consider the criteria listed below when considering the purchase of Internet resources.

- the improvement or enhancement that the resource will give to existing print materials
- the broad accessibility of the resource under present copyright laws and licensing agreements
- the compatibility of the resource with existing hardware about to be purchased or already in the Library and hardware on the University of Oregon campus
- the currency and relevancy of the resource's information, if deemed necessary for subject matter
- the user-friendliness of the resource

When possible, it is helpful to consult available reviews of Internet resources before their selection. Reviews can outline how well a resource meets specific criteria and can provide further insight regarding the resource's overall quality. Subject specialists should not necessarily exclude a title because it does not meet every individual criterion. However, subject specialists should attempt to select resources that adequately meet as many of the selection criteria as is possible.

Selection Tools: In addition to searching the Internet via various search engines, subject specialists may consult several sources for current reviews of Internet resources. These sources of selection, which do not constitute comprehensive coverage, include CRL News' regular feature on Internet resources geared for specific subjects, the column "Net Sightings, " featured in Database and Online, respectively, and the column "Internet Librarian," in American Libraries.

V. Copyright

The Library will comply with the existing copyright laws. The Library will also promote copyright compliance among its users and among its staff.

VI. Licensing

When applicable to Internet resources, the Library will negotiate and comply with vendor licensing agreements. Because this format increases the complexity of licensing agreements, subject specialists should inform the Head of Collection Development about Internet resources requiring a licensing agreement prior to selecting that resource.

VII. Provision of Access

The Library will maximize access to Internet resources through several means:

> cataloging of each resource
> regular updating of records when information, particularly the site's URL, changes;
> provision, maintenance, preparation, and loading of necessary software and hardware;
> appropriate staff and user support and training for in-building use

VIII. Duplication

Selecting an Internet resource that duplicates an existing print resource usually constitutes acceptable duplication because the site probably will incur no fee and a site's selection provides greater access than the single use point that a print resource may provide. The Library will duplicate print resources with fee-based Internet resources when:

> the resource has significant historical value
> one format is unstable
> a cost benefit for purchasing multiple formats exists
> multiple formats meet the different needs of user groups

IX. Deselection

Different subject areas obviously require different applications of generally accepted deselection principles. Nevertheless, ongoing deselection of Internet resources is a necessity because of the dynamic nature of such resources. These guidelines should provide some suggestions for when to deselect a resource:

1) an Internet resource is no longer available or maintained;
2) the currency and reliability of the resource's information has lost its value;
3) another Internet site or resource offers more comprehensive coverage.

X. Policy Review

Because of the complex and dynamic nature of providing access to Internet resources, the head of Collection Development and other librarians will need to review this policy regularly.

University of Wyoming
Coe Library
Laramie, Wyoming

Resources

I. Purpose

The University of Wyoming Libraries support the instructional and research programs of the University. Toward this aim, the Libraries collect or provide access to materials in multiple formats, including electronic formats available over the Internet. The challenges in providing access to electronic resources warrant a separate collection development policy focusing on their selection, acquisition, and provision of access.

II. Scope

This policy seeks to address the selection and acquisition of electronic resources accessible via the Internet, including:

- Electronic serials or collections of serials;
- Online bibliographic or numeric databases;
- Electronic reference tools, such as encyclopedias, directories, etc.; and
- Electronic monographs or collections of monographs.

This policy covers electronic resources for which the Libraries gain free access, access at a reduced rate because the Libraries subscribe to the print, or purchase access to an electronic-only version.

The Libraries will pursue the purchase of other types of resources as these develop in the future and meet the guidelines outlined herein. This policy also does not address offline electronic resources, such as CD-ROMs or microcomputer software, which are covered in other collection development policies.

III. Principal Access Point and Provision of Access

The inability of Libraries' current Public Access Catalog to provide embedded hot links means that, while the resources may be cataloged, the Libraries will provide access to electronic resources which it acquires and/or licenses via the Libraries' Web pages. The Libraries will maximize access to the Libraries' electronic resources through several means: cataloging of resources; necessary archiving and/or storage; provision, maintenance, preparation, and loading of necessary software and hardware; and appropriate staff and user support and training for optimal use. Additionally, subject bibliographers or branch libraries and collections may wish to provide links to these resources via appropriate Web pages.

IV. General Selection Principles

A. Selection Responsibility: Responsibility for selecting these materials falls to individual subject bibliographers and the Collection Development Officer as these materials fall into their regular selecting responsibilities. Other librarians and library users may suggest titles to appropriate subject bibliographers or the Collection Development Officer.

B. Funding: Many Internet resources are available free, though this situation will likely change over time. When purchase is necessary, the subject content will determine the individual fund.

Subject bibliographers and the Collection Development Officer will determine the appropriate individual funds to use for purchasing electronic resources. As with all other formats, the Libraries will consider other allocations for those titles deemed major purchases. The Libraries will also consider trial periods, though the requesting bibliographer should consider the extent to which the public should be encouraged to use a trial resource.

C. Adherence to Other Collection Development Guidelines: The purchase of electronic resources should follow present collecting policies whether general or subject specific. Specifically, their purchase should adhere to the chronological, geographical, language, and date of publication guidelines set forth in general or subject specific policies. As with other materials subject bibliographers should also:

- consider present curriculum and research needs,
- select materials which meet the standards the Libraries expect of all materials in regard to excellence, comprehensiveness, and authority,
- weigh the purchase of a particular title against other possible acquisitions from collection development budgets, and
- should not order or arrange trial uses of electronic resources but have Acquisitions do so.

D. Trial Uses of Internet Resources: The best way to evaluate Internet resources is to have staff and patrons use them. Such trials or pilot tests should be arranged by filling out a Request for Internet-Based Electronic Resources (a Word fill-in form is available in the Forms folder of Subject Bibliographer Stuff, distinguished by "L") and submitting it to the Collection Development Office. Once the Office is aware of the trial, the form will be sent to the Acquisitions Department, so that the Libraries adhere to vendor restrictions and time limits. The requesting bibliographer should inform colleagues and promote the trial to appropriate departments. At the end of the trial, the requesting bibliographer may propose purchase, subscription, or continuing use of a free resource by filling out another Request for Internet-Based Electronic Resources.

Trials are not required for electronic versions of current subscriptions; see special instructions in the section, "Internet-Based Versions of Print Subscriptions" (IV., F. below).

E. Specific Format Criteria: In addition to content, subject bibliographers should consider the following criteria in acquiring electronic resources:

- The improvement or enhancement that the resource will give to existing print materials.
- The compatibility of the resource with existing hardware in the Libraries and on the University of Wyoming campus. (Questions about compatibility should be referred to Library Technology Support.)
- The broad accessibility of the resource under present copyright laws and licensing agreements.
- The currency and relevancy of the resource's information, if deemed necessary for subject matter.
- The user-friendliness and flexibility of the resource.
- The necessity of archiving and/or availability of archives.

- IP limiting is the preferred method of controlling access. Given a choice of IP limits, Class B (UW in general) is preferred, Class C (specific UW buildings) is acceptable in rare circumstances, Class D (specific UW machines) is not acceptable.
- A title does not have to meet every individual criterion to be recommended. However, subject bibliographers should attempt to select resources that adequately meet as many of the selection criteria as is possible. Because this format increases the complexity of acquisition and access, subject bibliographers should fill out a Request for Internet-Based Electronic Resources when ordering electronic resources (as well as a Book Order Request Form or Serial Order Request Form, whichever is appropriate).

F. Internet-Based Versions of Print Subscriptions: A number of journal publishers are making electronic versions available for their print subscribers for free or for a small surcharge. Since the titles have already gone through the selection process, there is a shorter request form, Request of Internet-Based Versions of Print Subscriptions (or a Word fill-out form in Subject Bibliographer Stuff's Forms folder, distinguished by "S"), to arrange electronic access. Before completing this form, bibliographers should verify that the electronic version is complete (not just tables of contents) and what it costs.

V. Licensing

The Libraries will negotiate vendor licensing agreements in adherence the Principles for Licensing Electronic Resources (developed by The American Library Association (ALA), the Association of Research Libraries (ARL), and other library organizations). ARL also developed a practical guide, Licensing Electronic Resources, which provides basic questions to be answered before licensing products. In general, the Libraries have the following preferences for licensed electronic resources:

Electronic content should cost less than its print analog, unless there is substantial added value.

Costs for print and electronic formats should be separated and the Libraries should not have to purchase both.

Content and access costs should be separated. The Libraries should have flexibility in selecting appropriate access mechanisms (including local or remote server, resource sharing arrangements, etc.)

The purchasing power of UW's collections budget is declining; information providers should recognize this reality and control both initial costs and inflationary increases.

The Libraries prefer pricing based on the size of the actual community which will use the electronic information, or the actual recorded use (either unlimited simultaneous use or transaction-based licensing) as opposed to pricing based on the size of the total UW population.

The license should include permanent rights to information that has been paid for, in the event that a licensed database is subsequently cancelled or removed.

Information providers should employ a standard agreement that describes the rights of libraries and their authorized users in terms that are readable and explicit, and they should reflect realistic expectations concerning UW's ability to monitor use and discover abuse. Agreements should contain consistent business and legal provisions, including, for example, indemnification against third-party copyright infringement liability and permission to use records in personal bibliographic systems.

As a public institution with a broad mandate to serve the State of Wyoming, UW's "authorized users" include faculty, staff, students and all on-site and off-site users of the University.

The licensed content, plus any associated features and capabilities, should be accessible from all institutionally-supported computing platforms and networked environments; this access must be based on current standards (e.g., Z39.50 compliant) in use by the library community.

Licenses should permit fair use of all information for non-commercial, education, instructional, and research purposes by authorized users, including unlimited viewing, downloading and printing.

Information providers should be able to link their access control mechanisms to UW's authentication infrastructure; access to their products should not require individual passwords and/or user IDs.

UW use data should be available to UW as part of contractual provisions for a license and the confidentiality of individual users and their searches must be full protected.

Data formats should follow industry standards and must be fully documented. Data should be platform-independent and available in multiple formats (e.g., ASCII, PDF, SGML, etc.).

UW must be able to provide access from convenient workstations connected to a network infrastructure which is reasonably fast. System capacity and bandwidth should be adequate to provide response time comparable to that of existing CARL system databases.

Information providers must keep UW informed of format and content changes and coordinate their implementation with UW.

Licenses should clearly state archival responsibilities of the provider and the Libraries.

The appended Request for Internet-Based Electronic Resources (or the Word fill-in form in Subject Bibliographer Stuff's Forms folder) gathers the basic details necessary for licensing negotiation and compliance; a copy of the standard licensing agreement, when available, should be attached to the form in order to order the Internet resource. New University regulations requires the University's Legal Affairs Office to review all license agreements before the Vice President for Finance will sign the agreement.

VII. Duplicate Formats

Ordinarily, the Libraries can seldom afford to duplicate resources in multiple formats. Possible justifications for duplicating electronic and print subscriptions or multiple electronic formats include:

- A cost benefit for purchasing multiple formats exists.
- Multiple formats meet the different needs of user groups.
- The archived format of a resource will not operate with current technology.

VIII. Weeding

Different subject areas obviously require different applications of generally accepted weeding principles. Nevertheless, ongoing weeding of Internet resources is a necessity because of the dynamic nature of such resources. These guidelines provide some suggestions for when to weed a resource:

- An Internet resource is no longer available or maintained.
- A resource has difficulties maintaining the currency and reliability of its information.
- Another Internet site or resource offers more comprehensive coverage.

Decisions to weed an Internet resource should include the following:

- communicate to the Libraries' web technician to remove from the Libraries' Web pages,
- submit a Serial Cancellation Form to the Collection Development Office, and
- submit a Withdrawal form to the Cataloging Department, if the resource has been cataloged.

IX. Policy Review

Because of the complex and dynamic nature of providing access to electronic resources, the Collection Development Officer, the subject bibliographers, and other librarians will need to review this policy at least every two years.

6.3 Offline Electronic Resources

University of Oregon
University of Oregon Libraries
Eugene, Oregon

Offline Electronic Resources

I. Purpose

The University of Oregon Libraries supports the instructional and research programs of the University. Toward this aim, the Library collects or provides access to materials in multiple formats, including electronic formats. The challenges to providing access to off-line electronic resources warrant a separate collection development policy focusing on these materials. This policy will provide guidelines for the selection and acquisition of off-line electronic resources as well as the provision of access. Related collection development documents will address procedural concerns in detail.

II. Scope

This policy seeks to address the selection and acquisition of off-line electronic resources, primarily those monographic titles available on CD-ROM or floppy disk. These resources may be:

- numeric data files
- textual files
- bibliographic files
- graphic and multimedia files
- courseware/instructional files
- software needed specifically to utilize resources listed above.

The Library will pursue the purchase of other types of resources as these develop in the future and meet the guidelines outlined herein. This policy also does not address the following electronic resources, which may fall into more than one of the following categories:

- online bibliographic or full-text databases
- Internet resources
- electronic journals or serials

Collection development policies for online resources and electronic journals will address the selection, acquisition, and provision of access for these resources.

III. Location

The Knight Library Instructional Technology Center (ITC) will be the central location of most of these resources as well as the central access provider. Other libraries and collections, such as Science, Maps, AAA, Math, Music, Reference, Law, and Government Documents, also house and provide access to off-line electronic resources, appropriate for their individual missions.

IV. Electronic Resources Accompanying Other Formats

Floppy disks and CD-ROMs may accompany other formats—monographs, serials, films, videos, or audio recordings. When possible, the Library will purchase and provide access to these materials in compliance with this policy's guidelines. If off-line electronic resources accompany other primary formats, they will be shelved together in the appropriate location. Procedures for handling electronic resources that accompany print formats are provided in greater detail in a related document, Accompanying Off-line Electronic Resources.

V. General Selection Principles

Selection Responsibility: Responsibility for selecting these materials falls to individual subject specialists and the head of collection development as these materials fall into their regular selecting responsibility. The coordinator for the ITC as well as library users and other individuals will offer suggestions to appropriate subject specialists or the head of Collection Development.

Funding: Ordinarily, the subject content will determine the individual fund. Subject specialists and the head of collection development will determine the appropriate individual funds to use for purchasing off-line electronic resources. As with all other formats, the Library will consider other allocations for those titles deemed major purchases.

Adherence to Other Collection Development Guidelines: The purchase of off-line electronic resources should follow present collecting policies whether general or subject specific policies. Specifically their purchase should adhere to the chronological, geographical, language, and date of publication guidelines set forth in general or subject specific policies. As with other materials subject specialists should also 1) consider present curriculum and research needs, 2) select materials which meet the standards the Library expects of all materials in regard to excellence, comprehensiveness, and authoritativeness, and 3) weigh the purchase of a particular title against other possible acquisitions from material budgets.

Specific Format Criteria: In addition to content, subject specialists should closely consider the criteria listed below when considering the purchase of off-line electronic resources.

- the necessary amount of staff time to provide access, training, and assistance

- the improvement or enhancement that the resource will give to existing print materials
- the long-term viability of resources for preservation purposes
- the long-term usability of a resource's data (10 years or more)
- the broad accessibility of the resource under present copyright laws and licensing agreements
- the compatibility of the resource with existing hardware about to be purchased or already in the Library and hardware on the University of Oregon campus
- the availability and adequacy of documentation
- the currency of the resource's information, if deemed necessary for subject matter
- the user-friendliness of the resource
- the ability to network the resource if deemed appropriate
- the replacement policy of the publisher in the event of damage or theft.

It is particularly important to consult available published reviews of off-line electronic resources before their acquisition. Reviews can outline how well a resource meets specific criteria and can provide further insight regarding the resource's overall quality. Subject specialists should not necessarily exclude a title because it does not meet every individual criterion. However, subject specialists should attempt to select resources that adequately meet as many of the selection criteria as is possible. Because this format increases the complexity of acquisition and access, subject specialists should include the detailed list of pre-order guidelines when ordering off-line electronic resources. A sample of this detailed list is appended to this policy.

Selection Tools: In addition to subject-oriented reviewing sources and Choice reviews, subject specialists may consult several sources for current reviews of off-line electronic resources and for general information about the technology. Titles held by the UO Libraries include:

> CD-ROM News Extra
> CD-ROM Professional
> "CD-ROM Review," a regular feature of Library Journal Database
> "Multimedia Reviews," a monthly feature of Publishers Weekly
> Online and CD-ROM Review.

VI. Copyright

The Library will comply with the existing copyright laws. The Library will also promote copyright compliance among its users and among its staff.

VII. Licensing

The Library will negotiate and comply with vendor licensing agreements. An appended list of pre-order guidelines outline the necessary details for this negotiation and compliance. Because this format increases the complexity of licensing agreements, subject specialists should include the detailed list of pre-order guidelines and the necessary licensing agreement, when available, with any order for off-line electronic resources prior to ordering the title.

VIII. Provision of Access

The Library will maximize access to the Library's off-line electronic resources through several means:

> cataloging of each resource
> necessary storage
> provision, maintenance, preparation, and loading of necessary software and hardware
> appropriate staff and user support and training for in-building use
> circulation of resources according to ITC circulation procedures.

IX. Gifts

The Library will evaluate and accept gifts of off-line resources that meet the specific format criteria identified herein and that adhere to other collection development guidelines, whether general or subject specific. Gifts of off-line electronic resources should also follow the Library's gifts policy.

X. Replacements

The Library will replace off-line electronic resources using the same criteria for other formats: demand for the resource, cost, and availability from publishers or vendors.

XI. Conversion of Outmoded Off-line Electronic Resources

Off-line electronic resources may operate on computer software and hardware that becomes outdated or obsolete while the resource's information remains valuable. In such cases, the Library will attempt to convert or update off-line electronic resources to a useable format. When conversion of outmoded electronic resources is possible, the Library may decide to convert after examining copyright and licensing of the product, demand for the resource, historical significance and uniqueness of the resource (including cost of the conversion), and availability of the information in another format.

XII. Duplicates

The Library will purchase duplicate copies of off-line electronic resources when demonstrated need and other restrictions indicate that networking or other options for providing access are not adequate or available. The Library also will purchase duplicates of electronic resources or purchase duplicates of print resources in electronic format when:

> the resource has significant historical value
> one format is unstable
> a cost benefit for purchasing multiple formats exists
> multiple formats meet the different needs of user groups
> the archived format of a resource will not operate with current technology.

XIII. Policy Review

Because of the complex and dynamic nature of providing access to off-line resources, the head of Collection Development, the coordinator for the Instructional Technology Center, and other librarians will need to review this policy at least every two years.

Southern Connecticut State University
Hilton C. Buley Library
New Haven, Connecticut

Electronic Collection Development Policy

The purpose of acquiring electronic resources is to support instruction and research within the SCSU community. The goal of electronic resource collection development is to reach and maintain a balance between representation of all disciplines and the special needs of individual departments. As CD-ROM products come up for renewal, they are replaced with web-based equivalents. Preference is given to web-based products over CD-ROMs because of their greater accessibility both on and off campus. Among products available on the web, products that accommodate IP authentication from any SCSU IP, including the proxy server for remote access, are given preference over those requiring special client software on PCs with static IPs, or username/password access, for the same reason.

Whenever possible, a trial is arranged for evaluation of the product. Although evaluation is primarily the responsibility of the appropriate subject selector, all reference librarians investigate products during trial periods.

Decisions to acquire, cancel, or transfer a product to a new vendor are made by the Electronic Resources Coordinator in conjunction with Reference librarians, and other appropriate Library faculty.

Mohawk Valley Community College
Mohawk Valley Libraries
Utica, New York

Electronic Resources

Definition

"Electronic resources" shall be understood to refer to categories of materials or services which require computer access, either through a microcomputer or a mainframe. Examples include CD-ROM products, machine-readable datafiles (both local and remote), Internet resources, interactive media, and electronic journals.

Selection criteria

Among the criteria to be considered in the purchase of electronic resources are:

    Relevance to the curricula
    Relevance to the College's needs
    Accessibility and format
    User-friendliness
    Frequency of updates
    Availability of equipment and memory required to support the product
    Impact of the product on the library system
    Degree of technical support required
    Product reliability
    Price
    Number of simultaneous users allowed
    Campuses' accessibility

Trials

If the library selector desires to evaluate a new electronic product on a trial basis prior to purchase, he or she may request this through the Acquisitions Department.

License Agreements

Copies of all licensing agreements will be maintained by the Library.

Continuations

The ever-changing technologies in the area of electronic resources demand an annual review of the appropriateness of the collection. Each subscription, licensing, and/or agreement will be made for not longer than one year.

6.4 Online Electronic Resources

Brandeis University
Brandeis University Libraries
Waltham, Massachusetts

Basic Guidelines

The intellectual content of the electronic resource, whether purchased or free, must fit within the established parameters of the Brandeis University Libraries' collection development policies, the judgment of the relevant subject bibliographers, and the Brandeis University curriculum.

The electronic resource will provide sufficient added value over other formats.

The search interface must be powerful, flexible, user-friendly, and well-indexed, with numerous points of access.

Whenever possible, access to the electronic resource must meet these goals:

- Support remote users of library and information resources
- Deliver reliable remote access
- Be available 24 hours a day, 7 days a week
- Utilize a unified and intuitive interface
- The cost of the resource must be sustainable by the electronic resources budget for the foreseeable future.
- The technology and staff to deliver and support the resource is available at Brandeis University Libraries.
- The Libraries will participate in a consortial purchase for a desired resource when the agreement provides a significant price advantage over the cost as an individual institution.

The Libraries will purchase available backfiles of an electronic resource if affordable and deemed bibliographically essential for the collection.

Ideally the vendor (or some other reliable source) provides for archival access to the data.

The Libraries will maintain the stability and consistency of electronic titles offered to the Brandeis community whenever possible.

Format

The Libraries prefer Web delivery over CD-ROM unless the Web version fails to meet the basic criteria for a search interface (see point 3) or the cost differential between the formats is significant enough to be a factor.

If CD-ROM is the choice of format, the order of preferred access is:

Networked, remote access (WAN)
Networked, library-wide access (LAN)
Stand-alone (mounted on hard-drive or installed at use).

The resource employs (whenever possible) a user interface already familiar to the Brandeis community.

Ideally the format provides a single-search access to the entire electronic resource.

The resource is compatible across a wide variety of platforms (PC, Mac, etc.); the Libraries will only consider platform-dependent products if no other viable option is available and the resource is considered essential.

The Libraries will not support more than one version of an electronic resource (such as electronic and print) unless there are overriding and compelling reasons for maintaining multiple electronic formats.

When moving an electronic resource from one format to another, there must be compelling reasons to make the change; and the content of the new resource should be comparable or better than that of the existing format, unless others factors prevail.

Vendor and Licensing

The license must be in accordance with the Brandeis University Libraries' established electronic resource licensing policy.

The vendor should be stable and reliable, and offer technical support.

A change of vendors will occur only when a new vendor can deliver a superior search interface, enable greater and more reliable remote access at a reasonable cost, or provide other key factors, such as archival.

Dartmouth College Library
Hanover, New Hampshire

Introduction

Information in electronic format is integral to many academic disciplines represented in the Dartmouth College Library collection. However, problems and questions continually arise as we select, acquire, process and make these resources accessible.

The purpose of this policy is to outline the decision-making process, factors influencing the selection decision, the range of available formats and access options in Dartmouth's information environment. This policy is a response to the growing need among bibliographers for guidelines to assist them in answering questions raised in selecting, processing and making accessible information in electronic format.

This is a format-related guide intended as a collection management resource for bibliographers. It describes the subject's scope, Dartmouth's information environment, the types of electronic information considered. Finally, it presents a detailed outline of considerations in the decision-making process.

The task force's goal was to develop a useful policy for bibliographers. We suggest testing the policy's usefulness by having a bibliographer consult and use it when next considering the purchase of an electronic information resource. Through this, we hope to better understand from a collection management perspective what information is most helpful to bibliographers when selecting information in electronic format.

Dartmouth College Information Environment

The annual publication, Computing and Information Technologies, summarizes the campus information environment. Dartmouth has an impressive history of computing innovations, including the BASIC computer language, and a time-sharing system that served dozens of other educational institutions at its peak. The Kiewit Computation Center, built in 1966, serves as the administrative and support center for computing activities.

In 1984 Dartmouth first recommended the purchase of Macintosh personal computers to incoming students and began the process of wiring all buildings on campus for access to the campus network. This coincided with the Library's Online Catalog being made available experimentally on the network and the development of the Dartmouth Name Directory to facilitate electronic mail.

Today, Dartmouth is primarily an Apple campus. IBM-PCs and UNIX-based workstations are used as well, particularly at the Tuck, Thayer, and Medical schools. Apple computers running DOS and Windows-based applications are available. Undergraduate students are required to purchase Macintosh personal computers.

Users of Dartmouth's computing services can access the Internet, Usenet news groups, discussion groups, the Gopher system, and other resources. Participation in electronic bulletin board services and other online forums is commonplace. Blitzmail, the College's electronic mail service, has revolutionized campus communications.

The Online Catalog is one component of the Dartmouth College Information System (DCIS), under continuous development as a joint project of the Library and Computing Services. The Public File Server is the primary mechanism for shared electronic files, documents and programs, including Keyserver-controlled (shared) software.

Types and Formats of Materials

The types of electronic information in this policy include: bibliographic, text, numeric, graphic and multimedia files. The formats include tape-loaded products (for mounting on the campus network), cd-rom products (networked and stand-alone), and remotely-accessible files of many types available via Internet.

The software needed to run an electronic information product is within the scope of this policy. The policy excludes general-purpose applications such as word processing or database management software; it also excludes integrated library systems such as Innopac.

Materials selection is an intellectual decision best made by each bibliographer for his/her own particular subject areas. Consultation with colleagues and relevant Library groups may assist the bibliographer in answering the technical questions raised by selecting and acquiring information in electronic format.

Cooperative Arrangements

Electronic information resources are often very expensive. Their acquisition may involve negotiations with publishers or vendors, particularly when networking is involved.

Cooperative development and purchase arrangements negotiated with other institutions stretch our funds and make more services available to the Dartmouth community. At this writing, cooperative projects have been done and are being planned with Middlebury College and Williams College, respectively. The Director of Collection Services helps initiate and manage such arrangements.

Access Modes

For electronic information resources, bibliographers can provide one of two modes of access to the Library's users, local or remote. This section outlines issues and considerations in both cases.

Local Access to Resources

A.1. Access via the Network

This provides the broadest access to our users. When files are mounted using the existing DCIS/DCLOS interface, it also provides a familiar method of searching. This is often the preferred method of access, but licensing fees and mainframe storage costs necessitate a discretionary selection process.

As a general rule, the Library supports network access for materials of utility to the greatest number of Dartmouth users. Interdisciplinary materials of use to a variety of users in diverse locations also receive priority treatment. Those databases which provide enhanced bibliographic access to existing library collections [i.e. Early American Imprints, Marcive, Wilson Indexes] are also appropriate for networking campus-wide.

When bibliographers wish to recommend an electronic resource be networked on DCLOS, they should discuss the feasibilty of mounting the resource with the Director of Library Automation. If it is more appropriate to DCIS because of the need to use PAT or another search and retrieval software, they should discuss the proposal with the DCIS Project Director. Cost estimates for both the staff resources to mount the files and the disk space to store them should be assessed. If funding is available to support the acquisition, and the material can be networked within the Dartmouth environment, a proposal detailing costs and benefits should be submitted to the CMDC sub-committee which we propose in this document.

A.2. Access via the Fileserver

The Dartmouth Fileserver predates the existence of Gopher and other Worldwide Web servers widely available today on the Internet. Computing Services have set up a Gopher and a Mosaic Home Page at Dartmouth, and the Library has experimented with their utility as document storage mechanisms and as links to other resources.

For the present, resources that are useful to have on the network, but are kept as documents and are not indexed/searchable files, may be stored on the Public Fileserver/Library folder. Materials archived in this manner should be represented in the Online Catalog, with the necessary location to link the user to the resource.

B. Access via Networked CD-ROM

Resources that are of interest to a more limited clientele, or to a group of users primarily served by an individual library within the Dartmouth College Library, should be considered in a CD-ROM format. If access via one workstation is not sufficient to meet demand, or if providing ease of access to clientele linked by an existing local network is an important factor, the Bibliographer should consider purchasing a license agreement to network the CD-ROM product.

C. Access via Stand-Alone Workstation

Electronic products of interest to a limited number of users, or those difficult to network due to the size of the data, restrictive licensing agreements, specialized software needed for operation, prohibitive cost, etc., should be considered for purchase in a stand-alone workstation environment.

Remote Access to Resources

Bibliographers may also provide access to and inform users about electronic information resources located outside Dartmouth. Those resources include: catalogs; bibliographic, text, numeric, sound, image and data files; software; discussion lists, etc.

External data sources available via Telnet, Gopher, Mosaic are selected based upon expected utility and ease of access. Proven stability of the resource, and the host institution's intention to maintain an archive, are important factors for a bibliographer to consider when deciding to provide remote access. In general, if a desired resource is maintained and made accessible at a remote host site, it is preferable to provide a pointer to it within the Dartmouth College Information System rather than store archival files on-site.

In general, the provision of full bibliographic control via the library's Online Catalog is limited to materials that are owned and stored locally (including on the Library Fileserver). Resources that are pointed to will generally not be cataloged, unless the connection requires expenditure of materials funds.

A number of factors influence how access to external information is provided:
- means of access
- telnet, ftp, Gopher, Mosaic, Netscape, Wais
- hardware and software requirements to get and receive files
- file characteristics
- size, type—image, text, sound, data, etc.
- database search capabilities
- type of indexes
- expected frequency of potential use

This may help bibliographers decide if the resource should be made available in the Navigator (implies frequent use) or in the Gopher (less-than-regular use) options for saving text, viewing or browsing.

Bibliographers should refer identified external resources available through the Internet to the Internet Resources Subcommittee of LOSC. Subscription materials available over the Internet should be processed through normal acquisitions channels.

Selection Criteria

Making the Decision to Acquire Information in Electronic Format

Selecting an electronic information resource is similar to selecting other formats for the Library's collection. Bibliographers base selection decisions, regardless of format, on relevance to Dartmouth programs, the curriculum, and faculty and student research.

Cost is always a consideration because bibliographers must fund purchases from their respective materials budget, and they must continually balance the cost of information against importance and relevance to the collection.

Several bibliographers may share the cost of a purchase when they conclude a resource is relevant yet too expensive for one bibliographer's budget. Electronic information sources are often more expensive than print and may be appropriate candidates for central funding or split funding.

Points to Consider Before Purchase

- If there is a choice of formats, consider the advantages and disadvantages to be sure the electronic form is the most useful. Frequency of updates, inclusion of additional information, ability to manipulate data, and the ability to network all add value to the product.
- Consider only fully-documented products with well-known system requirements. Helpful sources in this regard: comments from relevant listservs, vendor presence in the Library community, vendor's reputation, other products owned by the Library from the same publisher or vendor.
- Consider whether the Library has the necessary staff resources and expertise to support the hardware and software, including installation, maintenance, troubleshooting etc.
- From a user services perspective, consider the staff time that may be needed to prepare user guides and to teach faculty and students how to use the product.
- Specify the type of hardware (Mac, IBM or compatible) and hard disk and RAM capacity required.
- Note any video or audio requirements.
- Based on any knowledge of the product gained from the literature, product reviews, conferences etc., evaluate the user interface, any additional product features (downloading, for example) and users' familiarity with the software.
- Investigate potential for saving and manipulating search results (i.e. printing, saving to a disk, to a hard disk, e-mail, or ftp). Also, can the results be imported into a word processing program?
- Check possible exposure to computer viruses resulting from a choice of media and access.
- Look at ways to access archival issues.
- Investigate ways to assure compliance (is monitoring software provided?) with license agreement or copyright requirements.

- Consider the level of access most appropriate for the product (should it be on the campus network? on a lan? etc.) and consult appropriate people or groups.
- In the case of compact disk databases, consider possible obstacles or constrictions: network speed, cd reader speed, printing bottlenecks.
- Note stability and adequacy of hardware; for example, high- capacity disk drives will be needed to read high-density disks.
- Decide on a location and necessary furniture for optimum access and use; investigate ergonomic considerations in setting up the workspaces
- If an electronic acquisition duplicates a print product currently received, consider whether the print subscription can be cancelled.
- If the product exists in electronic form in the library system, consider whether it could be networked instead of duplicated.

The Product

Are product reviews available?

Do relevant listservs exist to query colleagues?

Is the product user-friendly?

Can product quality and database content be easily appraised? (can one request a demo?)

What workspaces are necessary and appropriate?

What is the currency of content and frequency of updating?

Could information be supplied by other vendors? If so, what are the advantages and disadvantages of each, including cost?

The Vendor

What is the reputation of the vendor?

Do we have other products from the vendor and if so, what are bibliographers' impressions?

Are terms and conditions of contracts and access arrangements negotiable enough to meet Dartmouth's needs?

Is customer service and support available?

Necessary Equipment

What equipment—hardware, printer(s), specialized accessories such as a math co-processor—is needed to run the product?

Is existing hardware adequate or will new purchase(s) be necessary?

What software is needed?

What technical expertise and support is available?

Is new furniture needed to adequately house the product?

Service After the Sale

Is equipment maintenance/support/service available?

Is vendor support available after the sale?

What is known about hardware reliability?

Is documentation included and is it adequate?

The Bibliographer's Communication and Decision-Making Environment

Bibliographer and colleagues with whom he/she consults

Bibliographer's means of learning about electronic resources

- listservs
- newsgroups
- product reviews
- colleagues
- faculty and student recommendations
- Library committees and departments
- Library groups: LOSC, Internet Resources Subcommittee, Automation, Tecor
- Computing Services: IBM Specialists, Academic Computing Coordinators
- College Attorneys
- Budget

As noted previously, bibliographers fund purchases for the collection from their respective budgets. As the cost of electronic information may exceed the ability of one bibliographer to fund it, several bibliographers may collaborate on a purchase. In addition, the Director of Collection Services may be consulted to explore other funding possibilities. In the case of bibliographers working in a library associated with the professional schools, operating with acquisitions budgets separate from Arts and Sciences, these decisions rest with the Department Head, who may in turn consult with the Director of Collection Services.

Information Format and Type

- CD-ROM Databases
- hardware and software requirements
- stand-alone systems
- networked for one location
- networked across zones
- terms and conditions of use, including licensing and contracts
- Magnetic Tape Databases
- hardware and software requirements
- constituencies served
- terms and conditions of use, including licensing and contracts
- Remotely-Accessible Files
- files are accessible using various tools, including ftp,
- Gopher, Mosaic
- text, images and data — software and hardware
- requirements at the requestor's workstation

Types of Information Content

- bibliographic, text, numeric, graphic and multimedia
- Augmented Collection Services
- tables of contents providers and/or
- document delivery services

100

Information Access

Local Access

- Fileserver Resources
- Dartmouth Gopher
- DCLOS, DCIS

Remote Access

- Internet-accessible resources such as newsgroups
- Commercial online services
- pricing options: discounted for educational use, fixed-price, off-peak pricing

Access Tools

- ftp, Mosaic, Gopher, Wais, WWW, Veronica, etc.
- hardware and software requirements to gather and receive data

Licensing Agreements*

In general, it is the responsibility of the College Librarian or her/his designee to negotiate and sign licensing agreements. In the instance of simple CD-ROM agreements this responsibility may be delegated to the Unit Head in the holding library.

The Director of Collection Services will maintain a file containing copies of all licensing agreements and database contracts, regardless of the original Library signatory

The library unit which houses or provides access to an electronic resource is responsible for the day-to-day oversight of licensing requirements.

Final responsibility for compliance with licensing agreements rests with the College Librarian or her/his designee in consultation with appropriate College offices, as appropriate.

*derived from University of Southern California Library. Draft Collection Policy Statement #2 for Information in Electronic Formats.

Archival responsibilities

The Library's responsibility to preserve electronic information is equal to its responsibilities for collections of printed materials and other formats. Priority should be given to locally-produced and unique resources that are irreplaceable via standard commercial means. Attention should be given to electronic information in the development of a preservation plan for the Library.

Louisiana State University
Louisiana State University Libraries
Baton Rouge, Louisiana

Subject: Criteria and Guidelines for Acquiring and Providing Access to Electronic Resources

Purpose: To provide criteria and guidelines for acquiring and providing access to electronic resource titles.

Criteria and Guidelines for Acquiring and Providing Access to Electronic Resources

I. Introduction

This policy provides criteria and guidelines for acquiring and providing access to electronic resource titles. The purpose of acquiring these resources is to support the teaching, research and service missions of the University. They may be mounted on various automated delivery mechanisms for networked or single user access.

II. Selection Criteria

The following criteria should be followed in addition to the criteria set forth in the Libraries' Collection Development Policies:

1. The resource is a proven product, used at other academic libraries, and provided by an established producer/vendor.
2. The search software is compatible with other library systems where appropriate.
3. The licensing policies are in keeping with the library's distribution plans.
4. Priorities will be given to the following types of electronic resources:

   a. It is the only source available;

   b. It provides access to an aggregate of resources (e.g. Lexis/Nexis);

   c. The traditional format is difficult to use (e.g. Dissertation Abstracts);

   d. Keyword searching enhances information access (e.g. multiple volumes searchable in one file);

   e. Electronic format provides manipulatable data to customize research (e.g. statistics used with specific software to generate special reports, etc.);

   f. Electronic format provides enhanced capabilities (e.g. encyclopedia with bird songs for identification purposes; map images depicting special geographical features).

III. Delivery Mechanisms

Access to LSU Libraries' electronic resources can be provided via different mechanisms and should be specified in the proposal based on the following:

1. Single workstation

   a) Use will be limited to a small or specialized user community;

   b) Search/retrieval capabilities may require staff assistance;

   c) Space is not available on the LAN.

2. Library LAN

   a) The product is needed by simultaneous users;

   b) The license permits remote access;

   c) Security is needed for disk products.

3. Remote or Gateway Systems (contract-based)

   a) Access is limited to a gateway (e.g. Ingenta, Lexis/Nexis, etc.);

   b) A gateway provides the most efficient access in terms of reducing computer and staff resources required to maintain the local system.

IV. Responsibility for Recommendations

Purchase recommendations should follow established criteria in accordance with the following:

Gateways, Library LAN, Single Workstations, Library Web Resources:

Recommendations may originate with library departments, liaisons, staff, or users. They should be directed to the appropriate selector who will collaborate with Library Systems and others as appropriate. The final recommendation will then go to the Associate Dean for Collection Services when subscriptions are required or costs exceed $500. When nonsubscription costs range between $300 - $499, the Collection Development coordinator can make the decision. With lesser costs, the department recommending and housing the product may make the decision.

V. Guidelines

Guidelines in preparing recommendation proposals for new titles follow.

1. The proposed titles should meet the appropriate criteria defined in Section II and on the Selection Criteria Checklist.
2. When possible, titles should be tested on a trial basis to explore system compatibility and user response.
3. A proposal must be prepared for all electronic titles and submitted to the appropriate selector or administrator. The proposal must include:
    a. Selection Criteria Checklist

    b. Financial/Status Summary

    c. Access Checklist

4. Titles on Subscription

    a The Head of Serials Services will notify the Associate Dean for Collection Services when significant price changes occur as predetermined by the AD and the Head.

    b Changes to licenses must be approved by the Associate Dean for Collection Services when they result in a significant price change.

    c The Assistant Dean for Library Systems must approve changes to the delivery mechanism.

    d A product not renewed for network access may be continued on a single workstation basis with a department's own funds.

VI. Location of Physical Materials After Purchase

The source materials and physical pieces accompanying electronic resources will be housed in the following locations after purchase:

Location

   LAN Office

Reference Materials

Source materials for any products loaded on the Libraries' LAN (including CD-ROMs, DVD-ROMs, Floppy Disks required for installation), disk or paper guides which ONLY contain installation information.

Source materials for any products loaded on the Reference Standalone Computers (including CD-ROMs, DVD-ROMs, Floppy Disks required for installation), User Guides for any electronic products.

Rice University
Houston, Texas

Current Collection Policy:

Recognizing that one of the goals of the Fondren Library is to increase access to full-text scholarly information, the library is committed to acquiring and facilitating uses of their electronic, full-text resources.

Principal considerations for acquisition of full-text electronic resources include ability to provide access and guidance to the digital resources, to integrate them into library service programs, and to ensure that the advantages of the digital resource are significant enough to justify its selection in digital format.

Priority will be given to digital resources that offer significant added value over print equivalents by including search tools, more extensive content, multimedia components or by accommodating the ability to invoke linkages to local and/or related resources, to annotate text, to transfer information.

Resources that display the full text as well as afford manipulation of texts (searching, concordancing, annotating, generating word lists, etc.) are preferred. Moreover, electronic full-text resources should afford educational or personal use by offering flexible options for saving and printing.

Data formats should follow industry standards and be fully documented. Data should be platform-independent and preferably available in a multiplicity of formats (i.e., ASCII, SGML, PDF, etc.). Standard Generalized Markup Language (SGML) format, an international standard for encoding document format and content, is preferred since it affords more detailed and flexible access to the content of full-text resources.

Interfaces should be easy to master by ordinary users. For this reason, Windows or Mac interfaces are preferred over DOS or other command-based interfaces.

Full-text electronic resources should be hard drive and memory efficient in relation to their respective capabilities.

Resources should include their own search tools. If they do not, they should provide information about options for accessing the texts. Costs for added software, fonts, or other applications that afford use of the material should be factored in to the total cost of the resource.

Resources should be able to work with existing library equipment. This will vary depending upon its designated location.

Support for Full-Text Electronic Resources

Full-text resources are defined broadly to include text, hypertext, images, audio, or other multimedia components. The Electronic Text Center will provide support for full-text electronic resources, particularly in the humanities, that have been acquired by collection development librarians. Some full-text resources, particularly reference tools, statistical data, and resources of general interest will be supported by other library departments, including Reference, Government Publications and Special Resources, and Reserves, or will circulate with the general collection.

Full-text electronic resources with accompanying software require greater support, and therefore, will generally not circulate. Resources that do not require separate installation software may circulate with regular materials.

Reference or Government Publications and Special Resources will give priority to the support of bibliographic and reference tools or statistical information. The Electronic Text Center will give priority to the support of specialized full-text collections and specialized electronic resources.

The Electronic Text Center will provide access to non-commercial electronic texts, particularly as more electronic texts produced according to international standards become publicly available.

The Electronic Text Center will support a variety of applications which facilitate greater access to electronic texts. This includes applications for text analysis, text markup, computational linguistic and language learning, and multi-lingual word processing to afford greater flexibility in the use of full-text resources.

Because scholarship and educational use of electronic texts involves responding to these resources in various ways, the Electronic Text Center will support software for the creating of electronic resources. These applications include markup programs for HTML and SGML, digital imaging and image manipulation tools, optical character recognition software, and other multimedia applications.

The Electronic Text Center, in cooperation with Public Services, will be responsible for assessing the impact of full-text resources in both users and public service operations.

6.5 Electronic Journals

University of Oregon
University of Oregon Libraries
Eugene, Oregon

Electronic Journals

I. Purpose

The University of Oregon Libraries supports the instructional and research programs of the University. Toward this aim, the Library collects or provides access to materials in multiple formats, including electronic formats. The challenges to providing access to electronic journals warrant a separate collection development policy focusing on these materials. This policy will provide guidelines for the selection and acquisition of electronic journals as well as the provision of access. Related collection development documents will address procedural concerns in detail.

II. Scope

This policy seeks to address the selection and acquisition of electronic journals accessible via the Internet. This policy covers electronic journals for which the Library gains free access, access at a reduced rate because the Library subscribes to the print, or purchased access to an electronic-only version.

The Library will pursue the purchase of other types of resources as these develop in the future and meet the guidelines outlined herein. This policy also does not address the following electronic resources, which may fall into more than one of the following categories:

- online bibliographic or full-text databases
- offline electronic resources
- Internet resources (monographic in nature)

Collection development policies for online resources and offline electronic resources address the selection, acquisition, and provision of access for these materials.

III. Principal Access Point and Provision of Access

The Library will provide access to electronic journals which it acquires and/or licenses via the central Library Web page. The Library will maximize access to the Library's electronic journals through several means: cataloging of each e-journal, necessary archiving and/or storage, provision, maintenance, preparation, and loading of necessary software and hardware, and appropriate staff and user support and training for optimal use. Because the Library will catalog e-journals, there will be links to these resources via the Janus Webpac. Additionally, subject specialists or departmental libraries and collections may wish to provide links to these journals via appropriate Web pages.

IV. General Selection Principles

Selection Responsibility: Responsibility for selecting these materials falls to individual subject specialists and the head of collection development as these materials fall into their regular selecting responsibility. Other librarians and library users will offer suggestions to appropriate subject specialists or the head of collection development.

Funding: Ordinarily, the subject content will determine the individual fund. Subject specialists and the head of collection development will determine the appropriate individual funds to use for purchasing electronic journals. As with all other formats, the Library will consider other allocations for those titles deemed major purchases.

Adherence to Other Collection Development Guidelines: The purchase of electronic journals should follow present collecting policies whether general or subject specific policies. Specifically their purchase should adhere to the chronological, geographical, language, and date of publication guidelines set forth in general or subject specific policies. As with other materials subject specialists should also 1) consider present curriculum and research needs, 2) select materials which meet the standards the Library expects of all materials in regard to excellence, comprehensiveness, and authoritativeness, and 3) weigh the purchase of a particular title against other possible acquisitions from material budgets.

Specific Format Criteria: In addition to content, subject specialists should closely consider the criteria listed below when considering the purchase of electronic journals:

- if free, the improvement or enhancement that the resource will give to existing print materials
- the technical requirements necessary to provide access
- the broad accessibility of the resource under present copyright laws and licensing agreements
- the user-friendliness of the resource
- the necessity of archiving and/or availability of archives

It is particularly important to consult available published reviews of electronic journals before their acquisition. Reviews can outline how well a resource meets specific criteria and can provide further insight regarding the resource's overall quality. If reviews are not available, then subject specialists should make an effort to locate other pertinent information about the resource, possibly through listservs, and provide the names of contacts at comparable institutions who are using the resource so that Collection Development may explore possible issues and concerns about a resource.

Subject specialists should not necessarily exclude a title because it does not meet every individual criterion or because it automatically duplicates a print subscription. However, subject specialists should attempt to select resources that adequately meet as many of the selection criteria as is possible. Because this format increases the complexity of acquisition and access, subject specialists should include the detailed list of pre-order guidelines when ordering electronic journals. A sample of this detailed list is appended to this policy.

V. Licensing

The Library will negotiate and comply with vendor licensing agreements. An appended list of pre-order guidelines outline the necessary details for this negotiation and compliance. The Library will also promote compliance with licensing agreements among its users and among its staff. Because this format increases the complexity of licensing agreements, subject specialists should include the detailed list of pre-order guidelines and the necessary licensing agreement, when available, with any order for electronic journals prior to ordering the title.

VII. Duplicates

The Library will purchase electronic journals which duplicate print subscriptions when:

- one format is unstable
- a cost benefit for purchasing multiple formats exists
- multiple formats meet the different needs of user groups
- the archived format of a resource will not operate with current technology.

VIII. Policy Review

Because of the complex and dynamic nature of providing access to electronic journals, the head of Collection Development, the subject specialists, and other librarians will need to review this policy at least every two years.

University of Maryland
University of Maryland Libraries
College Park, Maryland

Appendix: Special Considerations for Electronic Journals

The selection of electronic journals raises special issues not found in the selection of print journals or in the selection of other electronic publications. This Appendix gathers together e-journal-specific issues scattered throughout the Collection Development Policy Statement: Electronic Publications. Before selecting an e-journal, selectors should address the following concerns.

General. The same selection criteria that apply to paper journals apply to electronic journals. They must be appropriate to our collections, support the research and teaching activity of the

University of Maryland, and be of a scholarly nature or likely to advance scholarly research or university education programs. Electronic versions of paper journals to which we subscribe are obvious candidates.

Access. Selectors should add to the collection only those electronic journals openly available to the campus community or accessible through IP address validation. Requirements for individual registration, passwords or other methods of unique individual authentication or authorization should be avoided. Services allowing users to voluntarily create profiles for notification of new content are not problematic.

Number of Issues. Publishers sometimes fail to make all issues of a journal available electronically; for example, publishers may publish issues online sporadically or temporarily. The selector should clarify with the publisher the number of issues a particular subscription covers and ensure that no gaps in coverage occur. Only journals that have a significant run of issues or that commit to making a significant run of issues available full-text in their entirety should be added to the collection. Likewise, titles available only temporarily (trial versions, for example) should not be selected.

Consistency with Print Version. The electronic version of a journal can differ substantially from its print counterpart; for example, an electronic publication may omit articles, illustrations, or reviews found in print. Conversely, the electronic version may have more current content or contain content not found in its print counterpart. If an electronic publication has a print counterpart, the selector should compare the versions to determine whether they are consistent. Online access should include the complete articles, chapters or essays, with accompanying graphics, tables, references, and text plus an official citation.

Currency. The selector should determine how quickly the most recent issue of an electronic journal becomes available in comparison with its print counterpart. Some electronic journals may lag as much as two months or more behind their print counterparts.

Funding. Electronic journals are funded through normal serials lines. This means that, unless new funds are made available for continuations, new e-journal subscriptions requiring additional funding must be balanced by the cancellation of other serials.

Pricing. The pricing structures of electronic journals vary significantly from vendor to vendor and from publication to publication. Selectors should watch for variations among pricing structures and note that these pricing structures can change rapidly.

Duration of Agreement. Selectors should pinpoint when a subscription starts and comes up for renewal. Not all vendors sell subscriptions that start at the time of payment. A publisher may also offer multi-year commitments which a selector should carefully review.

Non-Cancellation Clauses. Some license agreements contain non-cancellation clauses that require the Libraries to promise to maintain a subscription for a specified period of time. In exchange, the publisher or vendor will promise to cap price increases for the period of non-cancellation. To date, the Libraries have not purchased or licensed any products that require the acceptance of a non-cancellation clause.

Time Limits on Access to Back Issues. Many vendors provide all available past years of online content with an online subscription. Some vendors, however, may remove back issues received under a subscription from a Web site after a certain period of time has passed. Selectors should determine whether back issues are available and how long a vendor will commit to maintaining access to subscribed issues.

Bundling. A publisher who sells a title individually in print may only offer that title electronically as part of a package or bundle of titles. Examples of publishers who bundle journals include Elsevier, Academic Press and IEEE. When there is a choice between a package or individual purchase, the selector should evaluate the advantages of each and consult with other interested selectors where appropriate.

Access to Online Content Dated Prior to Subscription. While currently uncommon, some publishers divide content between "current content" and backfiles and charge an additional amount for access to backfiles. Selectors should determine whether a particular price includes backfiles and, if not, the cost of purchasing those backfiles. If a selector purchases publications as a package, he or she should determine the availability of backfiles for each publication.

Purchasing of Electronic Without Print. Publishers do not always allow access to electronic publications without a purchase of the print counterpart. In addition to a required print purchase, the publisher may also impose a surcharge for the electronic subscription. Others may treat the e-version as a separate entity. Particularly when initiating new subscriptions, selectors should consider the possible advantages of purchasing only e-versions of titles where possible.

Evaluation of Vendors. The Libraries currently have agreements with a number of aggregators to provide access to electronic journals. While selectors should always include in their evaluation an assessment of the product and services offered by these aggregators, many journals are available from multiple sources including direct purchase from the publisher.

University of Alabama
University of Alabama Libraries
Tuscaloosa, Alabama

Guidelines for Selection of Electronic Journals

Criteria

Electronic journals must be appropriate to our collections. The same selection criteria apply to electronic journals as to paper journals. Journals are selected based on their ability to support the research, teaching, and outreach activities of The University of Alabama; they must be of a scholarly nature or likely to advance scholarly research or university programs. Electronic versions of journals we subscribe to in paper are obvious candidates.

Generally, electronic journals are funded through normal serials lines. This means that new e-journal subscriptions or titles requiring additional funding must be balanced by cancellation of other serials or by identification of new funding.

Preference should be given to journals which have a significant run of issues or commit to making a significant run of issues available full-text. Sample issues of e-journals are not appropriate additions to the collection. If a selector is unsure whether a publisher will be making future issues available, it is wise to query the publisher or check back after a few more issues have been published. Implications of access to archives should be fully explored.

Preference should be given to journals which are openly available to the campus community (either with or without campus registration). The requirement of individual registration or password access is generally not acceptable.

Licenses must be submitted for approval through the Libraries' license review process.

Access to trial versions of journals will only be supported if ultimate selection of the title is deemed likely by the selector (or Collection Management). Titles which are available temporarily but which are expected to become inaccessible should not be added to the collection.

The Libraries' cooperative/consortial arrangements may influence the outcome of this criteria.

Boston College
Boston College Libraries
Chestnut Hill, Massachusetts

I. Purpose

The Boston College Libraries collect materials in areas and formats which support the instructional and research programs of the university. Electronic journals are rapidly becoming a significant format for publishing academic scholarship and communicating information. Their appearance has been accompanied by a number of concerns and issues regarding their selection, acquisition, and access. The policy guidelines which follow are meant to address some of the challenges they pose. Given the newness of this type of publication, this document is necessarily a work-in-progress, and will no doubt be revised to reflect technological developments and experience.

2. Definitions

For purposes of this policy, electronic journals will be defined as any serial publication that is available over the WWW, or through other internet technologies such gopher, ftp, telnet, or list-serv, and that offers a stable set of back issues. This definition excludes those e-journals which offer only the most recent issue(s), or table of contents, or table of contents and abstracts. The collection is defined as all those resources with records in the BC Libraries' online catalog. This definition excludes any resources listed in any BC Library web page but are not in the online catalog.

3. Access

Each electronic journal will receive a separate catalog record (or share one with its print version). The online catalog will serve as the official source of information about the BC Libraries' electronic journals collection. Additional access points may be available via library web pages like subject guides and the Selected E-Journals list. The WWW is the preferred means of e-journal access.

4. Selection

The selection of electronic journal titles will be the task of individual subject specialists who will be guided by their collection policies and subject expertise. In addition to content, the subject specialists

110

need to consider the following criteria before selecting any particular electronic journal for subscription and cataloging:

- Does the e-journal improve or enhance existing print material?
- Can the journals be easily accessed remotely and in the libraries with currently available technology?
- Does the publisher allow fair use and sufficient access under the license agreement?
- Is the e-journal user-friendly?
- Is there some provision for archiving back issues and is there an intent to continue to provide web-accessible back files?
- For e-journals accessed through subscription, do the BC Libraries own the published data?
- For free e-journals, is there sufficient evidence of stability and reliability of access to all the issues published?
- Is it indexed in appropriate sources?
- If it is the electronic counterpart of a print journal, does it provide all or an acceptably sufficient part of the print version's coverage?

No journal will meet all criteria, but those selected for the collections should meet as many as possible.

5. Other Desirable Features

- The color and background should facilitate optimal readability.
- It should be logically and clearly designed.
- The different sections should be plainly indicated.
- There should be a table of contents and/or an index that should link the relevant parts of the e-journal.
- If the e-journal's articles have hyper-text links to other data, to resources mentioned in works cited, bibliographies, footnotes etc, to e-mail addresses and so on, they should work.
- The e-journal site should be stable and be accessible at any time.
- If the e-journal provides graphics, audio, video, they should work well. They should also serve a real function and not be just padding or decoration.
- If there are graphics, they should not slow down transmission excessively.
- For some e-journals it might be appropriate if the reader can choose text-only.
- There is good technical support and maintenance for the e-journal.
- The server from which the journal is accessed is dependable and stable. Response time should be acceptable.
- Printing, downloading, and e-mailing are available and are easy to operate.
- Generally access to the e-journal should be managed by IP addresses. If a password must be used in conjunction with the IP address, then the publisher/vendor must permit it to be published on BC Libraries' homepage.
- It is important to determine what usage statistics will be made available by the publisher/vendor and their frequency.

6. Licensing

The BC Libraries will negotiate with e-journal publishers to achieve the best possible license agreements that best serves immediate user needs and helps continue the Libraries' collection program to increase and preserve research resources.

7. Consortia Acquisitions

Consortia acquisitions of electronic journal collections with other BLC and NERL libraries (and when advantageous to BC, with libraries from other groups) should be pursued as much as possible in order to achieve cost savings through coordinated purchasing.

8. Duplication

The acquisition of e-journals will not lead to withdrawal of other formats of the same title in the immediate future. A number of issues need to be resolved and the recognition of the digital format for journals as an essential means of scholarly communication needs to be more widespread among users before this format is selected to be the sole format for any particular journal title.

6.6 Disclaimer for Internet Links

Richmond Public Library
Richmond, Virginia

Disclaimer

We attempt to regularly maintain the Richmond Public Library web site (http://www.richmondpubliclibrary.org) and provide information that is complete, timely, accurate, and relevant to our mission and patrons; however we cannot provide guarantees. If you see something in a Richmond Public Library web site document that should be corrected or updated, please e-mail: webmaster@richmondpubliclibrary.org

Hypertext links to other web sites are for the convenience of users of the Richmond Public Library's web site and do not constitute any endorsement by the Richmond Public Library. These sites were initially visited before linking with them and are periodically checked. Richmond Public Library does not control their content, has not participated in the development of these other sites and does not exert any editorial or other control over these sites. If you find a link that is inactive or you have any questions or concerns about a link, please contact: webmaster@richmondpubliclibrary.org. Please be sure to identify the inactive link and the page on which it appears.

The Richmond Public Library does not warrant that its web site, the server that makes it available, or any links from its site to other web sites are free of viruses or other harmful components.

6.7 Archiving and Preservation

Cornell University
Cornell University Library
Ithaca, New York

Purpose

This document formalizes Cornell University Library's (CUL) continuing commitment to the long-term preservation of its diverse and extensive range of digital assets. CUL recognizes that a fully implemented digital preservation program has a reliable and sustainable digital archive at its core, compliant with prevailing standards and practice. This program contributes to the University's mission to enrich the intellectual life of the University by fostering information discovery and intellectual growth, nurturing creativity, partnering in the development and dissemination of new knowledge, and ensuring access to this corpus of information over time. CUL is committed to realizing this digital preservation program vision.

Mandate:

CUL's mandate for digital preservation is at least five-fold:

- Scholarship: Realizing Cornell University's mission led to the maintenance of a library system to support scholarship, teaching, and learning. As more resources and services associated with these functions become digital, CUL's responsibilities must expand to include the identification, stewardship, and preservation of designated digital content.
- Institutional records: The University has charged CUL with maintaining the University Archives by collecting and preserving university records, including those in electronic format.
- Legal obligations: The University has mandated responsibilities to preserve and maintain access to certain digital objects, as well as responsibilities as a designated land grant institution. Some legal obligations derived from Federal and State laws require us to maintain files in an archival fashion.
- Organizational commitment: CUL's commitment to digital preservation is explicitly cited in the Library's Goals and Objectives as Goal II, objective 1, which calls for establishing a common depository system capable of ensuring systematic management and long-term preservation of digital collections, and in Goal II, objective 6, which calls for working with the University to establish a program to archive the university's electronic records. CUL has identified developing an OAI S-compliant depository as a top priority.
- Consortial and contractual obligations: CUL has consortial obligations and contractual agreements to assume or share in the responsibility for preserving designated digital content.

Objectives

The primary intention of the digital preservation program is to preserve the intellectual and cultural heritage important to the University. The program's objectives are to:

- identify, through systematic selection, digital assets to be preserved across new generations of technologies
- include in the scope of the program materials that originated in digital form (born digital) and those that were converted to digital form through a digitization process

113

- protect CUL's digital investments through a fully-implemented digital preservation program
- demonstrate organizational commitment through the identification of sustainable funding for the program and its digital archive (the Common Depository System)
- identify and support the core working team to develop and operate the digital archive and provide requisite training and development as needed
- develop a cost-effective program through means such as, system-wide integration, shared responsibilities, and automating human-intensive efforts
- comply with prevailing community standards for digital preservation and access
- seek, expand, and develop digital preservation methods that are appropriate for Cornell and promote inter-institutional collaboration

Scope

The digital preservation program is responsible for identifying, securing, and providing the means to preserve and ensure ongoing access to selected digital assets. Not all of the digital content CUL creates or acquires will be preserved. Cornell commits to these classes of objects with associated preservation priorities and levels of commitment:

- Priority 1: born digital materials - Rigorous effort will be made to ensure preservation in perpetuity of material selected for preservation, both library resources and institutional records.
- Priority 2: digitized materials (no available analog) - Every reasonable step will be taken to preserve materials without a print analog, when redigitizing is not possible or no analog versions are located elsewhere. Also included are digitized materials that have annotations or other value-added features making them difficult or impossible to recreate.
- Priority 3: digitized materials (available analog) – Reasonable measures will be taken to extend the life of the digital objects with a readily available print analog. However, the cost of redigitizing as needed will be weighed against the cost of preserving the existing digital objects
- Priority 4: items and other materials – No preservation steps will be taken for ephemeral materials such as, materials scanned for E-reserve and Document Delivery, odds and ends of collections, portions of text, and content that is deemed unessential to the comprehensiveness of collections.

Operating Principles

CUL avows that the digital preservation program will:

- comply with the Open Archival Information System (OAIS) reference model standard in the development of the digital archive
- adhere to prevailing community-based standards in developing and maintaining its organizational and technological context
- participate in the development of digital preservation standards and their promulgation
- commit to ensuring that the digital archive is as interoperable as possible by utilizing open source options whenever feasible and to working with other organizations on core issues to enable interoperability

- define a sustainability plan for the digital archive that ensures its cost-effective, transparent, and auditable management over time
- develop the digital archive to maximize scalability, flexibility, and reliability
- ensure consistent, documented policies, procedures, and practices for the program and the operation of the digital archive within a distributed environment (across CUL and the university and beyond)
- employ appropriate storage management for digital content, utilizing on-line, near-line, and off-line storage as appropriate
- manage hardware, software, and storage media containing archival copies of digital content in accordance with environmental, quality control, security, and other standards and requirements
- establish procedures to meet archival requirements pertaining to the provenance, chain of custody, authenticity, and integrity (bit-level and content) of institutional records and assets
- define policies and procedures for the preservation and availability of digital assets respectful of intellectual property ownership and rights

Roles and Responsibilities

The traditional role of librarians and archivists has included preserving the intellectual record of the research community in analog formats. The same is true for research materials in digital form. The University Library has primary responsibility for digital preservation at Cornell, but digital preservation is a shared responsibility across the University. All responsible officers of the University, content creators, and disseminators with a custodial role for digital content identified for long-term preservation have a responsibility to actively contribute to the intent and priorities necessary to fulfill this policy.

Preservation

Digital preservation activities at CUL include:
- selecting material for long-term access based on scholarly value and technical capabilities
- securing digital assets through physical custody or other arrangements
- actively monitoring technology
- reviewing licenses for preservation implications
- promulgating good practice
- providing support services
- ensuring quality creation of digital materials
- negotiating for deposits
- responding to technology obsolescence through migration or other strategies
- establishing reliable, comprehensive, archival storage
- providing security for content and systems
- collaborating with other institutions to provide digital preservation services

In acquiring materials for the common depository, CUL must continually define and communicate levels of preservation appropriate to each type of format. Rather than limit inclusion in the digital preservation program to those formats with known and feasible preservation approaches, a level of preservation is associated with each format. The preservation level and the priority, as described above under Scope, determine the preservation strategy for materials. As new formats emerge, a level of difficulty required to preserve each type is assigned. The resources required to preserve are balanced against the overall need. This selection process applies to both new and existing content. CUL will review existing digital content for preservation as priorities dictate and resources allow.

Access/Use

Access to preserved digital content is provided using the most up to date technology available at the time of use. When retaining the look and feel is deemed necessary, CUL will seek to enable the original versions of the digital objects to be rendered over time. CUL complies with access restrictions as defined in relevant laws, regulations, licenses, and deposit agreements. Appropriate preservation plans to make rendering the original version possible are devised on a case-by-case basis and revised as needed. Without the preservation of digital materials, access would not be possible and essential cultural heritage materials would be at risk.

Challenges

There are recognized challenges in implementing an effective digital preservation program, such as:

- Rapid growth and evolution: Technology that enables the variety of formats and dissemination mechanisms changes rapidly. Establishing a program that is responsive to change is a huge challenge.
- Sustainability: The need for good cost models and affordable programs is widely acknowledged, yet still unaddressed. The scale is based on the level of commitment. CUL requires sufficient funding for startup and major improvements, as well as designated library funding to sustain ongoing preservation efforts. The program should reflect reasonable expectations of requisite resources, i.e., CUL should not promise more than can be delivered.
- Content provider partnerships: Working with creators and providers of crucial content to employ appropriate maintenance prior to deposit that will facilitate future preservation.
- Enabling full preservation: Moving from well-managed digital collections to preserved collections in the true sense of the term requires institutional effort, partnership development, and a financial commitment.
- Flexibility: To respond to evolving technological capabilities and changing user expectations, the digital archive must revise continually the definition of the dissemination information package (DIP) for delivery to an expanding array of content delivery platforms. These requirements must be met without jeopardizing the ongoing care of the digital content.

Cooperation/Collaboration

CUL is committed to collaborating within the University and with other institutions to: advance the development of the digital preservation program, share lessons learned with other digital preservation programs, extend the breadth of our available expertise, and extend the digital content that is available within a broad information community to CUL users through cooperative efforts.

Part IV
Reference Services:
Circulation and
Interlibrary Loan (ILL)

Chapter 7

CIRCULATION SERVICES POLICIES

LOANING AND BORROWING MATERIALS

7.1 Loaning Reference Material Guidelines

Chelmsford Public Library
Chelmsford, Massachusetts

LOANING OF REFERENCE MATERIALS:

Reference material will not circulate. Material in this area is considered to be important for ready access to patrons. Allowing it to circulate defeats the purpose of having a separate section for reference only. Patrons will be encouraged to photocopy if they need to have the printed material in hand.

Memorial Hall Library
Andover, Massachusetts

Reference books may be checked out overnight at the discretion of the reference librarian on duty. No volumes of sets, heavily used titles, or ready reference titles will be allowed to circulate. Staff will verify that the patron has a valid library card in good standing. Books will be checked out at the circulation desk for 1 day and should be returned as close to 9 am as possible. A note will be left in the Reference Notebook to alert the Head of Reference and the staff that the title has been borrowed.

Monroe Township Public Library
Monroe Township, New Jersey

CIRCULATION OF REFERENCE MATERIALS FOR USE OUTSIDE LIBRARY

In general, reference materials are maintained permanently inside the Library building so that they will be accessible to as many users as possible when the Library is open. Most reference tools cannot be taken from the building without causing severe inconvenience to other potential Library users. The reference needs of the majority are given priority over the needs of any individual. However, since some reference materials are in much less demand than others, these reference books and pamphlets may be borrowed for limited periods of time upon approval of the reference librarian or Library Director. Exceptions: Monroe Township employees may borrow any reference title, including a law book, provided that it is for official Township business and can be returned expeditiously. Any other exceptions must be approved by the Library Director.

Morton Grove Public Library
Morton Grove, Illinois

Reference books (following reference policy guidelines and at the discretion of the reference librarian on duty) may be checked out overnight. Items with circulating copies (even if they are earlier editions) will be excluded from this policy, since copies are available to library patrons. Reference books may be taken out between 8:15 PM and 8:45 PM, with corresponding allowances for weekend times.

Librarian must verify that the patron has a valid library card in his/her possession and is registered in Dynix. Also, verify that the patron has no outstanding fines or bills on his/her record. (If necessary, the circulation department can check for you.)

Give the book to the patron to check out at the Circulation Desk with Part 1 of "Reference Check-Out Form" paper-clipped to the inside of the book. Tape Part 2 of the form to the reference desk.

The Reference Check-Out Form taped to the reference desk alerts the librarian to the fact that the book is expected back at the reference desk by closing time on the following day. If the book is returned on time then sign Part 2 and give to patron. Part 1 may be discarded. Take the book to the Circulation Desk to discharge and resensitize. Finally, return the book to the reference shelf.

If the book is returned late, follow the steps as outlined above. In addition, accompany the patron to the Circulation Desk to see that the fine is paid. For current fine rates, see "Reference Check-Out Form."

If the book is not back the next day at opening, try and contact the patron. If contact cannot be made, or if the book is not returned by closing time on the second day, notify the Head of Circulation so that a note can be placed on the patron's record.

Some reference items may never be circulated. Examples include:

- Ready-Reference Materials
- Book or Periodical Indexes
- Expensive Materials ($200+)
- Frequently Used Materials
- Multi-Volume Sets
- Leased Items

Kent State University
Kent State University Libraries and Media Services
Kent, Ohio

Reference materials normally do not circulate, except overnight. At the discretion of a reference librarian, reference materials may be checked out for a very limited period of time to holders of valid Kent State University IDs or Courtesy Cards.

The following materials do not circulate at any time:

- Directories, almanacs, and encyclopedias in the Reference Collection
- Federal and state legal reporters and digests in the Reference Collection and Main tower stacks
- Foreign language dictionaries in the Reference Collection
- Loose-leaf materials in the Reference Collection and Main tower stacks
- May 4 Collection
- Reference Desk Collection
- Encyclopaedia Britannica, 9th and 11th editions
- National Union Catalog
- United States Congressional Serial Set

Weber State University
Stewart Library
Ogden, Utah

As a general rule, no reference items circulate. In justified circumstances, a loan may be granted under special permission. Permission should be granted first by a faculty librarian from public services. If none such is available, then any contracted staff member on duty may grant permission. Student workers are not authorized to grant such permission. A reference item may not be loaned if there is a duplicate copy available in the circulating collections or if its absence would seriously impair service to other patrons.

2. Length of Loan

Length of loan is negotiated between librarian and patron and depends on the intended purpose of the loan and the impact which the item's absence would have on service to others.

3. Eligible Borrowers

Anyone able to present a currently valid WSU identification card is eligible. Those not officially affiliated with WSU are ineligible.

4. Checkout Process

The patron must fill out a charge slip in two parts. The librarian making the transaction is responsible to ensure that every box is completed on the slip and that the information is legible.

This person should also initial the slip in case there is any question about the loan. The patron's WSU identification card must be clipped to one copy of the slip and held at the reference desk till the item is returned. The other copy of the slip should accompany the item.

Since many reference items have permanently sensitized theft detection devices implanted inside them, the patron will have to be accompanied through the building exit by a library employee.

5. Overdues

The Reference and Information Services Librarian is responsible for monitoring the reference circulation file, contacting patrons with overdue reference materials, and using all available means to secure their return as soon as possible after the items become overdue.

With exceptions listed below, books and other materials assigned to reference status in the Library may be loaned to students, faculty and staff of the college and through a district inter-library loan request, for a period of up to one week, subject to immediate recall.

Guidelines

Decisions about the availability of a specific item for loan (including district interlibrary loan requests) and the length of time of the loan are made by the reference librarians or by the Library/ Media Services Administrator in their absence. Factors to consider are the item's current use pattern, it's physical durability, the length of the information contained, and the relevance of the information to the borrower's needs.

Reference check out is carried out via a "Reference Check Out" slip filled out and signed or initialed by the librarian who has approved the loan. The Reference Check Out slip is maintained in the reference circulation file at the circulation desk.

The following reference materials do not circulate:

- Volumes from multi-volume encyclopedias, dictionaries or other sets
- The most recent edition of yearbooks and similar periodical publications
- Materials which, due to factors of size, cost or durability, require special handling or treatment (e.g., maps, atlases, globes, some art books)
- Materials which, in the judgment of the librarians, are in such frequent demand due to an assignment that the available copies should be on hand in the reference collection
- Materials which, in the judgment of the librarians, are in such frequent demand that the available copies should always be on hand in the reference collection (e.g., "Occupational Outlook Handbook", unabridged dictionary)

In the case of disagreement among the librarians as to the eligibility of an item for circulation, the item will not be loaned except for short-term classroom use.

Exceptions to all of the above may be made in cases where the item is needed for short-term (maximum two hours) use in a classroom setting.

Fees for lost or damaged Reference material while on loan are determined on an individual basis by a librarian.

Overdue reference material on special loan is charged 50 cents per hour per item to a maximum of $10.00. All Library open hours, including Saturday and Sunday, are used to compute fines. Fines are waived if the overdue material is returned within a 15-minute grace period.

7.2 Loan Periods and Renewal

Stillwater Public Library
Stillwater, Oklahoma

RENEWALS

Materials may be renewed in person, over the telephone, or from the Library's Internet web page. Items cannot be renewed from the web page if there are overdue items or $5.00 or more in fines. Library materials may be renewed two times. Interlibrary Loan materials may be renewed only once for five days. Longer renewal periods require the consent of the lending institution. The following materials may not be renewed:

- Materials on a teacher's card
- Items with holds/reserves
- Items previously renewed twice

Brandeis University
Brandeis University Libraries
Waltham, Massachusetts

Renewal Policy

Library books should be renewed on or before the due date. Patrons are expected to keep track of their own due dates and should not depend on overdue notices, which are sent out as a courtesy.

The Circulation Department views renewal of materials as an acknowledgement that the patron currently has these materials in their possession.

How to renew:

Brandeis University students, faculty and staff can renew library materials and monitor account information directly in LOUIS. For more information, please check the online renewals web page:

- http://www.library.brandeis.edu/access/renewals.html
- Renewals may also be made in person (renewal receipts are available), or by direct email to circulation@brandeis.edu.
- Material cannot be renewed over the phone, as the library cannot guarantee the accuracy of telephone transactions.

Materials may not be eligible for renewal for the following reasons:

- Books cannot be renewed if they have been recalled/requested.
- Items cannot be renewed if the borrower has overdue Interlibrary loan materials or long-overdue circulating items for which replacement charges have been assessed.

The Library is unable to extend loan periods on materials that have reached their renewal limit: five (5) renewals for internal Brandeis borrowers with month-long loan periods, two (2) for internal Brandeis borrowers with semester-long loan periods, and one (1) renewal for all other affiliated borrowers (i.e. Alumni, B.L.C. etc). Books that have reached their renewal limits can still be charged out for another cycle if first brought back to the Circulation Desk and checked in.

Why have renewal limits?

Renewal limits are needed to ensure that the collection is available to the entire community. Having more books on the Library's shelves increases the ability of borrowers to browse the collection and provides more immediate access to materials than our recall system provides. Renewal limits encourage borrowers to return books they are no longer actively using.

Renewal limits also serve as an inventory for circulating materials and helps us retrieve and salvage materials that have been improperly stored by borrowers.

Renewal limits allow both the Library and borrowers to identify lost or damaged books more quickly. As a result of periodic review of loan records, we have fewer missing books when borrowers leave the University.

Wheelock College
Wheelock College Library
Boston, Massachusetts

Renewals

Materials may be renewed once, if no one else has requested the item, and if the item is not overdue. Renewals can be handled over the phone or in person. Please call either the day before or on the day the item is due. Once an item is overdue, you must bring the item to the library to check it out for another borrowing period.

7.3 Fines and Overdues

Hamilton College
Burke Library
Clinton, New York

Fines

Books returned after the last day of final exams, are subject to a fine of $.20 per day to a maximum of $40.00 per book. After the book has been overdue for 80 days, the system will add this fine as a replacement charge to the patron's record, and it will not be refunded if the book is returned. The student will be billed for the book(s) by the College Business Office.

During the time between when the book becomes overdue and the billing letter is sent, a patron receives 7 overdue notices. The first notice is sent on the day after the due date. The second notice and all subsequent notices, are sent in 10 day intervals.

7.4 Lost or Forgotten Cards

Sarasota County Libraries
Sarasota, Florida

Lost or Forgotten Cards:

Persons are responsible for all materials borrowed on their card and agree to abide by library lending rules and all policies and regulations. If a person loses his/her library card there is a $1 replacement charge. Patrons should report lost or stolen cards immediately. Persons who must replace a card due to negligent care will be charged $1. Cards replaced due to normal wear and tear will not carry a fee.

Any patron, who presents material for checkout but cannot present a library card will be allowed to checkout materials provided a valid ID proving name and address is presented. A "message" stating show/replace card, will be added to the patron's record. The patron will be asked to present their card upon their next visit. If they are unable to, they will be asked to purchase a replacement card. If address has changed, proof of new address should be presented at this time.

Horsham Township Library
Horsham, Pennsylvania

Lost or forgotten cards

If a patron loses his/her library card, he should notify the library as soon as possible and request a replacement.

All patrons, adult and juvenile, are expected to bring their library cards with them if they intend to check out items. An individual who repeatedly ignores this expectation may be denied the privilege of checking out materials until they present their card at the library.

7.5 Replacement of Lost/Damaged Material

University of California–Irvine
University of California Irvine Libraries
Irvine, California
Reprinted with the permission of University of California Irvine

REPLACEMENT OF LOST OR DAMAGED ITEMS

A borrower, who does not return an item by the due date/time may be billed for the replacement cost of each item plus a $10 non-refundable processing fee per item. Material returned after billing is still subject to the $10 non-refundable processing fee per item.

All borrowers are subject to replacement charges if items are lost or damaged beyond repair. An item is considered lost when the borrower reports it lost, damaged or fails to return it (see 4.7 above). If a borrower returns an item for which payment has been made, the replacement cost may be refunded if the item has not yet been replaced or if the item is returned within one year of the invoice date. Accrued fines, if any, may be levied at that time.

A borrower may arrange to replace a lost or damaged book with an exact duplicate acceptable to the appropriate Subject Bibliographer. Charges for lost or damaged non-print material are the actual cost of the item. The charges will include a billing charge and binding costs if necessary. Charges for a lost or damaged Humanities & Social Sciences books are a minimum of $50. Charges for lost or damaged science, technology and medical books and the replacement of bound periodicals are a minimum of $75.

Missoula Public Library
Missoula, Montana

Damaged and Lost Material? All Library materials are inspected upon return. Those materials deemed by Library staff to be damaged but not destroyed will be assessed a repair charge. The repair charge is $5.00 for damaged books that can be repaired in-house. Those materials deemed destroyed/unusable will be assessed a destroyed or lost material charge. If lost material is returned in acceptable condition, replacement cost will be refunded minus the handling fee and any additional charges incurred by the Missoula Public Library. The charge will be the retail or stated default price of the book, plus a $10.00 handling charge. Exceptions – $1.00 for TOT books, no handling charge for paperbacks.

7.6 Borrowing Privileges

Carbondale Public Library
Carbondale, Illinois

Use of Library Card

A valid* library card must be presented when borrowing library materials. Valid cards include:

a Carbondale Public Library card
a resident card from any Illinois public library

*A valid card must show an expiration date.

Patrons may access the library catalog via the Internet and place holds on items. To access information about an individual account or renew materials requires a PIN number. Patrons must come into the library to register for this service and select a PIN number. It will not be issued over the telephone. A parent/guardian must accompany any minor under age 16 applying for a PIN number.

Carbondale resident card holders may use their card at any public library in Shawnee Library System. However, the policies, fines, and fees of that library will apply when borrowing materials whether on-site or through interlibrary loan.

With the new law, nonresidents (including nonresidents who own property within the city limits of Carbondale) are eligible to use their Carbondale Public Library card at any Shawnee System library.

Fines on a patron record must be under $1.00 to be eligible to borrow materials. This includes fines incurred at another public library.

Registered patrons who do not have their card with them when borrowing materials may show proof of identification. However, this privilege may not be abused. A patron who habitually "forgets" their card will be asked to come back with the card or replace it if it is lost.

Lost cards should be reported immediately. There is a fee of $1.25 to replace a lost card.

Patrons are responsible for all items checked out on their card. This includes any fines or fees due to late return, damage to or loss of an item. It is suggested that patrons not allow others to use their card.

Individuals who reside in a community (within Shawnee Library System) that taxes itself for library service but whose library does not participate in the Shawnee Library System automated database are eligible to receive service as a reciprocal patron. However, their home library is responsible for issuing them a library card.

Grinnell College
Grinnell, Iowa

Number of items loaned: Faculty and staff loans should be limited to not more than 75 volumes at any one time (not including interlibrary loan volumes). Loans in excess of this number to any one individual impair the libraries' collections and the ability of students and other faculty to use them. Although library materials can be recalled, few library users actually do so, preferring to use only those items which are in the libraries when they are required. There are also many users who browse shelves for relevant books, rather than searching for items in the catalog. The latter individuals are particularly disadvantaged when a faculty member's scholarly interests result in a large number of books on a particular focused subject being absent from the shelves. Finally, in our collective experience, we judge that 75 volumes borrowed from the libraries at any one time are adequate to support active teaching and research requirements.

San Jose Public Library and San Jose State University Library
San Jose, California

Library users have certain distinct borrowing privileges depending on their current status as University staff/faculty/student, SJSU staff, or general public, and that status may change from semester to semester or throughout the year.

A one record/one card policy does the following:
- Minimizes duplication of patron records and limits errors when establishing borrowing privileges.
- Avoids having users obtain a new library card each time their status changes.

Requirements & Guidelines

At the beginning of each University session, enrollment verification will be downloaded from Student Information Services to determine which Library customers have University faculty, staff, or student status.

All users who are not currently enrolled at SJSU or employed by either the University or the Library are designated as Public Library customers.

Exceptions due to enrollment issues (i.e., Master's candidates, students completing pending course-work, etc.) are handled on an individual basis by the circulation department.

Patrons may only use their own library card to access library resources including public access computers, music listening rooms, and checking out materials. The only exception is parents using their children's card and vice versa.

7.7 Nonaffiliated Patron Privileges

Whitman County Library
Colfax, Washington

NON-RESIDENT SERVICE: Basic questions are answered for all customers. If a customer resides outside the Whitman County Library District and their request will consume an inor-dinate amount of time or research, they will be advised of and assessed a $30 per hour non-resident reference fee.

Hamilton College
Burke Library
Clinton, New York

Area Residents, Area College Students and Summer Programs

Area residents, area college students and most summer program participants may check out up to 20 books for a period of 28 days. Books may be renewed twice. These patrons may not recall a book from another borrower. Fines are assessed at $.50 per day per book up to the maximum of $40.00 per book. Recalls are fined at $5.00 per day per book up to the maximum ($40.00).

7.8 Library Card Privileges

Glen Ellyn Public Library
Glen Ellyn, Illinois

Company Cards

Any corporation, partnership, sole proprietorship or unit of government located in the Village of Glen Ellyn is eligible for a library card free of charge at the Glen Ellyn Public Library under the following conditions:

- An officer of the organization requests a Library card and designates as many as three individuals who are authorized to use the card.
- The organization agrees to be responsible for all materials checked out on the card.
- The library card is used solely for business purposes.

The library card remains on file at the Library and is requested by the authorized individuals each time they visit the Library.

All such cards carry full borrowing privileges for business materials only at the Glen Ellyn Public Library and are valid for one year.

Wheelock College
Wheelock College Library
Boston, Massachusetts

To check out materials from the Wheelock College Library, all patrons must have a valid Wheelock College ID or a valid Fenway Libraries Online (FLO) library card.

The following people are eligible for Fenway Libraries Online (FLO) library cards:
- Wheelock students, faculty, administrators and staff.
- Non-matriculating Wheelock Associate Degree and Graduate students enrolled in courses during the current semester.
- Wheelock alumni with a valid Library/Resource Center card for the current year. If you do not have a Library card, please come to the Library Circulation desk. You will be required to register and pay a $20 alumni fee.
- Students, faculty, administrators and staff from FLO libraries with FLO cards (FLO member patrons who do not have cards must register at their own institutions).
- Students, faculty and staff with a valid ID from a Fenway Libraries Consortium institution (Hebrew College, Simmons College, Suffolk University, Brookline Public Library and U. Mass. Boston).

- Guest borrowers with a valid Library/Resource Center card for the current year. If you do not have a Library card, please come to the Library Circulation desk. You will be required to register and pay a $50 fee.

7.9 Borrowing Privileges for Alumni and Family of Staff

Brandeis University
Brandeis University Libraries
Waltham, Massachusetts

Family Cards

Spouses, domestic partners and children (age 13 or older) of Brandeis faculty and staff may obtain a borrowing card from the Brandeis University Libraries. The Brandeis faculty or staff member assumes responsibility for all material and fines. Cards expire at the end of each academic year. When family members register to borrow for the first time they must be accompanied by the Brandeis faculty or staff member. The Brandeis faculty or staff member will present their University ID to circulation staff and must co-sign for the family card. Library privileges cover the right to borrow Brandeis books only and do not include BLC cards, Interlibrary Loan, or off-campus access to subscription databases.

Hamilton College
Burke Library
Clinton, New York

Spouses and Children of College Employees, and Alumni

Spouses and children of college employees and Alumni have the same borrowing privileges as college employees, and may borrow up to 50 books. Fines for overdue books and recalls are the same as those for Hamilton students.

7.10 Academic Faculty and Staff Borrowing Privileges

Bucknell University
Bertrand Library
Lewisburg, Pennsylvania

Faculty and Staff

The following borrowing policies recognize research needs for Bucknell faculty and administrators while ensuring availability of materials to students. These guidelines reflect reasonable and consistent policies that also allow for individual circumstances and exceptions when needed.

This policy applies to current and retired faculty and all staff of Bucknell University, including adjunct and summer faculty. Faculty/staff who separate from the university may apply for a community borrower card if residing in Union, Snyder or Northumberland counties.

Loan Periods

Faculty/staff may borrow most books for an extended period of one academic year, provided items are not recalled by other Bucknell faculty, students, spouses, staff, or for Reserves. Academic-year loans are due at the end of each spring semester and must be returned or renewed at that time. There are no phone renewals. Faculty are encouraged to return books before the due date if they are not using the items regularly for teaching and research purposes, so that other users have immediate access to them. Exceptions to the academic-year loan period follow:

3-Week Loan Audio Cassettes, Maps, Compact Discs, Multimedia, Phonograph Records
3-Day Loan Videos & DVD's

Materials that do not circulate include reference books, periodicals, microform, and scores. Faculty who need videos for longer than three days may request an extension at the Circulation Desk.

Total Items a Borrower May Charge

Bucknell identification cards must be presented to charge library materials, and borrowers are responsible for all items charged on their accounts. Faculty and staff may have as many as 100 items charged at any one time. Only 4 videos/DVDs may be borrowed under most circumstances; exceptions may be negotiated with library staff.

Renewals

Faculty/staff may renew items, provided they are not recalled, including the items loaned for three weeks. Items must be brought to the Circulation Desk; there are no phone or online renewals because of the extended loan period.

Recalls

Items are subject to recall after the borrower has had them for seven days. Recalls are requests by current Bucknell faculty, staff, spouses, students or Reserves for material charged to another borrower. Email notices specifying a new due date will be issued when items are recalled . Penalties (fines) of $1.00/day/item will accrue on overdue items as well as blocking of further borrowing privileges until items are returned. Faculty/staff who are planning to be away from campus for a week or more should make appropriate arrangements for the return of recalled items to avoid penalties.

Overdue and Lost Items

Faculty/staff are not charged fines for overdue items unless they have been recalled (see above). Overdue notices are sent as a courtesy to our borrowers. A $15.00 processing fee and an appropriate replacement charge will be assessed for lost or damaged items, and charges will be forwarded to the employee's accommodation account.

Hamilton College
Burke Library
Clinton, New York

Faculty, Administrators and Staff

Faculty, Administrators and Staff may check out an unlimited number of books for the semester. If a book is 80 days overdue, it will be declared missing, and replaced. The borrower's departmental library book budget will be charged for the replacement.

University of Minnesota–Duluth
University of Minnesota Duluth Library
Duluth, Minnesota

Borrowing Privileges for Courtesy Card Users

Courtesy cards are available to adult residents of the Duluth regional area, allowing checkout of items from the UMD Library circulating collections. If you are a community resident, please present a driver's license or state I.D. when applying for a courtesy card. If your photo I.D. does not show your current address, we will ask you to present a bill addressed to you at your current address.

Courtesy cards are also available for students and faculty of area postsecondary educational institutions. We will ask you to present a photo I.D. in addition to a student or faculty I.D. from your college or university.

High school students working on advanced-level research must bring a photo I.D. and a letter of recommendation from their high school librarian or teacher requesting one-time use of the UMD Library for a specific research assignment. Teachers and high school librarians should make sure that the student has attempted to complete the research at his or her school and public libraries before requesting checkout of materials from the UMD Library.

Summer visitors to UMD who are temporarily residing in UMD campus residences are extended borrowing privileges at the UMD Library during their stay.

Please show your photo ID along with your UMD Library courtesy card when you check out items. This is for your protection in the event that you lose your card. We want to make sure that the materials that leave the Library in your name are truly in your possession.

Be aware that overdue materials or outstanding fines will cause your borrowing privileges to become blocked. If this happens, return overdue materials and see a Circulation supervisor to pay your fines. If an item becomes more than 45 days overdue, it will be billed as unreturned. The fee will include an overdue fine, replacement cost, plus $15 for processing.

7.11 Reciprocal Borrowing

Sarasota County Libraries
Sarasota, Florida

Free Reciprocal Borrowing Agreements

Manatee County Agreement

Manatee County residents may receive a free Sarasota County library card by presenting their Manatee County library card and one form of identification with their current address. Manatee reciprocal cards are valid for one year and will be renewed as long as the reciprocal agreement is in effect. Materials borrowed from a Sarasota County Library must be returned to a Sarasota County Library. A courier system has not been established between the two counties. Manatee County reciprocal borrowers must abide by the same policies and procedures regarding overdue fines and replacement fees as Sarasota County borrowers.

Charlotte County Agreement

Charlotte County residents may receive a free Sarasota County library card by presenting their Charlotte County library card and one form of identification with their current address. Charlotte reciprocal cards will expire on June 30, each year and will be renewed as long as the reciprocal agreement is in effect. Materials borrowed from a Sarasota County Library must be returned to a Sarasota County Library. A courier system has not been established between the two counties. Charlotte reciprocal borrowers must abide by the same policies and procedures regarding overdue fines and replacement fees as Sarasota County borrowers.

TBLC Agreement (Tampa Bay Library Consortium)

Libraries who are members of TBLC's reciprocal borrowing agreement have agreed to allow patrons from participating libraries to check out materials free of charge. Patrons may use their own library card, with a reciprocal borrowing sticker attached, to check out materials.

TBLC Borrower Responsibilities:
- Present home library card to a reciprocal borrowing library to register for library privileges in that library system.
- Be in good standing at your local library.
- Be informed and abide by the rules and polices of the participating libraries you use.
- Assume responsibility for all materials borrowed on your cards, including payment for lost/damaged materials, overdue fines or other fees.
- Return materials to any participating library in a timely manner according to the rules of the lending library.

Culver-Union Township Public Library
Culver, Indiana

Any Indiana resident age 18 or over that is not attending a secondary school and has a public library card at another Indiana public library may obtain a reciprocal borrowing card at the Culver-Union Township Public Library. The applicant's library card from another Indiana public library must be shown, along with other applicable identification, in order to obtain the reciprocal card. The applicant must also be in good standing (i.e. non-excessive overdue materials and/or fines) at that library.

HOLDS, RESERVES, REQUESTS, AND RECALLS POLICIES

7.12 General Guidelines

Grinnell College
Grinnell, Iowa

The Grinnell College Libraries' reserve policies apply to the libraries' reserve collection to the extent that it functions as an extension of classroom readings or reflects an individual student's right to reproduce copyrighted works for personal scholastic use under the doctrine of fair use. The policies apply both to placing original works on reserve as well as to reproducing the work by either photocopying or digitizing it.

Libraries may reproduce materials for reserve use for the convenience of students both in preparing class assignments and in pursuing collateral educational activities that the college sponsors, such as independent study or research, under the conditions specified below.

Library reserves are intended to be a means of extending the classroom by making complementary or supplementary readings available to students. Such reserve readings may not constitute the universe of written material assigned for a course. The Grinnell College Libraries reserve the right to decline to place materials on reserve which violate this principle.

Books:

(a) Owned by the Grinnell College Libraries may be placed on library reserve without restrictions.

(b) Not owned by the Libraries: The libraries will initiate expedited orders to purchase any books required for course reserves. Pending the receipt of books so ordered the libraries may place personal copies belonging to instructors or photocopies on reserve. Personal copies or photocopies will be removed from reserve when the library-purchased copies are received.

Note: The national interlibrary loan code prohibits borrowing books from other libraries for the purpose of placing them on reserve at the borrowing institution.

Course textbooks: Upon the request of an instructor the libraries will purchase one copy of any course text from the College Bookstore and place that copy on library reserve. Such textbooks are placed on reserve as an occasional convenience—as, for example, when a student is in the library, needs to consult the course text, and has accidentally left it at a residence hall. The normal expectation is that each student will have purchased a copy of the primary textbook(s) required for a course. Personal copies of textbooks in an instructor's possession may be placed on reserve in a temporary exigency, such as when the bookstore may not have received enough copies of a text for all students in a class and the libraries have been unable to purchase a copy.

Course packets: May not be placed on library reserve, because this violates the college's agreement with XanEdu, the producer of the course packets. Moreover, case law indicates that course packets may not be placed on library reserve as a means of evading their purchase and (thereby) the payment of royalties to copyright owners. As a temporary measure, a copy of a course packet may be placed on library reserve during such time as an insufficient number of copies are available through the College Bookstore for all students in a class.

Chapters in books:

(a) Owned by the Grinnell College Libraries: The book may be placed on library reserve. If class size justifies, the libraries will order any needed additional copies. Pending the receipt of those additional copies, personal copies belonging to instructors may be placed on library reserve.

(b) Not owned by the libraries: A copy of the chapter may be placed on electronic reserve. The libraries will expedite an immediate order for the book in which the chapter appears. If a copy of the book cannot be purchased by the libraries, and it is desired to place the chapter in question on e-reserve for more than one semester, copyright permission must be obtained (see below).

Articles:

(a) In serials/periodicals owned by the Grinnell College Libraries: The volume or issue in which the article appears may be placed on physical reserve an indefinite number of times. If it is desired to place such an article on electronic reserve, this may be done for one semester. Thereafter copyright permission must be obtained for each such electronic-reserve use—as in section (c) below.

(b) In serials/periodicals to which the libraries have licensed access to electronic versions: The libraries will provide electronic links to the articles in question through the course reserve lists in Innopac.

(c) In serials/periodicals which the Grinnell College Libraries do not own and to which the libraries do not have licensed electronic access: A copy may be placed on electronic reserve for one semester. Thereafter, copyright permission must be obtained for each use. The libraries will obtain such permission on behalf of Grinnell College, provided that such permission can be obtained from the Copyright Clearance Center (or similar royalty-collection agency) and the copyright royalty charged does not exceed $150 for individual item or a cumulative total of $1000 for all the items on reserve for a particular course. Absent these two conditions, obtaining of copyright permission and paying a copyright royalty in excess of the specified limits will be the responsibility of the instructor, the department or the concentration—or an arrangement may be negotiated directly with the Librarian of the College.

Videos and recordings:

(a) Owned by the Grinnell College Libraries: May be placed on reserve in the Burling Library Listening Room. Copying is not permitted.

(b) Not owned by the Grinnell College Libraries: The libraries will initiate expedited orders to purchase any videos or recordings required for course reserves. Pending the receipt of videos or recordings so ordered the libraries may place personal copies belonging to instructors on reserve.

Personal copies will be removed from reserve when the library-purchased copy is received. Neither videos rented by instructors at video rental outlets nor off-the-air recordings may be placed on reserve.

Exceptions: In unusual circumstances temporary exceptions to these policies may be made by the Librarian of the College.

7.13 Holds on Materials

Culver-Union Township Public Library
Culver, Indiana

A hold may be placed on items that are currently checked out or otherwise temporarily unavailable for immediate check out. When the item does become available, a person with a hold will be notified and will have an opportunity to check out the item. Holds will be processed on a first-come, first-served basis; i.e., the person who first placed a hold on an item will be the first one to have an opportunity to check out the item when it becomes available, and so forth. Persons that are notified that a hold is ready for them to check out will be given a minimum of three days to pick up the item. If the item is not picked up after three days, the item may be returned to shelf or, if there are other holds on the item, the next person on hold may be notified and given an opportunity to pick up the item.

7.14 E-Reserves on Materials

University of Wisconsin–Platteville
Elton S. Karrmann Library
Platteville, Wisconsin

General Information

Electronic Reserves consists of scanned chapters of books, journal articles, notes, exams, syllabi, etc. and are available to students of the University of Wisconsin–Platteville and can be accessed either on or off campus. Not all reserves are available electronically and this may require students to physically come to the Karrmann Library. Electronic reserves may be printed once for personal use according to fair use provisions of the US Copyright Act of 1976, Section 107.

The Karrmann Library catalog contains a listing of all items currently on reserve and may be searched by instructor, department or course number. Since reserves are sometimes used in multiple classes, an instructor search is most effective. From the title list most reserves are available by clicking on the appropriate link or title. Electronic reserves are available off campus through the university proxy server. You will be prompted to enter your NDS username and password for access.

Adobe Acrobat Reader must be installed in order to view electronic reserves.

Guidelines

Library materials are purchased and intended for nonprofit educational use by students and faculty of the University of Wisconsin–Platteville. All library materials are acquired with the understanding that there will be multiple uses of a limited number of copies. Libraries frequently pay a premium institutional subscription price for journals for the privilege of supporting multiple academic users. The purpose of print and electronic reserves is to facilitate the availability of supplementary materials for class use. The Karrmann Library reserves collection contains both copyrighted material and non-copyrighted material in both electronic and print formats. Copyrighted material is covered by the fair use provisions of the US Copyright Act. The reserve collection includes materials owned by the library, instructor or other unit of the university that owns a lawfully obtained copy.

Whenever possible, materials to be copied or scanned will be purchased by the library. To ensure fair use compliance, electronic files will be deleted and paper files will be returned to the instructor or destroyed at the end of each academic year.

The Karrmann Library will place the following item types on electronic reserve:

- A single chapter from a book
- A single article from an issue of a journal
- One short story, essay or poem from a collective work
- One chart, graph, diagram, drawing, cartoon or picture from a book journal or newspaper
- A short excerpt of a work, which is not divided into chapters or articles.
- Student papers if permission has been obtained
- Material that violates any of these guidelines will not knowingly be made available.

Instructions for Instructors

Follow the requirements below when submitting your course reserves:

- Follow the guidelines mentioned above
- Complete the "Course Reserve Form" available at Circulation Desk
- Make sure to copy the COMPLETE article
- Do not staple articles
- Avoid black borders
- Submit requests at least one week before it is needed for class
- Indicate the complete bibliographic citation on the front page of each reserved item. This does not apply to exams, syllabi, or items you have written
- Copy on one side only
- Allow at least ¾ inch margins
- Large documents may need to be divided into several files
- Use the same title on the reserved material as you use in the class syllabus

University of Rhode Island
University of Rhode Island University Libraries
Kingston, Rhode Island

What is Electronic Reserves?

The Electronic Reserves system is a service which uses image scanning technology to provide electronic document delivery for some reserve readings. The service allows students to search, view, and print reserve course materials online. Using the Internet, students can search the "Course Reserves" section of the HELIN library catalog then click on any item marked "Electronic Copy Available" to access the material. Students must enter their name and valid library card number for security and copyright compliance.

Where is E-Reserves available?

Electronic Reserves is currently available at the University Library in Kingston and the URI Providence Campus Library only. It is not yet available at the Pell Marine Science Library (Narragansett).

What can be placed on E-Reserves?

Items that may be placed on Electronic Reserves are:

Instructor generated material (i.e. class notes, past exams, homework, etc.)

Journal articles which can be linked through the ProQuest databases or the Expanded Academic Index database. (Complete citation information must be provided.**)

Other print materials, providing the instructor has met copyright requirements.

**Processing materials for Electronic Reserves is more time consuming and uses more man hours than the traditional Reserves process. Therefore, we ask that instructors request only those items that will be receiving the highest use from students.

How do instructors submit material for E-Reserves?

After reading the Reserves Policies and Procedures, complete and sign a Reserve List Request Form. Submit this form along with your material to the Reserves Office.

Due to the additional processing procedures required for E-Reserves, material must be submitted 2 weeks prior to the date needed for class use.

Instructors should indicate on the traditional "Reserve List Request" form those items they would like available electronically.

Original paper copies submitted for E-Reserves must be:

> New, clear, clean copies OR saved on a disk in .PDF, .TIF, .GIF, JPEG, or .DOC format.
> NO staples, folds or creases please.
> Less than 30 pages per item. (Keep in mind large files are difficult to download/print.)
> One-sided copies only. (No double-sided copies.)
> All pages should be numbered to insure proper sequence.

7.15 Reserve Material Loan Periods

University of Louisiana–Lafayette
Edith Garland Dupré Library
Lafayette, Louisiana

Loan Periods

There are four types of loan periods: two-hour library-use-only, one day, three day and seven day. The loan period for materials is designated by the instructor who places the material on reserve. No renewals of any kind are allowed.

- Two-hour Reserves: Restricted to use within the library and two hours at a time per person.
- One-Day Reserves: Materials may be checked out at any time during the day and can be returned at any time during hours of operation the following day.
- Three-Day Reserves: materials may be checked out for three days and returned at any time during hours of operation on the third day.
- Seven-Day Reserves: materials may be checked out for seven days and returned at any time during hours of operation on the seventh day.

University of Texas–El Paso
University Library
El Paso, Texas

Loan Options:
- 1 Hour 1 Day
- 2 Hours 2 Days
- 3 Hours 3 Days

Materials processed for the Reserves Collection are handled on first come first served basis.

Materials received 10 to 15 days prior to the start of a new semester will be processed before classes begin.

The anticipated turn around time for processing materials, being added to the Reserves Collections or scanned into the online system, is 48 hours. Large numbers of materials received within a short span of time may affect the turn around time needed to complete the processing, therefore the library encourages faculty to submit materials to the Reserves Unit as early as possible.

Faculty have the option and right to remove any materials, which they have placed on Reserve, from the Reserves Unit of Circulation or the online system. They need to come and request the materials which they can take with them. Books owned by the library will be returned to the stacks when no longer needed as a reserve item and their location in the library will be reflected in the online public catalog. Faculty owned items, removed from Reserves, will be purged promptly from the Library's databases so that access is not available to library users. Scanned articles will be deleted or rendered inaccessible, once the faculty member has requested this action.

7.16 Reserves on Course Materials

San Jose Public Library and San Jose State University Library
San Jose, California

Statement of Policy & Text

San Jose State University has the right to place any library materials within the University Library Collections into the Course Reserve Collection.

Course Reserves are any portion of the University collection that a University faculty member has requested be placed on reserve.

These materials must be required for use in a scheduled University class or a University-approved examination, and the request must serve a legitimate academic purpose. (Defined in Section 2.1.29 of the Operating Agreement—see References below.)

The University shall retain the right to determine the rules and regulations that govern any particular material placed in the Reserve Collection, including the time period allowed for such Library material to be used.

Any such rules and regulations must apply uniformly and be enforced in the same manner for both the general public and University library users.

Limitations on the use of Course Reserves are specified in the Requirements & Guidelines section below.

Need for the Policy

Course Reserves support the instructional requirements of specific courses offered by SJSU. They ensure supplementary course materials that are assigned by SJSU students during the designated semester.

Requirements & Guidelines

Materials for Academic Reserves:
*   Are selected by SJSU faculty.
*   May be either SJSU-owned, the instructor's personal material, or online/electronic formatted material.

- Are not renewable and holds are not allowed.
- Cannot be checked out by patrons with temporary borrower status
- Can only be checked out at King Library and must be returned to the King Library Course Reserves Desk.

Loan Periods for Course Reserves are established based on the type of material and the urgency of the need. Load periods are limited to one of the following:
- 2 hours
- I day
- 3 days

Check-out limits for Course Reserves material are:
- 2 books/CDs/Videos and/or
- 5 personal folders

Fines: Course Reserves materials are fined based on loan periods:
- $1 per hour for 2 hour loans.
- $5 per day for 1- to 3-day loans.
- $20.00 is the maximum charge per item.
- Replacement Fee for Course Reserves materials is $80.00 plus accrued fines.

Recall of materials: Any SJSU-owned library materials may be recalled from any King Library user for placement on Course Reserve.

Public library card holders in the new King Library will:

Have access to the University-owned Course Reserve print and audiovisual collection, subject to the same limitations, terms and conditions as University students.

Not have access to an instructor's personal material or Electronic Reserves.

Alverno College
Alverno Library
Milwaukee, Wisconsin

COURSE RESERVES GUIDELINES

Reserves are materials needed by students for class work which have high and short term use, thus limiting the loan period so that all students may access them. Materials for use by college faculty and staff for short term, high use may also be placed on reserve. Reserves can include:
- Videos, those taped in class, those taped legally off-air, those personally owned by faculty/staff, and those held in the Alverno College Library collection
- Photocopies and reprints of periodical articles, as supplied by faculty/staff
- Specific issues of highly used periodicals held in the Library's collection
- Books owned by faculty/staff and those held in the Library's collection
- Computer software owned by faculty/staff and those held in the Library's collection
- Other types of audiovisual materials owned by faculty/staff and those held in the Library's collection. Education tests and computer software held in the Library's collection are generally placed on permanent reserve.

Items that will not be placed on reserve include:

Items owned by another institution, e.g., other libraries, video rental stores, etc.

Copyright and Reserves provides copyright guidelines for print and electronic reserves material.

Materials to be placed on reserve may be left at the Alverno College Library's Circulation/ Reserves Desk and must be accompanied by completed (yellow) reserve cards. If multiple copies of a title are being placed on reserve at the same time for a single class, only one card needs to be filled out.

Reserve materials will be processed as soon as possible. To avoid student frustration the library recommends that reserve materials be delivered to the library for processing 24 hours in advance of the time when they will be needed or expected by students. In the best of all possible worlds materials should be placed on reserve before they are mentioned as being on reserve in class.

Materials no longer needed for class reserves should be removed as soon as possible.

The library also offers some reserves material in PDF format which can be viewed both on campus and off campus using a personal computer. See the library's Electronic Reserves Guidelines for more information.

7.17 Reserves on Print Materials

Monroe Township Public Library
Monroe Township, New Jersey

Monroe Township Library cardholders can reserve books and electronic media. There is a nominal service charge for reserves.

Books may be reserved:

    a) in the Library by completing a reserve card.
    b) by phone.
    c) electronically by completing the reserve form on the Library's web page.

Reserves will be held for 10 days from the date the notice is mailed. After that time, a book not claimed is returned to the shelf or given to the next patron.

Stillwater Public Library
Stillwater, Texas

RESERVES/HOLDS

Patrons may reserve items that are listed in the online card catalog as checked out, having other holds, or in-process. Reservations cannot be placed on an item that is currently in the Library. Patrons must have a valid library card to place reserves. There is a limit of 15 requests for reserves per patron at any time. Reserves are not accepted for patrons who have overdue materials or $5.00 or more in fines.

Staff will attempt to contact patrons for at least three days when an item is available before removing their name from the reserved item. Reserve items will be held for three days after patron is notified of availability.

7.18 Proxy Authorization Guidelines

University of Illinois at Urbana-Champaign
University Library
Urbana, Illinois

PROXY AUTHORIZATION

UIUC faculty members, graduate students, and other library borrowers with extenuating circumstances may authorize another library borrower to charge out Library materials for them. This authorization is usually extended to students who are assisting a faculty member or a graduate student in his or her research, but a spouse, staff member, etc. can be designated as a proxy patron. Also, a library borrower can designate more than one proxy. Library materials will receive faculty or graduate loan periods. The length of the authorization is specified for up to one year. The individual is responsible for all library materials charged to their account, including those materials that his or her proxy checked out.

To obtain authorization, the faculty member or graduate student must complete and sign a "Proxy Form" available in the Main Circulation Office, Room 203 Main Library. The application form requires both the faculty or graduate student's and proxy's identification numbers and signatures.

The patron authorized to check out library materials for another individual must present his/her I-card or courtesy card at the desk and tell the staff member that he/she is checking out materials for another library borrower. A special proxy card will no longer be issued.

Brandeis University
Brandeis University Libraries
Waltham, Massachusetts

Proxy Policy

Proxy cards are a convenience offered by the library to current Brandeis University faculty and administrators only. In order to issue a proxy card, the faculty or administrator must have a library account of his/her own, which initially involves appearing at the library in person to register.

Once the faculty member or administrator establishes a library account (see General Circulation Department Policies), s/he may request a supply of proxy cards to issue to his/ her research assistants as s/he feels necessary, with the following in mind:

- The faculty/administrator is responsible for all items borrowed on his/her account, including but not limited to renewal, return and replacement of the materials.

- The proxy must have a valid Brandeis ID or library borrower's card, which must be presented before any materials can be checked out.
- The professor has an obligation to notify the library if the researcher's status changes during the school year.
- All proxy cards must have expiration dates.
- Get a proxy card here. [PDF file]

Researchers to whom the proxy cards are issued must obey the following rules:

- The card is for the convenience of the faculty member and not for personal use of the proxy.
- Proxies are required to inform the library of changes to their status and contact information.

Proxy card records will be reviewed each semester and declared inactive as necessary. The cards are housed at the library and are only valid when a current Brandeis ID or library card is provided during checkout. Proxy cards do not have to be submitted in person by the professor. However, any card submitted by a researcher will not be available for immediate use until its validity is first verified by telephone with the professor.

The circulation loan period for Main Library materials checked out by proxy is equivalent to the faculty loan period: a semester loan with two additional renewals. Science Library books circulate monthly with up to five renewals.

7.19 Recalls on Materials

University of Illinois at Urbana-Champaign
University Library
Urbana, Illinois

Recalling an item from another borrower: While borrowers cannot initiate recalls online, they may request to have a UIUC item recalled from another borrower by inquiring at any library public service point or by calling the Library Telephone Center at 333-8400. Library staff can only recall a UIUC item from another borrower if there are no other available copies anywhere in the statewide online catalog. Items owned by other ILCSO Libraries cannot be recalled without prior permission of the owning library.

If another borrower recalls an item that you have checked out, you will receive a "recall notice" in the mail. This notice informs you that the loan period for the item has been shortened and that the material must be returned by a certain date. This date is usually 15 days from the date the item was recalled. The Library's recall policy insures that library materials are equitably available. FAILURE TO RESPOND TO A RECALL WILL RESULT IN A $5.00/DAY (maximum $25.00/item) FINE. This fine applies to ALL borrowers, even those—such as faculty and staff—who are not charged processing fees. One day after the recall due date, your borrowing privileges will be automatically blocked until the recalled item is returned.

University of California Irvine
University of California Irvine Libraries
Irvine, California
Reprinted with permission of University of California Irvine

RECALLS/HOLDS

Any borrower with a valid library card may place a recall or hold on material that is checked out to another borrower, except:

Reserve materials
Bound serials checked out on special loan
Materials being searched
Material for which a bill has been generated
In-Process material
On order material
Materials under consideration for purchase

If an item is recalled, the new due date will be ten days from the date the recall was placed, unless the original due date is sooner.

Borrowers will be mailed or e-mailed a recall notice with the new due date and a courtesy overdue recall notice. Failure to receive recall and overdue notices does not exempt a borrower from fines or a lost book bill. Home and e-mail addresses may be changed in ANTPAC Web or at any Loan Desk.

Faculty and teaching assistants who want to reserve media for specific classroom show dates are encouraged to complete a MRC "Media Use Form," rather than placing a hold or recall.

Brandeis University
Brandeis University Libraries
Waltham, Massachusetts

Recall Policy

The recall and request services are available to Brandeis students, faculty and staff only.

The library collection is a shared collection owned by the University for use by the entire community, not just one individual or group. Because of this, all books are subject to recall or request. Original borrowers are expected to honor the recall request in order to assure the collection's accessibility to all patrons.

If a book is on loan and is due within 14 days of the current date, patrons may place a hold request on the item. A hold request does not shorten the original borrower's loan period but serves as a flag in the computer system, which appears when the item is checked in and indicates to the Circulation Staff that the book needs to be set aside for a patron.

If a book is due more than 14 days from the current date, the patron may recall the item from the current borrower. The original borrower's loan period will be reduced and s/he will have a maximum of 14 days for use of the recalled material. Recalled items are subject to fines of $2.00 per day. Recalls should be made in person at the Circulation Desk.

Patrons are notified by phone or email when their requested or recalled item has arrived and will have 10 days to pick up the item before it is re-shelved.

Tulane University
Howard-Tilton Memorial Library
New Orleans, Louisiana

Recalls & holds

To maximize access to the library's collection, all library material checked out to patrons is subject to recall. Recalls may be placed after a patron has had an item for at least two weeks. The loan period is shortened and a notice is sent to the patron notifying them of the new due date.

The patron will have ten days to return the item to the library. After ten days the library charges $1.00 a day in overdue fines. Yes, one dollar a day. One day, one dollar. The idea is to get people to take recalls seriously. Any patron with an outstanding recall will be blocked from library privileges until the item has been returned. So check your mailbox, be sure the library has your correct address and check your record online every week or so.

The returned item will be held for the patron who has initiated the recall for ten days. If the patron does not pick up the material in ten days, it will be sent back to the stacks.

Faculty members are also subject to recalls and to any applicable recall fines.

Items that are at the bindery or on reserve cannot be recalled.

Holds can be placed on items that are soon to fall due, or are overdue. When a hold is placed it will block other patrons from checking the item out or renewing their loan.

Please note: The Access Services staff cannot and will not give out the name of the patron who has the library material that is being recalled.

7.20 Forms: Reserve Requests

St. Charles Community College
St. Charles Community College Library
St. Peters, Missouri

Library Reserve Request

Instructor: _____ Phone/Email: _____

Course Title: _____ Course #: _____

Year/Semester: _____

In the columns below, list the material you wish to place on reserve status. Write the title, indicate the format, and check out time.

Formats: A=Article   B=Book   V=Video   O=Other

Lending Periods: 2 hours   24 hours   3 days   7 days

Title		Call#	Format	Checkout
			A B V O	2hr 3D 7D

_____

_____

_____

_____

_____

_____

_____

_____

_____

_____

Bucknell University
Bertrand Library
Lewisburg, Pennsylvania

Reserves Request

Course (include section if there are more than one Ex: BIOL 355):

Instructor's Name:

Instructor's Phone:

Email:

Semester:

Call Number	Title	Date to Remove (If prior to end of semester)	Loan Period			Material Type			
			2h	3h	Overnight	VHS	DVD	Personal Copy	Library Owned Book

Please fill out all applicable sections to insure timely processing

Comments/Additional Information:

145

PLEASE NOTE:

Overnight loans are due back by 10:30 AM the next morning.

The Reserve Room is designed to accommodate primarily REQUIRED readings. General guidelines as endorsed by the ULC suggest a maximum of 25 items per course.

Make sure the library owns the material you wish to place on reserve. If an item needs to be ordered, please do so online here.

Titles on your syllabus should match the titles in our catalog to avoid confusion.

Reserve requests will usually be processed in **3-5 working days.** Requests will be processed in the order in which they were received.

If a loan period you require is not listed, please see the reserve manager for other arrangements.

7.21 Form: E-Reserve Request

University of California Bakersfield
Walter W. Stiern Library
Bakersfield, California

Electronic Reserve Request Form

This form is for use by CSUB faculty to submit requests for items (e.g. photocopies, articles, class notes, etc.) to be placed on Electronic Reserve. These items will be available to students (with valid CSUB Runnercard) on the Internet. Items for Electronic Reserve must be submitted on clean 8 1/2" x 11" single-sided white paper at least three weeks prior to the date students will need access to them. For formats other than scanned items, please use Hardcopy Reserve Request Form.

Please submit a course syllabus with Reserve lists of ten or more items.

This section is necessary for the initial setup of the Electronic Reserve Course Page.

Please complete all fields.

Instructor name: _____

Campus phone: _____

Campus address: (e.g.DDH100)_____ Campus email address: _____

Course number: (e.g.Anth 100) _____ Course name:_____

Quarter: FALL WINTER SPRING SUMMER PERMANENT Year: _____

Please note: The Library follows the Fair Use Guidelines of the Federal Copyright Law. This means we can accept: one chapter from a book and/or one article from a specific journal issue. If you have questions about copyright compliance, please contact us for further information.

Please submit a separate form for each course and return forms to Circulation Manager.

Questions?

Please list all Electronic Reserve items submitted for the class specified above. Please list author, title, and source for each item. Use reverse for additional space. *(Examples in italics)*

PLEASE ALLOW AT LEAST THREE WEEKS PROCESSING TIME

Author Title of Item Source/date

Smith, J. "Coral Aggression" Fish v.2, #5, May 2000, pp1-10

(article)_____

_____

Jones, J.P. "Violence on the Reef" Oceans. Harper, 1998, chapter 1, pp 1-17

(book chapter)

_____

_____

_____

_____

_____

COPYRIGHT

7.22 Course Reserves Copyright

University of Central Florida
University of Central Florida Libraries
Orlando, Florida

The UCF Libraries' Circulation Department, including the main library and other branches of UCF Libraries, provide course reserve services to support the teaching activities of the University. All reserve materials must comply with copyright laws. Any item for which the UCF faculty or staff has obtained written permission from the copyright holder, materials that fall within fair use, and any work in the public domain may be placed on reserve. Current fair use guidelines do not cover the use of material beyond one semester. At the end of each semester, all materials on reserve will be removed from reserve.

Faculty or staff placing materials on reserve are responsible for verifying that those items are copyright compliant. To assist in determining whether copyright permission is required, please consult the UCF Libraries Copyright Decision Tree. When required, written permission must be obtained. UCF Libraries' staff may require proof that materials placed on reserve do not violate copyright guidelines.

To date, there is no university-wide infrastructure for the University to process and/or pay for copyright permissions. Individual faculty members may check with their departments, or obtain permissions on an individual basis.

University of Texas at Arlington
University of Texas at Arlington Libraries
Arlington, Texas

Built upon "UT System Rules of Thumb for Reserves"

Reserve copies should be a small part of the materials required for a course and obtained legally by the faculty member or the library through purchase, license, interlibrary loan, fair use, etc. CONFU (Conference on Fair Use) guidelines stipulate that reserve articles should not substitute for the purchase of a textbook.

Copies of copyrighted materials placed on reserve can be: a single article or chapter; a short story, poem or essay; or a few graphs, charts or pictures.

Reserve copies should include any copyright notice on the original, complete citation and attributions to the source, and a section 108(f)(l) notice that reads, "Copying, displaying and distributing copyrighted works may infringe the owner's copyright."

Access to copies, whether paper or electronic, should be limited to students enrolled in the class and administrative staff as needed. Access is to be terminated at the end of the class term.

Copies of copyrighted materials that will be used repeatedly by the same instructor for the same class requires permission from the copyright holder. Generally the first semester a copy is placed on reserve, permission will not be required unless there is some factor that negates it falling under fair use guidelines.

If permission has to be sought, one (1) copy will be placed on reserve (either electronic or paper–the faculty member may choose). Once permission is received additional paper copies may be placed on reserve if so desired. The following credit line should go on copied material authorized by the Copyright Clearance Center: "Reproduced with permission of the copyright holder via the Copyright Clearance Center."

If permission is denied or the royalty charge excessive, the copy will be removed from reserve and returned to the faculty member. If the original work is owned by the Library, it may be placed on reserve in place of the copy.

If the original work is placed on reserve (a book or journal issue for example) then copyright permission does not have to be sought.

If an article to be placed on reserve is already available electronically and our licensing agreement allows, we will point to that location from the reserve list instead of scanning and posting the article.

Photocopies of entire works and coursepacks will not be placed on reserve.

7.23 E-Reserves Copyright

University of Minnesota Duluth
UMD Library
Duluth, Minnesota

RESERVE - Electronic

Duplications made for Electronic Reserve are governed by the US Code Title 17 Chapter 1 Sec. 107 Limitations on exclusive rights: Fair use. Reserve Processing staff, acting in the best interest of the Library, reserves the right to refuse a processing request if, in their judgment, fulfillment of the request would involve violation of the copyright law.

The UMD Library Reserve Processing staff will, at the request of UMD faculty or staff, place on electronic reserve duplications from copyrighted materials owned by the library since library materials are acquired with the understanding that there will be multiple uses of a limited number of copies.

Requests for duplications from materials not owned by the UMD Library will be placed on reserve as "fair use" as determined by the requesting faculty or staff or with proof of copyright clearance from the copyright holder. Faculty and staff will be encouraged to complete a Fair Use Worksheet, which is available on the Campus Copyright Information Site. Use of duplications determined to be in excess of fair use will require a purchase of the original by the UMD Library, permission from the copyright holder or payment of copyright fees.

Reserve Processing staff will assist in obtaining copyright permission and/or arranging for the payment of copyright fees for duplications determined not to be fair use. Copyright clearance will be sought using the Copyright Clearance Center ECCS (Electronic Course Content Service) account. In instances when the cost is prohibitive, a single copy will be placed on traditional reserve with payment through the CCC TRS (Transactional Reporting Service) account.

Duplications of lecture notes, exams or items in the public domain will be placed on electronic reserve.

Papers submitted for course work will be placed on electronic reserve when accompanied by a written permission form signed by the student. They will remain on reserve for the time period indicated by the requesting faculty unless an earlier time period is specified on the permission form.

A copyright statement will be placed on each electronic reserve item to indicate the material may be protected by the copyright law.

Electronic files will be removed from the reserve system as soon as time permits following the end of the term indicated by the requesting faculty or staff.

University of Texas System
Austin, Texas

INTRODUCTION

Many college, university, and school libraries have established reserve operations for readings and other materials that support the instructional requirements of specific courses. Some educational institutions are now providing electronic reserve systems that allow storage of electronic versions of materials that students may retrieve on a computer screen, and from which they may print a copy for their personal study. When materials are included as a matter of fair use, electronic reserve systems should constitute an ad hoc or supplemental source of information for students, beyond a textbook or other materials. If included with permission from the copyright owner, however, the scope and range of materials is potentially unlimited, depending upon the permission granted. Although fair use is determined on a case-by-case basis, the following guidelines identify an understanding of fair use for the reproduction, distribution, display, and performance of materials in the context of creating and using an electronic reserve system.

Making materials accessible through electronic reserve systems raises significant copyright issues. Electronic reserve operations include the making of a digital version of text, the distribution and display of that version at workstations, and downloading and printing of copies. The complexities of the electronic environment, and the growing potential for implicating copyright infringements, raise the need for a fresh understanding of fair use. These guidelines are not intended to burden the facilitation of reserves unduly, but instead offer a workable path that educators and librarians may follow in order to exercise a meaningful application of fair use, while also acknowledging and respecting the interests of copyright owners.

These guidelines focus generally on the traditional domain of reserve rooms, particularly copies of journal articles and book chapters, and their accompanying graphics. Nevertheless, they are not meant to apply exclusively to textual materials and may be instructive for the fair use of other media. The guidelines also focus on the use of the complete article or the entire book chapter. Using only brief excerpts from such works would most likely also be fair use, possibly without all of the restrictions or conditions set forth in these guidelines. Operators of reserve systems should also provide safeguards for the integrity of the text and the author's reputation, including verification that the text is correctly scanned.

The guidelines address only those materials protected by copyright and for which the institution has not obtained permission before including them in an electronic reserve system. The limitations and conditions set forth in these guidelines need not apply to materials in the public domain—such as works of the U.S. government or works on which copyright has expired—or to works for which the institution has obtained permission for inclusion in the electronic reserve system. License agreements may govern the uses of some materials. Persons responsible for electronic reserve systems should refer to applicable license terms for guidance. If an instructor arranges for students to acquire a work by some means that includes permission from the copyright owner, the instructor should not include that same work on an electronic reserve system as a matter of fair use.

These guidelines are the outgrowth of negotiations among diverse parties attending the Conference on Fair Use ("CONFU") meetings sponsored by the Information Infrastructure Task Force's Working Group on Intellectual Property Rights. While endorsements of any guidelines by all conference participants is unlikely, these guidelines have been endorsed by the organizations whose names appear at the end. These guidelines are in furtherance of the Working Group's objective of encouraging negotiated guidelines of fair use.

This introduction is an integral part of these guidelines and should be included with the guidelines wherever they may be reprinted or adopted by a library, academic institution, or other organization or association. No copyright protection of these guidelines is claimed by any person or entity, and anyone is free to reproduce and distribute this document without permission.

A. SCOPE OF MATERIAL

1. In accordance with fair use (Section 107 of the U.S. Copyright Act), electronic reserve systems may include copyrighted materials at the request of a course instructor.

2. Electronic reserve systems may include short items (such as an article from a journal, a chapter from a book or conference proceedings, or a poem from a collected work) or excerpts from longer items. "Longer items" may include articles, chapters, poems, and other works that are of such length as to constitute a substantial portion of a book, journal, or other work of which they may be a part. "Short items" may include articles, chapters, poems, and other works of a customary length and structure as to be a small part of a book, journal, or other work, even if that work may be marketed individually.

3. Electronic reserve systems should not include any material unless the instructor, the library, or another unit of the educational institution possesses a lawfully obtained copy.

4. The total amount of material included in electronic reserve systems for a specific course as a matter of fair use should be a small proportion of the total assigned reading for a particular course.

B. NOTICES AND ATTRIBUTIONS

1. On a preliminary or introductory screen, electronic reserve systems should display a notice, consistent with the notice described in Section 108(f)(1) of the Copyright Act. The notice should include additional language cautioning against further electronic distribution of the digital work.

2. If a notice of copyright appears on the copy of a work that is included in an electronic reserve system, the following statement shall appear at some place where users will likely see it in connection with access to the particular work:
   "The work from which this copy is made includes this notice: [restate the elements of the statutory copyright notice: e.g., Copyright 1996, XXX Corp.]"

3. Materials included in electronic reserve systems should include appropriate citations or attributions to their sources.

C. ACCESS AND USE

1. Electronic reserve systems should be structured to limit access to students registered in the course for which the items have been placed on reserve, and to instructors and staff responsible for the course or the electronic system.

2. The appropriate methods for limiting access will depend on available technology. Solely to suggest and not to prescribe options for implementation, possible methods for limiting access may include one or more of the following or other appropriate methods:
   a) individual password controls or verification of a student's registration status; or
   b) password system for each class; or
   c) retrieval of works by course number or instructor name, but not by author or title of the work; or
   d) access limited to workstations that are ordinarily used by, or are accessible to, only enrolled students or appropriate staff or faculty.

3. Students should not be charged specifically or directly for access to electronic reserve systems.

D. STORAGE AND REUSE

1. Permission from the copyright holder is required if the item is to be reused in a subsequent academic term for the same course offered by the same instructor, or if the item is a standard assigned or optional reading for an individual course taught in multiple sections by many instructors.
2. Material may be retained in electronic form while permission is being sought or until the next academic term in which the material might be used, but in no event for more than three calendar years, including the year in which the materials are last used.
3. Short-term access to materials included on electronic reserve systems in previous academic terms may be provided to students who have not completed the course.

7.24 Forms: Sample Copyright Permission Letters

St. Charles Community College
St. Charles Community College Library
St. Peters, Missouri

Copyright Permission Sample Letter

Date

Copyright Holder/Publisher [This portion to be filed out by LRC staff]
Street Address
City, State Zip
Attn: Copyrights and Permissions Department

Dear Sir or Madam:

Regarding the following title and information, I would like permission to retain a copy the following material on reserve in the library at St. Charles Community College.

[This portion to be filled out by instructor or requesting department.]

Author or Editor: _____

Article or Chapter: _____

Periodical or Book Title: _____

For Periodical: Volume #_____ Issue Date: _____ Pages: _____ ISSN: _____

For Book: Copyright date: _____ Pages: _____ ISBN: _____

Number of copies to be placed on reserve: _____

Time item will remain on reserve until: _____

The copy will be used exclusively for educational purpose, with no direct or indirect commercial advantage, and will include a notice of copyright for students enrolled in my class.

Thank you for considering my request; I am looking forward to your reply. If you have any questions, contact Gwen Bell, Secretary for Learning Resources, at the address listed below, by phone at 636-922-8470, or by email gbell@stchas.edu.

Sincerely,

[Signature of instructor]

University of California

University of California Policy on the Reproduction of Copyrighted Materials for Teaching and Research

The following is a sample letter to a copyright owner (in this example a publisher) requesting permission to copy:

Date

Material Permissions Department
Academic Book Company
200 Park Avenue
New York, New York 10016

Dear Sir/Madam:

I would like permission to copy the following for use in my class (name of class) (next semester) or (next semester and subsequent semesters during which the course is offered.)

Title: Ethics and the Law, Second Edition

Copyright: Academic Book Co., 1965, 1971.

Author: John Smith

Material to be duplicated: Chapter 9 (photocopy enclosed).

Number of Copies: 50

Distribution: The material will be distributed to students in my class and they will pay only the cost of the photocopying.

Type of reprint: Photocopy

Use: The chapter will be used as supplementary teaching materials.

I have enclosed a self-addressed envelope for your convenience in replying to this request.

Sincerely,

Faculty Member

PRIVACY OF CIRCULATION AND LIBRARY RECORDS

7.25 General Policy Guidelines

University of Illinois at Urbana–Champaign
University Library
Urbana, Illinois

POLICY ON CONFIDENTIALITY OF LIBRARY RECORDS

In consideration of:

Council of the American Library Association's strong recommendation that the responsible officers of each library formally adopt a policy with regard to confidentiality of library patron records;

ALA Policy Manual 54.15—Code of Ethics, point 3, which states "Librarians must protect each user's right to privacy with respect to information sought or received, and to materials consulted, borrowed or acquired";

Family Education Rights and Privacy Act of 1974, which prevents schools from distributing students educational records to third parties without a student's consent; and

Illinois Library Records Confidentiality Act, P.A. 83-179, effective January 1, 1984 which states: "The registration and circulation records of a library are confidential information. Except pursuant to a court order, no person shall publish or make any information contained in such records available to the public."

The UIUC Library formally recognizes:

That all records identifying the names, social security numbers, or I.D. number of library patrons are confidential in nature;

That such records are not to be revealed to anyone other than the patron in question without either the express written permission of the patron in question or the adherence to proper legal and University procedures regarding required access to such information;

That library employees are encouraged not to keep records with personally identifiable information, unless that information is necessary, and to destroy such records as soon as possible.

That the confidentiality of patron records requires that such records should be consulted by library employees only for LEGITIMATE purposes such as locating or recalling library materials, processing overdue notices and fines, adding or deleting names to the database, making collection development decisions, resolving billing matters, or investigating violations of Library circulation policies, including but not limited to, the following:

- expired I.D. number with overdue items still charged
- patrons who repeatedly claim to have returned books
- patrons who have manipulated the system to set their own due dates outside the Library's established patron loan periods
- patrons with outstanding Library accounts who have been referred to collection
- Library employees may not view patron records for such purposes as idle curiosity, personal interest, or general monitoring.

Special requests for confidential information to be used for research purposes shall be addressed to the University Librarian.

EXAMPLES OF REQUESTS FOR LIBRARY INFORMATION THAT IS CONFIDENTIAL AND MUST NOT BE HONORED. This list is intended to provide examples of possible violations of confidentiality of library information and is by no means inclusive. Any request for confidential information from patron records coming from a law enforcement officer or investigative agent of the state or federal governments MUST be referred to the University Librarian.

CIRCULATION AND PATRON RECORDS
- A request for the circulation records of a faculty, student, staff or other library card holder by someone else.
- A request by a faculty member for the identity of students who borrowed reserve items.

- A request to review the circulation records of a student suspected of plagiarism.
- A request to see interlibrary loan borrowing records.
- A request for addresses, phone numbers, I.D. numbers or other personal information contained in the borrower database.
- A request to see a list of individuals who are not members of the university community but who have been granted library borrowing privileges.
- A request by a parent for information such as fines or other fees by the library to Students Accounts Receivable without the student's permission.

OTHER EXAMPLES

- A request for the name of the person who has signed out a particular item.
- A request to review the identity of persons who have used a study room, listening room, study carrel or CD-ROM workstation.
- A request to reveal the nature of a library user's reference request or database search.
- A request for the names of persons who have used audio-visual materials.
- A request for a list of items photocopied for or faxed to a particular Library user.
- A request for a list of suggested acquisitions submitted by a particular Library user.
- A request from law enforcement authorities for the identity of anyone conducting research on a particular subject.

Santa Monica Public Library
Santa Monica, California
Personally Identifiable Information

Santa Monica Public Library will collect only the information needed to contact library users, such as mailing address, email address, phone number, etc., in order to ensure the proper notification, lending, and return of library materials and the collection of fines. Records will be retained for the shortest length of time necessary to facilitate library operations.

Individuals may choose to submit their names, email addresses, postal addresses or telephone numbers in order to receive library services, such as registering for library cards, ordering materials, receiving personal responses to questions, receiving Library promotional materials, or being added to specific mailing lists. The Library does not sell, rent or otherwise distribute information to outside companies or organizations. However, library records may be subject to disclosure to law enforcement officials under provisions of the USA PATRIOT Act Uniting and Strengthening America by Providing Appropriate Tools Required to Intercept and Obstruct Terrorism Act (USA PATRIOT Act) and under some circumstances librarians may be forbidden to disclose that certain records have been requested or obtained.

Email reference questions submitted to the Library will be retained for no more than three months. Questions are retained only for the purpose of statistics and to assist with follow up queries from clients. The questions themselves and any personal information such as names, email addresses, telephone and fax numbers submitted with the questions are confidential and are treated as other library user information under provisions the Confidentiality of Library Records policy above.

Fresno County Public Library
Fresno, California
Registration & Circulation

By law (California Government Code Section 6267), circulation and registration records of Library users are confidential. The Library collects only that information needed to verify the identity of borrowers, to enable contact for Library operations purposes, and for minors, contact information for a parent or legally responsible adult. The Library takes reasonable steps to safeguard this registration data and to prevent unauthorized access to it.

Upon request, the Library will provide information to parents and guardians about fines, fees, or other charges incurred by their minor children.

Users have the right to access their personal information and to verify its accuracy through "My Account" in the Library catalog. A library card number and PIN are required to access your records which include materials currently checked out, holds to be filled, money owed, and personal reading lists in "My List."

Records of items borrowed are maintained electronically. Links between users and the items they borrow are broken after the items are returned. Records of fines and fees may be retained for several years according to Fresno County and San Joaquin Valley Library System policies. "My List" is managed by each individual user, but lists inactive for 90 days are purged. Circulation system back-up is maintained as necessary to allow data rebuild in the event of system problems.

University of Michigan
University Library
Ann Arbor, Michigan

Circulation

It is the policy of the Library that the privacy of all borrowers of library materials shall be respected. The Library will not reveal the names of individual borrowers nor reveal what books are, or have been, charged to any individual.

When library users need books that are on loan, the units with circulation responsibility will assist them by calling in those books as soon as the guaranteed loan period (usually three weeks) has ended. If the books desired are in a renewal period, they will be recalled immediately.

Washington University in St. Louis
University Libraries
St. Louis, Missouri

Confidentiality of Washington University Library Records

Consistent with federal and state law and university policy, the Washington University Libraries treat as confidential all records that identify the library material borrowed, used, or requested by an individual, and all other records identifying individual library users (collectively "library records"). Except as specified below, the Libraries will not release library records.

Library records may be released in these circumstances:

The individual identified in a library record may request a copy of that record from full-time circulation staff. If the records are readily available and do not identify any other individual, circulation staff may provide the individual with copies of his/her own library records.

If it appears to a member of the faculty or administration that a student may have violated School or University academic integrity policies, that member of the faculty or administration may request library records relevant to determining whether such a violation has occurred by contacting the Judicial Administrator or a school's Academic Integrity Officer (collectively, "academic integrity officers"). If an academic integrity officer determines that certain library records are likely to be relevant to determining whether the student has violated academic integrity rules, the officer shall ask the Head of Access to provide specified records. With the authorization of an academic integrity officer, the Head of Access shall make the records available to the requesting member of the faculty or administration. The library records shall remain confidential and may be used only in connection with the academic integrity inquiry.

Upon receipt of a court order, the Libraries must produce library records as directed by the court. Unless otherwise precluded by law, the Libraries will inform library users that their records have been accessed.

All requests for library records shall be directed to the Head of Access (or other individual designated by the Dean). Items may be recalled if they are needed by others. When an item is needed urgently, full-time circulation staff shall, upon special request, inform the borrower that another patron or library unit needs the material.

7.26 Procedures Protecting Patron Confidentiality

Keene State College
Mason Library
Keene, New Hampshire

Staff Procedures:

If anyone approaches library staff alleging to be a law enforcement official requesting information, staff members should refer the law enforcement official to the Library Director, the Assistant Director, or the Circulation Librarian. The Library Director, Assistant Director, or Circulation Librarian will ask to see official identification and photocopy the ID.

If a law enforcement official presents a subpoena, the library staff member should direct that person to the Library Director, the Assistant Director, or the Circulation Librarian who will, in turn, forward it to the University System's General Counsel Office.

If a library staff member is presented with a search warrant, they should immediately contact the Library Director, the Assistant Director, or the Circulation Librarian who will also contact the University System's General Counsel Office.

Keep a detailed record of the legal requests and give that record to the Library Director.

The Library Director will keep a record of all legal requests and of all costs incurred by any search and/or seizures.

If a "Gag Order" is in effect, report the contact only to the Library Director. A search warrant presented under the US Patriot Act typically contains language restricting the dissemination of information about the search warrant. This language is referred to as the "Gag Order."

If a "Gag Order" is not in effect, the Library Director will notify the President of the College, the University System's General Counsel Office, and the American Library Association.

Emergency Disclosures of Information: If in the normal course of business, the library staff observes behavior or receives a communication, which may be reasonably construed to be a threat of imminent danger to life and limb of the general public or the staff, they should contact local law enforcement agencies immediately. They should then contact their supervisor and the Library Director and fill out an Incident Report.

Santa Monica Public Library
Santa Monica, California

Procedures for Handling Requests for Library Records

Library staff who are approached by a law enforcement officer or agent with any request or court order to examine or obtain the library records of any library user will ask for identification and direct the officer or agent to the City Librarian or other designated person in charge. The City Librarian or the designated person in charge will review the request or search warrant and seek the advice of the City Attorney.

Search warrants signed by the court are immediately enforceable. Staff will request identification and a copy of the warrant. Staff may request that the agent or officers direct inquiries through the City Librarian or the designated person in charge. The City Librarian or designated person in charge may request time to fax the warrant to the City Attorney for verification. If the officer or agent wishes to immediately enforce the search warrant, staff should not interfere but should proceed to notify the City Librarian or designated person in charge of the search.

7.27 Patriot Act Privacy Guidelines

Keene State College
Mason Library
Keene, New Hampshire

About the USA Patriot Act of 2001

Libraries are facing a dilemma of having the responsibility of protecting the privacy of our patrons while responding to legitimate national security concerns. On October 25, 2001, Congress passed the Uniting and Strengthening America by Providing Appropriate Tools Required to Intercept and Obstruct Terrorism" (USA PATRIOT) Act. The Act broadly expands law enforcement's surveillance and investigative powers.

HR-3162 became Public Law 107-56: in response to the events of 9/11/01.

For additional information, see the American Library Association's Office for Intellectual Freedom.

The USA Patriot Act overrides New Hampshire confidentiality laws protecting library records and the library will comply with it. The library's policy relating to privacy and confidentiality of information has not changed as a result of the act.

Access to patron information under the Act may include, but not be limited to, the following records:

> Database search records
> Circulation records
> Computer use records
> Interlibrary loan records
> Reference interviews

Libraries or librarians served with a search warrant issued under FISA (Foreign Intelligence Security Act) rules may not disclose, under penalty of law, the existence of the warrant or the fact that records were produced as a result of the warrant. Staff cannot tell a patron that his or her records were given to the FBI or that he or she is the subject of an FBI investigation, nor speak to coworkers, the media, or other government officials about the inquiry. Such requests can be reported to a higher authority within the library and the University System of New Hampshire's General Counsel only.

Gleason Public Library
Carlisle, Massachusetts

The Gleason Public Library strives to protect the privacy of library patrons' free access to information to the fullest extent of the law.

The Library will ask for and retain only that information necessary to perform user services. The Library keeps no permanent record of items checked out, Internet sites visited, electronic databases used, or searches performed by patrons; any data stored (either intentionally or incidentally) on our computer network, consortia servers, or individual machines is protected by MA Law (MGL Chapter 78, Section 7).

All staff members must support this policy of privacy. Only authorized library staff may access personal data stored in the library's computer system and files for the purpose of performing library work.

The Library is not to reveal the borrowing records, reserve or fine records to any person other than the owner to which they are assigned, unless authorized by that individual*. No records can be made available to any inquiries, governmental or otherwise, unless a subpoena has been served by a court of competent jurisdiction and the library administration has consulted with legal counsel to determine if it is proper to release the requested information.

However, Library patrons should be aware that provisions in the USA Patriot Act (Public Law 107-56) may require the Library to provide Federal officials with information about individuals' use of library resources pursuant to a subpoena. Other portions under the USA Patriot Act also specify that no delay is possible and that the library workers are prohibited from informing the patron that information regarding their records has been subpoenaed.

While the Library will endeavor to protect the privacy of patrons' use of Library computers and borrowing practices, absolute privacy is not guaranteed. Please take note that library computers and collection stacks (containing books, magazines, and media) are located in public areas, which must be shared by all library users. In addition, the Library cannot and does not guarantee that every task completed via its network is unconditionally private and secure.

The Gleason Public Library is committed to the American Library Association's (ALA) Library Bill of Rights and its Freedom to Read Statement. According to the ALA, in a library, the right to privacy is the right to inquiry without having the subject of one's interest examined and scrutinized. Confidentiality exists when a library is in possession of personally identifiable information about users and keeps that information private on their behalf. Recognizing the role of the library as a center for free and uninhibited access to information of a democratic society, the library staff must vigilantly guard their patrons' privacy and freedom of inquiry, honoring their trust and confidence. This policy is based on recommendations of the American Library Association and Massachusetts General Laws Chapter 78, Section 7 which states, That part of the records of a public library which reveals the identity and intellectual pursuits of a person using such library shall not be a public record as defined by clause Twenty-sixth of section seven of chapter four.

*The Library understands that special circumstances in the case of minors may arise, in which staff must release information relating to misplaced items, due dates, fines, or lost/damaged items to the legal guardian of that minor.

Chapter 8

INTERLIBRARY LOAN REQUEST POLICIES

PATRON BORROWING GUIDELINES

8.1 General Statement

Bridgewater Public Library
Bridgewater, Massachusetts

WHAT IS INTERLIBRARY LOAN?

An interlibrary loan is a transaction in which library material, or a copy of the material, is made available by one library to another upon request, not including material shared among SAILS member libraries.

The purpose of interlibrary loan is to obtain library material not available in the Bridgewater Public Library or SAILS, and to loan material found at the Bridgewater Public Library to non-SAILS libraries.

Interlibrary loan service is essential to the vitality of libraries of all types and sizes as a means of greatly expanding the range of materials available to users. Lending between libraries is in the public interest and should be encouraged. Interlibrary loan should serve as an adjunct to, not a substitute for, collection development at the local level.

Tazewell County Public Library
Tazewell, Virginia

DEFINITION AND PURPOSE

Interlibrary Loan (ILL) is the process by which a library requests material from, or supplies material to, another library. In the interest of providing quality service, libraries have an obligation to obtain material to meet the informational needs of users when local resources do not meet those needs. Tazewell County Public Library (TCPL) recognizes that the sharing of material between libraries is an integral element in the provision of library service and believes it to be essential to the vitality of all libraries.

GOVERNANCE

Interlibrary loan policies of this library are governed by the American Library Association's Interlibrary Loan Code for the United States (2001), the Virginia Interlibrary Loan Code (1989), the Copyright Law, Title 17, U.S. Code, HAL's Reciprocal Borrowing Agreement (2000), and by the regulations of lending libraries. TCPL also works in cooperation with SWING and other groups of libraries to make resources available for patron use. Within the limits of the policy set forth here, TCPL will offer to obtain for patrons requested materials not available in the collections of this system. TCPL will consider such factors as geographic proximity, type of library, and lending fees when determining to which library an interlibrary loan request will be made, when there is a choice.

University of Albany–State University of New York
University Libraries
Albany, New York

Mission statement: The mission of the Interlibrary Loan Department is to support the research and teaching needs of the University at Albany academic community, by expanding the range of materials available for scholarship beyond the physical and electronic collections of the University Libraries. The department provides article delivery and short term loans from a vast network of libraries and document suppliers on a local, statewide, national, and international basis.

University of Nevada Reno
University Libraries
Reno, Nevada

Interlibrary loan is a transaction in which library material, or a copy of the library material, is made available by one library to another upon request. When library materials are not available in the University of Nevada, Reno Libraries, library users may request those items through Document Delivery Services. An interlibrary loan transaction has two components: borrowing and lending. This policy addresses the borrowing component.

Document Delivery Services abides by the American Library Association's National Interlibrary Loan Code for the United States, 2001 and the specific policies of lending libraries. In addition, Document Delivery Services complies with the Copyright Act of 1976 (Title 17 of the United States Code) and guidelines developed by the National Commission on New Technological Uses of Copyrighted Works, known as the CONTU guidelines, as described in the Library of Congress' Copyright Publication number 21.

8.2 Verifying Bibliographic Citations

Florida International University
Florida International University Libraries
Miami, Florida

Why do I need to verify a citation?

Verified ILL citations will reduce the time you must wait for a response from the ILL Office. Citations which are correct have a better chance of being filled than do citations which are incorrect or incomplete. Be aware that citations from unverified sources, such as bibliographies at the end of chapters or articles, are more likely to be wrong than are citations from a verified source. Consult a verified source, such as an index, an abstract, or an online source supported by a library, in order to be assured that your citation is as good as you can make it.

How do I verify a citation?

There are many sources to be found in the library which should help you to verify your citation. Begin your verification at the Reference Desk if you are unsure about where next to proceed. Or, you may choose one or more of the following options as a starting point:

The FIU Library Catalog will help you to verify FIU Library ownership of books, journals, magazines, newspapers, government documents, audio-visual materials, or many other materials in the Catalog. The Articles and Subject sections will help you to access indexes and abstracts in order to find articles in journals, newspapers, and magazines.

The FIU Library provides electronic access to Full Text Materials available via indexes and abstracts, as well as to Electronic Journals to which the library subscribes. Also, electronic access to information by Subject or in Alphabetical Order is available.

Books published before 1968 can be found in several places, primarily in the National Union Catalog. This multi-hundred volume work, a catalog of research libraries in the United States and Canada, is found in the Reference Collection. There are 3 sets of "NUC's" —

Pre-1956 Imprints, listing books printed before 1956

Supplement to the Pre-1956 Imprints, listing books printed before 1956 which were not listed in the Pre-1956 Imprints

1956–1967 Imprints, listing books published from 1956 until 1967

Books published after 1968 to the present can be found in the SUS Catalog and FirstSearch, both available in WebLUIS.

Union catalogs, which list materials owned by a library on a specific subject or by groups of libraries on one or more subjects, can be found in the FIU Libraries in print format and microform. Visit the Union Catalogs in Print and Microform web guide to assist you with your research and citation verification needs.

For older and/or those difficult-to-find journal, magazine, and newspaper titles, use the Union List of Serials, found in the Reference Department [call number = Z6945 .U45 1956].

8.3 Requesting Material

Bridgewater Public Library
Bridgewater, Massachusetts

To request a book you will need the author, title and if possible, the year of publication. Subject requests are also accepted.

To request a periodical article you will need the title of the journal, date, page numbers, author and title of the article. The source of the information must also be included (index, bibliography, etc.)

A "need by" date should be indicated, if applicable, and whether a non-circulating copy of the requested materials is acceptable if no circulating copy can be borrowed.

To avoid delays, fill out the forms as completely as possible. Please do not use abbreviations. If you don't have all of the information, we will still try to fill your request, but may not be successful.

Tempe Public Library
Tempe, Arizona

An interlibrary borrowing request is initiated by submitting a completed ILL request form to the Reference or Computer Access Center service desks. Requests will also be accepted by telephone from any Tempe Public Library cardholder in good standing. When requesting an item for interlibrary loan, the following information will assist library staff in locating and requesting the item: exact title of the item, author or editor's full name, publisher, and date of publication.

8.4 Number of Requests Allowed

University of South Carolina
University of South Carolina Libraries
Columbia, South Carolina

Interlibrary loan (ILL) is a service through which books or journal articles not owned by the University Libraries may be obtained from other libraries or commercial document suppliers. This service is available at no cost to faculty members, currently-enrolled students, University staff, current members of the Thomas Cooper Society and current members of the Carolina Alumni Association. Persons affiliated with the School of Medicine, the Law School, or the University's Regional and Four-Year campuses should use their respective Interlibrary Loan departments.

The number of interlibrary loan requests in progress at one time is limited according to patron category, as approved by the University Faculty Committee on Libraries. Please plan your research activities accordingly. If there are special circumstances surrounding your research, any of the Interlibrary Loan Department staff members will be happy to discuss them with you. The limits are as follows:

Faculty: 100 active requests

Graduate students: 50 active requests

Staff: 25 active requests

Undergraduates: 10 active requests

Current members of the Thomas Cooper Society: 5 active requests

Current members of the Carolina Alumni Association: 3 active requests

Please check the library catalog to be certain that the material you need is not already held by the University Libraries (Business, Columbia Annex, Education, Film, Government Documents, Law, Maps, Math, Microforms, Music, Rare Books and Special Collections, Science, South Caroliniana, and Thomas Cooper). We do not accept requests for items held by the University Libraries.

Please note that we do not accept orders for textbooks and other classroom materials that are available at the USC bookstore for currently-offered courses.

Tempe Public Library
Tempe, Arizona

A library user may have up to three (3) outstanding interlibrary loan transactions at any one time. This includes requests that are pending as well as materials that the user currently has borrowed through interlibrary loan.

8.5 Procedure for Rush Requests

Florida International University
Florida International University Libraries
Miami, Florida

Due to the labor intensive and costly nature associated with this service, a maximum of 5 Rush requests per week per person will be accepted. Please limit and prioritize your rush requests to those materials you truly need urgently and within a short period of time. Your requests are important, and a 24-hour turnaround request will be forwarded to potential lending libraries. Rush requests for books are not eligible for this service, but the requests will be processed with all due speed.

University of Louisville
University Libraries
Louisville, Kentucky

Rush Requests

Rush options for interlibrary loan will be left to each interlibrary loan department. Costs for rush charges are fixed, however.

8.6 Reasons to Refuse ILL Request

Florida International University
Florida International University Libraries
Miami, Florida

What if FIU owns the book or journal I need?

ILL service is not available for books owned by the FIU Libraries, including books and other materials currently checked out by another patron. If you need a book which is currently checked out to another patron, the Circulation Desk will be able to hold the book for you when it is returned or recall it immediately. Inquire at the Circulation Desk for details. If the book or periodical is not on the shelf when you look for it, please check again. Materials used by patrons within the library will be reshelved to the correct location. If the book is listed in the FIU Library Catalog as being "lost", "missing", or "at bindery", ILL will process your request. Articles in issues of journals and magazines owned by the FIU Libraries are not available through ILL. Requests for articles from periodical issues which are charged out or enroute to the bindery will be processed. Search in the FIU Library Catalog to verify holdings.

University of Albany–State University of New York
University Libraries
Albany, New York

Books: If a book is available through the University Libraries, it is not ordered through Interlibrary Loan if it is on the shelf or accessible through the reserve system. However, if the book is checked out you may chose either to recall it at the Circulation Desk or to order it through Interlibrary Loan. If you decide to order the book through ILL, please indicate in the notes field in the ILLiad book order form that our copy is checked out.

8.7 Patron Eligibility

Tempe Public Library
Tempe, Arizona

Interlibrary loan service is available to any library user in good standing (i.e., card is not blocked for fines, overdue materials, or incorrect address) that has been issued a current Tempe Public Library borrower's card.

Tazewell County Public Library
Tazewell, Virginia

Eligibility

Patrons must have a valid TCPL borrower's card and be in good standing (accounts free of fines or overdue materials) to request material via ILL. Faculty and students of local colleges are encouraged to borrow material for their academic research through their own institutions. Non-residents are encouraged to request ILL service through their local public libraries. All transactions are from library to library.

Athens-Limestone Public Library
Athens, Alabama

The Interlibrary Loan librarian will verify all loan requests for specific titles in Library Management Network, Alabama Library Catalog, and other resources as needed. As much bibliographic data as possible is needed from the patron in order for a request to be processed. Requests will not be accepted from patrons who have overdue materials and/or owe fines or other charges. Overdue and fine records will be checked before a loan request is sent to another library.

Florida International University
Florida International University Libraries
Miami, Florida

Who can use ILL?

Interlibrary Loan is available to any faculty (including retirees), staff, and currently enrolled FIU or SUS students.

FIU Alumni are ineligible to receive ILL services, and are encouraged to seek this service from the nearest public library.

Why aren't FIU Alumni eligible for ILL service?

Because the purpose of ILL in an academic library is one of research and instructional support for faculty and enrolled students. Please contact the nearest public library for assistance.

University of Nevada–Reno
University Libraries
Reno, Nevada

Eligible Users

Library users with valid University of Nevada, Reno library cards may use the service as follows:

University of Nevada, Reno faculty, staff, graduate students, and undergraduate students are eligible for the service.

University and Community College of Nevada System (non-University of Nevada, Reno affiliated) faculty and staff may use the service for $3 per request plus any associated fees.

Community Borrowers may use the service for $10 per request plus any associated fees.

Colgate University
Colgate University Libraries
Hamilton, New York

Who Is Eligible to Borrow?

ILL services are freely available to current Colgate University faculty, students, staff and administrators.

Persons Who Are Not Colgate Faculty, Current Students or Staff:

Responsibilities to current faculty, staff, and students always take precedence. The heavy demand for interlibrary loan services for our primary clientele limits our abilities to provide similar services to others, and it is typical for academic libraries to provide no interlibrary loan services to others. However, within the limitations of our primary responsibilities and subject to responsible stewardship of materials lent to us by other libraries, the Colgate University Libraries wish to establish as generous and helpful a policy as possible.

From the beginning of the fall semester to the end of the spring semester, interlibrary loan services are available only to currently registered or employed students, faculty and staff; and to faculty and staff emeriti of Colgate University.

During the summer months, however, interlibrary loan privileges are extended to Colgate alumni or alumnae and to visiting scholars under the following provisions:

Alumni or alumnae:

Alumni or alumnae who wish to secure interlibrary loan privileges for the summer months must establish a $50.00 deposit account. Monies in deposit accounts are refundable at the end of the summer, less any unpaid fees or assessments for damage or loss of items.

Alumni or alumnae who wish to secure interlibrary loan privileges for the summer months must sign a statement accepting responsibility for payment for any lost or damaged materials in amounts established by the lending library.

Alumni or alumnae will pay in advance a $10.00 service charge for each item requested. If the lending library levies charges for borrowing privileges, these charges will be paid by the alumnus or alumna upon receipt of the material. Any unpaid charges will be deducted from the deposit account.

Overdue status on any Colgate-owned or interlibrary loan item will result in an immediate block on all borrowing. ILL privileges will be revoked if any ILL is kept more than two weeks overdue.

All payments must be made by check, payable to Colgate University. Interlibrary loan personnel are not authorized to accept any other method of payment. Refunds from deposit accounts will be made by a voucher redeemable at the cashier's window in Colgate Hall.

Alumni or alumnae may request visiting scholar status through the Dean's office as appropriate.

Visiting scholars:

Visiting scholars who wish to secure interlibrary loan privileges for the summer months must present a letter from the Office of the Dean of the Faculty establishing status as a visiting scholar. Interlibrary loan personnel can supply a form which, upon validation by the Office of the Dean of the Faculty, will meet this requirement.

Visiting scholars who wish to secure interlibrary loan privileges for the summer months must establish a $50.00 deposit account. Monies in deposit accounts are refundable at the end of the summer, less any unpaid fees or assessments for damage or loss of items.

Visiting scholars who wish to secure interlibrary loan privileges for the summer months must sign a statement accepting responsibility for payment for any lost or damaged materials in amounts established by the lending library.

If the lending library levies charges for borrowing privileges, these charges will be paid by the visiting scholar upon receipt of the material. Any unpaid charges will be deducted from the deposit account.

Overdue status on any Colgate-owned or interlibrary loan item will result in an immediate block on all borrowing. ILL privileges will be revoked if any ILL is kept more than two weeks overdue.

All payments must be made by check, payable to Colgate University. Interlibrary loan personnel are not authorized to accept any other method of payment. Refunds from deposit accounts will be made by a voucher redeemable at the cashier's window in Colgate Hall.

8.8 Failure to Pick Up Material

Tempe Public Library
Tempe, Arizona

Library users who request an item via interlibrary loan and fail to pick it up upon notification by a library staff member will be assessed a fee of $5.00 for each unclaimed item, in addition to any fees or charges assessed by the lending library.

Tazewell County Public Library
Tazewell, Virginia

ILL is a costly service and TCPL cannot afford to borrow material for patrons who do not claim material borrowed for them. TCPL will, therefore, assess a $5.00 fine for each unclaimed item.

8.9 Charges and Fees

University of Kentucky
University of Kentucky Libraries
Lexington, Kentucky

COSTS

The Library absorbs up to $30 for acquiring reproductions of articles/chapters/papers or for the loan of material acquired through Interlibrary Loan. If cost exceeds $30 the ILL staff will contact the patron to see if they are willing to absorb the extra cost. Fax or rush service may often generate extra costs from the supplying library. All expenses associated with the complete reproduction of an item (replacing the loan of a requested item) that becomes the property of the patron will be passed on to the patron. Patrons will be held responsible for any fees incurred by overdue, damaged or lost items while borrowed material is in their possession.

Tazewell County Public Library
Tazewell, Virginia

TCPL provides ILL service at no charge. Fees for photocopying and occasionally other charges may be assessed by the lending library. Such charges will be passed on to the patron. TCPL will obtain authorization from the patron before ordering material for which there is a charge. Patrons using rental microfilm must pay rental fees at the time of placing the request.

TCPL assesses fines for the late return of ILL material at the rate of $1 per day per item with no maximum fine. The lending library will assess repair or replacement charges if materials are returned damaged or are lost. In order to insure the effectiveness of ILL service, it is necessary to maintain good relations with cooperating libraries. Loan periods and use restrictions set by the lending library must be strictly observed. Abuse of ILL privileges (failure to return material on time or to pay fees for late return, damage or loss) may result in loss of these and other library privileges.

Athens-Limestone Public Library
Athens, Alabama

At the time of the initial request, patrons will be told that they will be responsible for payment of any photocopy, postage, or insurance charges on the books or other materials borrowed from other libraries. Postage charges are made only on the return trip of the material, and are not charged on books borrowed from Athens State University (ASU). When a patron fails to pick up and pay charges on an interlibrary loan, the cost of the postage will be attached to their record.

Hershey Public Library
Hershey, Pennsylvania

Most usual fees associated with ILL service, such as database searching and shipping, are paid by the library. Borrowers are responsible for any unusual fees charged by the lending library but will be contacted for approval before such items are requested. Borrowers are also responsible for any charges incurred for lost or damaged items, for overdue charges at a cost of $.50 per item per day and for photocopying fees where applicable.

University of Nevada–Reno
University Libraries
Reno, Nevada

Fees for Services

Interlibrary borrowing and document delivery services are provided to UNR faculty, staff, and students at no cost to the requester.

University and Community College System of Nevada faculty and staff (non-University of Nevada, Reno affiliated) are charged $3.00 per request for books and periodical articles plus any associated fees. Associated fees may include charges assessed by lending libraries for borrowing materials or supplying photocopies, or charges billed by commercial document delivery suppliers.

Community Borrowers are charged $10.00 per request for books and periodical articles plus any associated fees. Associated fees may include charges assessed by lending libraries for borrowing materials or supplying photocopies, or charges billed by commercial document delivery suppliers.

Alverno College
Alvervo College Library
Milwaukee, Wisconsin

There is no charge for libraries with which Alverno has reciprocal agreements unless special handling is required. Any billing that is necessary will be invoiced with materials. A $10.00 surcharge will be added for RUSH requests to Alverno.

8.10 Overdue or Lost ILL Material Charges and Fees

Rutgers University
Rutgers University Libraries
Newark, New Jersey

Interlibrary loan materials are subject to the same fines as materials owned by Rutgers University Libraries. Overdue Recall fines are assessed at $5 per day up to a maximum fine of $50. Replacement charges for lost materials are assessed at $102 per item when interlibrary loan materials are seven days overdue. You may pay fines in the following manner:

by check or cash at the circulation desks of Alexander, Chang, Douglass, Kilmer, Library of Science and Medicine, Camden, Dana (Newark) libraries; by Knight Express car at Alexander Library; or by credit card at a cashier's office if you are on academic hold.

The University reserves the right to hold transcripts and diplomas if you do not pay your obligations, and to forward delinquent accounts to collection agencies and to levy a collection fee.

Mohawk Valley Community College
Mohawk Valley Libraries
Utica, New York

Materials borrowed through interlibrary loan for our users are the property of the lending library, not of MVCC. If materials are not returned within two weeks after the due date, a hold will be put on student's grades, registration, and transcript. For ILL items that are lost, borrowers are responsible for the replacement cost, which is determined by the lending library.

Bridgewater Public Library
Bridgewater, Massachusetts

Payment must be made for materials lost or damaged while charged out to the borrower. No refunds will be made for lost and paid interlibrary loan materials that are subsequently found.

University of Kentucky
University of Kentucky Libraries
Lexington, Kentucky

Borrowed items kept overdue by patrons create critical problems for Interlibrary Loan service. Lending libraries may cease to lend to our institution for any other researchers until all overdue material is returned. Costly fines and replacement fees could also be incurred. Items kept overdue will result in a block of your use of the ILLiad service until the overdue is resolved. The Interlibrary Loan Unit will not hesitate to seek the help of academic advisors or departmental chairs in resolving these problems.

Alverno College
Alverno College Library
Milwaukee, Wisconsin

Borrowers not returning Interlibrary Loan books are not subject to current Alverno College Library overdue charges. However, if the patron is delinquent in returning any borrowed materials, the patron will be charged for the replacement cost of the material. Cost will be determined at the discretion of the lending institution.

Clarke Public Library
Athens Regional Library System
Athens, Georgia

Borrowers are expected to return ILL materials by the date due. Failure to do so jeopardizes the borrowing status of the entire Library System. Delinquent borrowers will be charged an overdue fine (see Fines/Fees Schedule) and will be blocked from use of other library services until the materials are returned. Fines may be excused by library staff in individual cases; i.e., illness or death in the borrower's family.

The borrower assumes responsibility for all ILL charges and replacement or repair costs if materials are lost or damaged. All Library System services will be suspended for patrons who fail to pay ILL charges over the amount set on Fines/Fees Schedule. ILL privileges will be revoked for patrons who consistently fail to return books promptly.

LENDING LIBRARY GUIDELINES

8.11 Materials Available from Lender

Aurora Public Library
Aurora, Illinois

The following materials are available for the Interlibrary Loan from the Aurora Public Library:
   a. Circulating books
   b. Circulating periodicals
   c. Sheet music
   d. Audio-visual materials
   e. Photocopies from non-circulating materials

Colorado State University Pueblo
University Library
Pueblo, Colorado

Circulating Materials: Books, government documents, theses, cds/audio cassettes, videos/dvds, maps. There is a 5-week lending period for returnable items, with renewals usually granted. The CSU-Pueblo Library is a partial government depository since 1965, and has a limited number of state documents, all circulating. Theses are available for loan if there is a second copy available for a 5-week period subject to renewal. Maps and limited microfiche are also available for loan.

Society for the Interdisciplinary Study of Social Imagery (SISSI) Conference Proceedings: Whole proceedings are not lent, but articles and Tables of Contents will be supplied to any requesting library. For more Conference information and some tables of contents, see: http://chass.colostate-pueblo.edu/sissi/, the SISSI web site.

Articles: At this time, color copies are not available.

Non-Circulating Materials: Reference, Reserve, and Rare Books Collections, records, most microforms, bound periodicals.

Delivery Policy: The department uses US Mail, Colorado Courier System, and will fax and Ariel requested articles. The department will mail materials to distance education students at their home or office, or send articles to distance students' WebView accounts.

Weber State University
Stewart Library
Ogden, Utah

Interlibrary Lending

1. Request
   A. The WSU Library lends to any requesting institution submitting its request on appropriate interlibrary loan forms or through the OCLC-ILL subsystem. Priority is given to requests from Utah libraries and BCR-AMIGOS network libraries.

2. Non-Circulating Items
   A. Media, reserve, microform and reference materials are designated as non-circulating and will not be lent through interlibrary loan. Material located in the Curriculum Library, Archives and Special Collections cannot be loaned but may be photocopied at the discretion of the individual responsible for those collections.

3. Journals
   A. Photocopies of articles are provided in lieu of loaning journal volumes and/or issues.

4. Loan Periods
   A. Monographs are lent through Interlibrary Loan for four weeks use.
   B. Two week renewals of monographs are allowed if they have not been requested by a WSU Library patron.
   C. Items lent through Interlibrary Loan that are not requested by a WSU patron will be recalled.

5. Overdue Material
   A. Overdue notices are sent on items that are not returned. Borrowing libraries will be billed for replacement cost of material that is two months overdue.

6. Restriction on Use
   A. Borrowing privileges may be revoked if an institution consistently damages or fails to replace lost WSU material or if restrictions placed on borrowed items are ignored.

8.12 Borrowing Items and Returning Items to Lender

University of South Carolina
University of South Carolina Libraries
Columbia, South Carolina

Materials obtained through interlibrary loan are for your exclusive use and are your responsibility from the time they are picked up at the Circulation Desk until they are returned. We recommend that you return your materials directly to the Interlibrary Loan Department. You will be responsible for any late fees, replacement costs of lost material, and cost of damages billed to us by lenders.

Abuse of the interlibrary loan service can result in the loss of your interlibrary loan borrowing privileges and also may result in suspension of your circulation privileges. If you are a USC student, your registration activity may also be placed on hold for failure to return interlibrary loan books. Failure to return materials on time can damage the library's relationship with the libraries from which we acquire materials and may prevent us from borrowing from those libraries in the future.

The lending library, not our Interlibrary Loan Department staff, sets the conditions for each loan. We cannot change these conditions, and we ask patrons to honor them.

The lending library may restrict the use of materials to use within the library only, and may also disallow copying or renewal. Restrictions are noted on the ILL Express! label on the front of your borrowed item. The lending library has the right to recall a loan at any time.

The due date for loans is three weeks from the date the item is processed in the Interlibrary Loan office, unless otherwise noted. Materials should be returned to the Interlibrary Loan office or to the Thomas Cooper Library Circulation Desk, on or before the date indicated on the item.

We do not recommend returning interlibrary loan material to drop boxes.

Please do not remove the ILL Express! identification bands that are placed on all borrowed items. We need them so that we can correctly identify your materials and process them for return to the lending institutions.

University of Louisville
University Libraries
Lexington, Kentucky

Returning Materials

Materials obtained through Ekstrom Interlibrary Loan should NOT be placed in book drops. Interlibrary Loan materials should be returned directly to the Circulation Desk.

Materials obtained through Kornhauser Interlibrary Loan may be placed in book drops or returned to the circulation desk.

8.13 Materials Unavailable

Aurora Public Library
Aurora, Illinois

The following materials will not be available for Interlibrary Loan:
a. Reference materials
b. Special local history & genealogy materials
c. Microfilm or Microfiche
d. Framed art prints
e. Sculptures
f. Bound periodicals

Tempe Public Library
Tempe, Arizona

In order to insure that local Tempe Public Library users have access to the latest materials, the following items will not be loaned via interlibrary loan: popular books published within the last year; books with long reserve lists; items designated as "high demand"; audio-visual materials (videos and sound recordings); software; reference material (e.g. directories, encyclopedia sets, indexes, standard library reference tools); bound or current issues of magazines and newspapers; and rare, archival, manuscript or fragile items.

8.14 Materials Available

University of Albany State University of New York
University Libraries
Albany, New York

In general, materials in the following categories are easily obtainable:
- Books printed since 1900 (except for certain current year imprints)
- Microforms of newspapers and back runs of periodicals
- Articles from scholarly journals and from periodicals in general
- Government documents
- Patents
- Some dissertations (availability is unpredictable)

California State University Northridge
Oviatt Library
Northridge, California

Materials available

Items which normally circulate, such as books and theses, and some materials reproduced in microform, such as newspapers, can be borrowed. Photocopies of non-circulating materials, primarily periodical articles, can be requested in accordance with the copyright law. Items owned by CSUN library but declared Officially Missing by the Circulation Department can also be requested.

8.15 Periodical Articles Available

Hershey Public Library
Hershey, Pennsylvania

Most libraries will not lend entire magazines, but may provide photocopies of individual articles for a fee. When requesting magazine articles, patrons are responsible for photocopying charges of at least $.10 per page. Because many libraries impose a minimum photocopying fee of $5.00 to $20.00 per article, maximum charges you are willing to pay must be included on request forms before requests can be processed. We will always, however, attempt to fill requests at the least possible cost.

University of Albany–State University of New York
University Libraries
Albany, New York

Articles: If an article is available from our print collections or from one of the online full text services to which we subscribe, we will not go forward with your request as an interlibrary loan transaction. The only exception is if the article is owned in hard copy only and if the article is missing from the journal or if the journal volume is at the bindery.

Dominican University of California
Archbishop Alemany Library
San Rafael, California

Individual journal articles require the COMPLETE journal title; no abbreviations (i.e.: Do not list DAI or ECT.) Many journals have the same initials, so you will need to include all words listed in the title. Without the volume number, issue number, correct date, and article title, processing your request can be unnecessarily delayed. If the citation you are using does not have all the required information, or if you have trouble locating either one or both, the volume or issue numbers, please ask a reference librarian to help you before submitting your request.

Once you are certain of your information and ready to fill in the online ILL form, select and click on the appropriate form at the top of this page, complete, and submit.

Note: Because all information requested from the patron must be converted into electronic form before the interlibrary loan transaction can occur, the Library would appreciate your avoidance of paper forms.

8.16 Materials Difficult to Borrow

University of Texas at Arlington
University Libraries
Arlington, Texas

You cannot request course textbooks through Interlibrary Loan. Faculty cannot request materials through ILL for the purpose of placing them on Reserve.

University of Albany–State University of New York
University Libraries
Albany, New York

In general, items from these categories are more difficult to obtain:

- Books printed before 1900 and/or rare books
- Manuscripts
- Materials published exclusively in some other countries
- Paper editions of newspapers or magazines
- Audio-visual material
- Current year imprints
- Reference materials and other non-circulating materials

Bridgewater Public Library
Bridgewater, Massachusetts

Materials which will not be borrowed:

Material owned by the Bridgewater Public Library or SAILS and temporarily in use

Titles on the New York Times or Publisher's Weekly bestseller lists

Multiple copies of a title for class or other group use

Inexpensive paperbacks in print

Titles not yet published

Tempe Public Library
Tempe, Arizona

Some types of materials are not available for lending by other libraries and, consequently, the following will not be requested on interlibrary loan: audio-visual materials (videos, and sound recordings); reference material (e.g. directories, encyclopedia sets, indexes, standard library reference tools); bound volumes or individual issues of magazines and newspapers; software; rare, archival, manuscript or fragile items; popular books published within the last year; and books currently in the collection of the Tempe Public Library which are not listed as lost or missing.

Tazewell County Public Library
Tazewell, Virginia

TCPL will not borrow:
1) an item which is already owned by TCPL unless it is long overdue or lost
2) textbooks
3) material determined to be in violation of copyright law
4) more than 5 items for one patron at any one time

Athens-Limestone Public Library
Athens, Alabama

Best sellers and high demand titles published within the current calendar year cannot be requested. The local library will attempt to purchase as many of these titles as budget permits.

Bridgewater Public Library
Bridgewater, Massachusetts

- Most libraries will not ordinarily lend the following types of materials:
- Newly published material
- Old, rare or valuable material
- Reference and genealogical material
- Audio and videocassettes, sound recordings, and motion picture films
- Entire issues of periodicals
- Material in high demand at the lending library; curriculum material, including textbooks
- Scripts, screen plays, libretti, and scores
- Multi-volume sets

University of Nevada–Reno
University Libraries
Reno, Nevada

What Cannot Be Requested

Non-circulating materials in the University Libraries are not eligible to be requested. The University Libraries' materials that are checked out cannot be requested; instead, checked-out materials can be recalled. Exceptions will be considered on a case-by-case basis.

Materials are loaned at the discretion of the lending library. High use materials may not be available. Materials with current year imprints are not always available; the Document Delivery Services Supervisor will let the user know if a specific title would be available.

The following items are usually not available for loan: Rare, fragile, or valuable materials; A-V materials; computer software; reference materials; entire issues or volumes of periodicals; multiple volume sets; and other non-circulating items. Textbooks for current university classes will not be requested by Document Delivery Services.

DDS is unable to supply copies of entire issues of journals due to the cost of purchasing royalty-paid articles. Users are asked to prioritize needed articles from a single issue and DDS will order as many as possible with a maximum total cost of $100.

Some universities do no lend their masters theses and doctoral dissertations. Document Delivery Services staff will check universities' policies to determine whether theses and dissertations can be borrowed. Most dissertations are available for purchase from University Microfilms International through the online database Dissertation Abstracts located on the Libraries' web site.

Because the National Judicial College Library, Truckee Meadows Community College Library, the Desert Research Institute Library, and the Washoe County Library are geographically close to the university, materials located at those libraries are not eligible to be requested through interlibrary loan.

8.17 Form: Article Interlibrary Loan Request

Wheelock College
Wheelock College Library

If an **article** is not available at the Wheelock College Library use the form below to request the item through InterLibrary Loan. You may also print the paper form (pdf) and submit it to the Reference Librarian on floor 1M of the Library.

Name:
Library Barcode Number:
Phone Number:
Email (required):
Patron Status:
Article Title:
Article Author:
Journal Title:
Journal Vol. and No.
Year/Date:
Page numbers:
Citation Source:
I will no longer need this item after:
Additional notes/special requests:

8.18 Lending Charges

Aurora Public Library
Aurora, Illinois

The Aurora Public Library shall not charge other libraries fees for use of its materials.

The Aurora Public Library shall not charge other libraries fines for overdue Aurora Public Library materials.

Tempe Public Library
Tempe, Arizona

There will be no charge to lend materials from the Tempe Public Library's collection to other libraries nor will charges be assessed for overdue items. If an item is not returned by the borrowing library to the Tempe Public Library, the borrowing library is responsible for the replacement cost of the item.

Colorado State University–Pueblo
University Library
Pueblo, Colorado

Charges/Payment: There are no charges to borrow materials. The department is an IFM participant.

Weber State University
Stewart Library
Ogden, Utah

Charges

A. The Library does not charge for interlibrary loan lending or photocopies. However, reciprocal charges will be assessed to those libraries charging WSU for interlibrary loans or photocopies.

Long Beach City College
Long Beach City College Library
Long Beach, California

CHARGES FOR LENDING SERVICES

A. Book Fees (Loan Fees)
  1. Institutions who charge us ILL fees Same as their fees
  2. For-Profit Organizations $10.00
  3. Reciprocal Institutions $ 0 (and no additional charges)
  4. Non-profit Organizations $ 0 (and no additional charges)
  5. Additional Charges
     a) First Class postal fee $ 5.00
     b) Rush delivery service $10.00
        Example: Federal Express
     c) International First Class postal fee $ 8.00

B. Photocopy Fees
  1. Institutions who charge us ILL fees
     First 50 pages $10.00 / article
     Each additional page $ .50 / page
  2. Reciprocal Institutions $ 0 (and no additional charges)

3. Non-profit Organizations $ 0 (and no additional charges)
4. Additional Charges
   For-profit organization service fee $ 5.00
   Fax Transmission (25 pgs max) $ 5.00
   Rush Fax Transmission (25 pgs max) $15.00

Note: Microfilm, microfiche, bound and unbound materials cannot be loaned out.

8.19 Renewals

Tempe Public Library
Tempe, Arizona

Library users are encouraged to return materials at the end of the loan period so that materials are not absent from the lending library for an unreasonable length of time. Renewals are only permitted if the lending library allows such an extension. Requests to renew an item must be submitted two days in advance of the due date for the item. Materials received through interlibrary loan may not be renewed or requested again for at least six months.

Florida International University
Florida International University Libraries
Miami, Florida

Are renewals possible?

Books obtained through Interlibrary Loan are not owned by the FIU Library, and the lending library has the right to deny a renewal request, grant a renewal request, or recall the book before the due date. (We have the same right, in the opposite direction.) Before contacting the ILL Office to request a renewal, you will need to look at the yellow band wrapped onto the book. If the "Renewal not allowed" section is check-marked, a renewal request is not possible. If this section is not check-marked, a renewal is not guaranteed, and we will submit a request if you contact the ILL Office at least 5 business days before the due date listed on the yellow band. Sufficient time will be needed for the lending library to decide about your renewal request. If the renewal request is denied, the book must be returned on the original due date. Since the FIU Library does not own the book, we have no jurisdiction over lending libraries' due dates.

University of Texas at Arlington
University Libraries
Arlington, Texas

Can I renew the material?

If an item is not marked "No Renewal", and it has not already been renewed once, you can request a renewal through ILL Online. You will get a new due date that is 14 days after the original due date unless we contact you to tell you differently. If the lending library cannot renew the item, you will return the item immediately.

Some items cannot be renewed.

- Items marked "No Renewal"
- Items that have already been renewed once
- Overdue items

University of Kentucky
University of Kentucky Libraries
Lexington, Kentucky

Please make reading your interlibrary loan material a priority in your research. Renewals are granted at the discretion of the lending library and are not routinely given. If a renewal is necessary, submit an electronic renewal request using ILLiad or ask at the Interlibrary Loan office in person or by phone. An additional two weeks will be requested. If the institution does not grant the renewal, the item must be returned immediately. Only one renewal will be requested per item.

8.20 Loan Periods

Falmouth Public Library
Falmouth, Massachusetts

The loan period for books is established by the lending library. Most items circulate for 2 weeks. The due date is indicated on the white label or white band on the front cover. When a periodical article is requested, the lending library sends a photocopy, which the borrower may keep. To maintain good relations with cooperating libraries, books borrowed via Interlibrary Loan should be returned to the circulation desk on or before the due date.

California State University Northridge
Oviatt Library
Northridge, California

Duration of Loans and returning materials

Lending libraries determine any conditions regarding the use of their materials, including the loan period which is normally two weeks for all patrons (including faculty), usually with no renewals allowed. The loan period begins on the date the material arrives at CSUN, so any delays in picking it up results in less use time for you. Renewals should be requested only when absolutely necessary, and must be made before the due date. Other restrictions may include "for Use in the Library Only", and "Photocopying Not Permitted". Be sure to leave the identification band on the cover of the book and do not return ILL materials to the Circulation Department or a book drop. All materials borrowed through Interlibrary Loan must be returned to the Interlibrary Loan Office for special processing. Late return of materials jeopardizes our Interlibrary Loan relationship with other libraries, and we may refuse further Interlibrary Loan service to anyone who disregards due dates, lender restrictions and CSUN policy.

BORROWING LIBRARY GUIDELINES

8.21 Item Arrival Notification

Bridgewater Public Library
Bridgewater, Massachusetts

Patrons are notified by telephone when the material arrives. Items are kept at the Service Desk for three days after the patron is notified. Periodical articles are kept at the Information Desk for one week.

Hershey Public Library
Hershey, Pennsylvania

Patrons will be notified by telephone when materials are ready to be picked up at the library. While library staff will attempt to speak directly with the borrower, it is often necessary to leave a message either with another individual answering at the number listed on the request form, or on an answering machine. We recommend that messages be checked regularly as we are unable to request a previously received item for a period of six months. Patrons will also be notified if we cannot obtain an item. At this time we are unable to offer email notification.

Florida International University
Florida International University Libraries
Miami, Florida

How do I know that my materials have arrived?

You will receive notification by email — please remember to provide your email address on all ILL forms (electronic and paper forms). If you do not have email, you may request an email account from FIU's UTS (University Technology Services). If you do not have email, book arrivals will be notified by telephone and will be held for you at the library until the due date assigned by the lending library has been reached; photocopied articles are mailed whenever possible only to campus addresses, otherwise notification will be made by telephone and the article will be held for you at the library. Materials may be picked up at the following campus locations: [Lists]

University of Nevada–Reno
University Libraries
Reno, Nevada

Notification When Materials Arrive

Document Delivery Services notifies users when materials arrive via e-mail, Campus Mail, or U.S. Mail depending on address information stored in their library card circulation records

8.22 Turnaround Time

Bridgewater Public Library
Bridgewater, Massachusetts

The Bridgewater Public Library belongs to the SAILS network. Requests can be placed electronically to several different library systems in Massachusetts and are delivered by van. It can take two or three weeks to receive an item from a Massachusetts library, or if we have to go out of state, it can take longer to complete the process.

Service will be given as quickly and inexpensively as possible.

Tazewell County Public Library
Tazewell, Virginia

Time required to receive requested material can vary considerably, depending on availability of material, location of the lending library, and shipping method. Some materials may arrive in 2-3 days, while others may take weeks or months. When making his ILL request, the patron should indicate any deadline for receipt of material and whether material will not be needed after a given date. Requests will be processed in the order in which they are received. If a patron has an urgent need, he must specify his deadline on his request form to receive priority processing.

University of Texas at Arlington
University Libraries
Arlington, Texas

When will the material arrive?

Your materials will usually arrive within 2 weeks. Items that are very recently published, unusual, or in a format other than a book or photocopy can take longer. ILL offices around the US usually don't operate during weekends and holiday periods, so at those times there can be delays.

But, materials that are available from libraries in the State of Texas can arrive in less than 2 weeks.

If you have special needs requiring fast delivery, talk to the ILL staff about your situation and include your deadline on the request forms. We will try to meet your deadline. When your deadline is reached, we will stop trying to locate your material and let you know the situation. There may be an extra charge for fast delivery. Contact the ILL Office for more information about extra charges.

Feel free to contact the ILL Office to ask about the status of your request. If your material has not arrived and you have not heard from us within two weeks of placing your request, contact us to ask about it.

Falmouth Public Library
Falmouth, Massachusetts

Interlibrary Loan orders take from 2-4 weeks, sometimes longer, so please be sure to plan ahead. Photocopy requests are usually filled within a week. We cannot guarantee delivery within a specific period of time. You will be notified by phone or by postcard as soon as the material arrives. Items may be picked up at the Circulation Desks.

University of Montana
University of Montana Libraries–Missoula
Missoula, Montana

Although turnaround times can vary considerably depending upon the type of request, the accuracy of the citation and the time of year, the following guidelines for delivery times can be used when planning research:

Materials that must be shipped via U.S. Mail

> 7-15 days

Reproduced material

> 3-10 days

During peak times of the semester more time is needed. Requestors should note their time constraints on the ILL form under NOT WANTED AFTER DATE.

Requests are processed in the order they are received. Large numbers of requests from one patron can monopolize the system. These requests will be processed at five per day. Therefore, the patron is expected to prioritize their requests and recognize that they will be processed as time permits.

8.23 Recalls

Rutgers University
Rutgers University Libraries
Newark, New Jersey

Interlibrary loan materials checked out to you may be recalled by the lending library. Rutgers University Libraries recall fines will apply if the item is not returned within the newly established due date, seven days from the date of recall. Your borrowing privileges will be suspended if recall fines are owed or interlibrary loan books are overdue.

Dominican University of California
Archbishop Alemany Library
San Rafael, California

Can a borrowed book be recalled early?

Yes, if the lending library recalls the book at any time during the loan period, we must comply immediately with the recall request.

8.24 Copyright Restrictions

Long Beach City College
Long Beach City College Library
Long Beach, California

A. Compliance with copyright laws is the responsibility of the borrowing library. An indication of copyright compliance must be indicated on their ILL request. We will not fulfill requests that do not have copyright compliance on them. If the request sent to us through the mail, the fax, or Ariel, does not have copyright compliance; we will mail the request back to the borrowing library. If the request is sent through OCLC, we will provide a conditional response: "We cannot supply this title unless copyright compliance is indicated on your request."

B. Our Lending Department reserves the right to refuse any requests for photocopies, which it believes, would constitute a violation of copyright laws.

University of South Carolina
University of South Carolina Libraries
Columbia, South Carolina

Fair use, as determined by U.S. Copyright law, Title 17, Copyrights, United States Code section 107, allows for the reproduction of copyrighted material for criticism, comment, news reporting, teaching (including multiple copies for classroom use), scholarship, or research. The categories used in determining fair use are:

    (1) the purpose and character of the use, including whether such use is of a commercial nature or is for nonprofit educational purposes;

    (2) the nature of the copyrighted work;

    (3) the amount and substantiality of the portion used in relation to the copyrighted work as a whole; and

    (4) the effect of the use upon the potential market for or value of the copyrighted work.

U.S. copyright law, Title 17, Copyrights, United States Code, strictly limits the ability of the Interlibrary Loan staff to obtain journal articles. Under section 108(d), "Limitation on exclusive rights: Reproduction by libraries and archives," libraries are authorized to furnish a photocopy. 108(d) reads:

"The rights of reproduction and distribution under this section apply to a copy, made from the collection of a library or archives where the user makes his or her request or from that of another library or archives, of no more than one article or other contribution to a copyrighted collection or periodical issue, or to a copy or phonorecord of a small part of any other copyrighted work, if-

    (1) the copy or phonorecord becomes the property of the user, and the library or archives has had no notice that the copy or phonorecord would be used for any purpose other than private study, scholarship, or research; and

    (2) the library or archives displays prominently, at the place where orders are accepted, and includes on its order form, a warning of copyright in accordance with requirements that the Register of Copyrights shall prescribe by regulation."

If a user requests more than one article from one issue of a journal, the Interlibrary Loan Department staff must pay a copyright fee through the Copyright Clearance Center or must purchase the article from a commercial vendor. If a user makes a request for, or later uses, a photocopy for purposes in excess of "fair use," that user may be liable for copyright infringement. The Interlibrary Loan Department staff reserves the right to refuse to accept a copying order if, in our judgment, fulfillment of that order would involve violation of the copyright law.

The National Commission on New Technological Uses of Copyrighted Works (CONTU) has developed a set of guidelines to assist libraries in fulfilling their duties while adhering to copyright law. CONTU guidelines (or the "suggestion of five") permits the copying during a calendar year of no more than five articles from a single journal title, not owned by the library, dated within the past five years. This means that the Interlibrary Loan Department staff can order a total of only 5 articles from a single journal title dated within the past 5 years regardless of how many users request articles from the same journal title. For articles obtained in excess of this number, the Library must pay a fee to the Copyright Clearance Center or must purchase the articles from a commercial vendor. The Interlibrary Loan Department staff reserves the right to restrict such purchases.

University of Nevada–Reno
University Libraries
Reno, Nevada

On occasion, library users will submit several requests for photocopies of journal articles from a single journal title during the course of the year. Document Delivery Services operates under copyright law guidelines, known as the CONTU Guidelines, which prohibit the library from requesting more than five articles within a calendar year from any one journal title published in the previous five years. Filled requests over the five-article limit are subject to royalty fees. Document Delivery Services will pay royalty fees to the Copyright Clearance Center or purchase the article from a commercial vendor, if possible. If neither of these options is available, Document Delivery Services may not be able to request the article.

8.25 Confidentiality of Patron ILL Records

Humboldt State University
Humboldt State University Library
Arcata, California

Documentation of requests is retained as necessary for the Library to comply with auditing, copyright or other regulations. Because of the software the Library uses this documentation will include names of borrowers. Personal information provided in order to request ILL service might be forwarded on to other library lenders. In some cases, information about requests may be shared with other library staff for collection development purposes; however, it remains confidential within the library.

California State Polytechnic University Pomona
Cal Poly Pomona University Library
Pomona, California

Document Delivery/Interlibrary Loan

Documentation of requests is retained as necessary for the Library to comply with auditing, copyright or other regulations. Because of the software the Library uses this documentation will include names of borrowers. Personal information provided in order to request ILL service might be forwarded on to other library lenders. In some cases, information about requests may be shared with other library staff for collection development and fine collection purposes; however, it remains confidential within the library.

University of Michigan
University of Michigan Libraries
Ann Arbor, Michigan

Interlibrary Loan/Document Delivery

Requestors of interlibrary loan and document delivery services receive the same protection in terms of confidentiality of their requests. In some cases, information about requests is shared with other library staff for collection development purposes; it remains confidential within the library. Documentation of requests may be retained as necessary for the Library to comply with auditing, copyright or other regulations.

Part V
Reference Services: Query Categories, Resources, and Assistance Offered

Chapter 9

SPECIFIC QUERY CATEGORY POLICIES

MEDICAL, LEGAL, FINANCIAL, AND TAX

9.1 Medical

Bridgewater Public Library
Bridgewater, Massachusetts

Medical Information: For telephone inquiries, correct spellings and brief dictionary or descriptions from published sources are provided. These sources will be quoted verbatim with sources and date cited. Staff does not provide medical advice, interpretation, evaluation, or assistance in self-diagnosis. Drug information will not be provided on the telephone based on physical description. Patrons should be encouraged to contact their physicians, pharmacists, or other health care professionals. Patrons will be introduced to online health databases, when appropriate. The Library reference staff may also contact a medical library for additional consumer health information.

Memorial Hall Library
Andover, Massachusetts

The library does not provide advice in the areas of medicine, law, and taxes. Under no circumstances will a staff member offer advice in medical, legal, or tax areas, no matter how commonplace the question seems to be. Complicated legal searches will not be undertaken nor will personal interpretations of legal matters be offered. Referrals will be made to the Lawrence Law Library in its role as the NMRLS Legal Reference Center.

Brief definitions and descriptions from authoritative sources will be provided in response to requests for medical information. These sources will be quoted verbatim with no personal interpretation. The patron will be informed of the sources from which the information is taken. Every effort will be made to use authoritative, current online sources when using the Internet.

Specific tax forms and publications will not be suggested. Patrons need to know the number of the forms they need. If more information is required, the patron will be encouraged to examine the library's collections or be referred to another source.

St. Joseph County Public Library
South Bend, Indiana

Medical Questions

a. Because Library staff members are not health care professionals, they cannot offer medical advice or an interpretation of medical information. Interpretation is defined as the explanation of what is not immediately plain, explicit, or unmistakable. Prognoses will not be read over the telephone.

b. Staff members will assist customers in the library in finding information about a disease or medical condition using print and non-print sources.

c. Staff members may read a definition over the telephone of a medical term or description of a disease or condition from an available source. The source will be cited, and quoted verbatim. When the definition is difficult to understand, staff will define terms used in the definition or description by using other sources, but will not give an interpretation of the term.

d. Staff members may read brief information over the telephone about prescription drugs from the Physicians' Desk Reference and other drug dictionaries when the name of the drug is given. The source will be cited and quoted verbatim with no interpretation. Terms used in the text will be defined by using another source. Staff will not identify a drug from a physical description, nor give recommended dosages.

e. Staff members will advise customers to consult a medical specialist when additional information is needed; however, they will not recommend a specific physician.

f. Staff members will refer customers to other health agencies in the area when these resources seem most appropriate to answer the customer's needs.

g. Before or after a reference telephone transaction, the customer will be informed that staff members are reading from the best available library sources; there may be other authorities or more current information.

Ryerson University
Ryerson University Libraries
Toronto, Ontario, Canada

Reference staff does not interpret information, such as legal, medical, financial, statistical information or class assignments.

Recommendations Regarding Library Patrons' Purchases of Sources

Reference staff refers patrons to standard reviews of the work in question and advise the patron to examine the library copy, if available; generally, staff members do not make recommendations regarding such purchases.

9.2 Legal

St. Joseph County Public Library
South Bend, Indiana

Legal Questions

   a. Because library staff members are not attorneys they can not offer legal advice or any interpretation of the law or legal terms. Interpretation is defined as the explanation of what is not immediately plain, explicit, or unmistakable. Although staff members will be as helpful as possible in locating and providing necessary legal materials, it is the responsibility of the customer to determine what the law "means."
   b. Staff members may read over the telephone a definition found in a law dictionary.
   c. Staff members will direct customers to the U.S. Code, the Indiana Code, the Municipal Code and other legal resources.
   d. Staff members may assist customers in the use of legal materials, explaining their organization and format.
   e. Staff members will advise customers to consult an attorney when additional information is needed; however, they will not recommend a specific attorney.
   f. Staff members will refer customers to local law libraries to research specific case law.
   g. Before or after a reference telephone transaction, the customer will be informed that staff members are reading from the best available library sources; there may be other authorities or more current information.

Palm Beach County Library System
West Palm Beach, Florida

About Legal Research

The Palm Beach County Library System holds legal materials such as statutes, codes, and regulations for local, state and federal law, with the largest collection at the Main Library. The Library also owns helpful resources such as legal encyclopedias, self-help guides, and books of legal forms. In addition, our Legal Research Web page contains links to a wide variety of online legal resources to assist users with their information needs.

Due to the specialized nature of legal research, legal searches, except for specific citations, cannot be provided because of possible misinterpretation of material by either patron or staff. [Palm Beach County PPM CLO-800, Reference Services] Our legal reference policy is based on the American Library Association's Guidelines for Medical, Legal, and Business Responses at General Reference Desk. Given these guidelines, reference staff will:

   • Look up specific citations
   • Explain what types of materials are available and show patrons how to use them
   • Refer patrons to legal self-help guides
   • Refer patrons to outside agencies such as the Legal Aid Society and the Bar Association

- Please make use of the print and online resources available through the Palm Beach County Library System, and be sure to contact a reference librarian if you have any questions about these materials.

9.3 Financial

St. Joseph County Public Library
South Bend, Indiana

Financial, Tax, and Other Professional Services Questions

Staff should use the full range of reference interview skills when working with customers on these topics. Customers should be encouraged to consult professionals in the appropriate field rather than to rely on printed sources alone. Brief definitions and descriptions can be read verbatim from published sources in answer to telephoned inquiries. Additionally, callers should be encouraged to come to the library to avail themselves of a variety of sources to make informed decisions. Staff do not interpret, give opinions, advise, or make appraisals.

University of Wisconsin–River Falls
Chalmer Davee Library
River Falls, Wisconsin

Medical, Legal, Tax or Consumer Advice. Librarians do not offer medical, legal, or tax advice or recommend particular consumer products, but will give patrons the appropriate sources to assist them in finding information.

9.4 Tax

Schiller Park Public Library
Schiller Park, Illinois

The Library provides, from January 1st to April 15th, free copies of the most popular IRS and State of Illinois tax forms and a reproducible master tax form book. Copies from the reproducible books are $.10 per page, copied by the patron. Users are encouraged to seek professional tax consultants with their tax questions, because the Library staff does not provide any tax advice including information regarding tax form usage.

EDUCATIONAL

9.5 Assignments/Homework

Memorial Hall Library
Andover, Massachusetts

Questions related to school assignments will be treated like any other request for reference assistance. Every effort will be made to satisfactorily answer a student's questions and provide the sources for information and the instruction needed to use those sources. If a student has a printed school assignment, it is helpful to ask permission to copy the assignment and pass it on to the Young Adult librarians so that they can set some books aside for the assignment or contact the teacher for further explanation.

If staff has used a good resource for the assignment they will pass the resources on to the next shift rather than rely on them to redo the search. If every effort has been made by the reference staff and the student to locate information without results, the student will be encouraged to return to the teacher for further instructions or an altered assignment. A note to this effect may be given to the student if the reference staff member feels it is justified.

Ryerson University
Ryerson University Libraries
Toronto, Ontario, Canada

Class Assignments

Staff members help patrons locate information for class assignments. When a class assignment creates a concern, the subject librarian is responsible for seeing that the instructor is contacted about the present and possible future class assignments. Subject librarians will also give background information to reference staff to efficiently handle assignment related queries.

9.6 Literary Criticism Evaluations

Glenview Public Library
Glenview, Illinois

Critical Analysis of Literary Works

Librarians cannot provide personal critical analyses, interpretations, or judgments regarding the merit of literary or other works.

Washington County Public Library
Abingdon, Virginia

Critical Analyses of Literary Works

Staff members should not provide personal critical analyses, interpretations, or judgments regarding the merit of literary or other works (including the patron's own writing efforts).

APPRAISALS

9.7 Books and Collectibles

Newark Public Library
Newark New Jersey

Collectibles, antiques and works of fine art: Financial appraisals of collectibles (antiques, rare books, coins, stamps, etc.) and fine arts are not within the purview of the Library's reference service. Values as they are stated in published price guides are provided. For additional information patrons may pursue further research on their own at the Library or be referred to appropriate professional services.

Schiller Park Public Library
Schiller Park, Illinois

We direct patrons to appraisers and price lists, but do not appraise rare books, antiques or collectibles. In the case of a telephone request, the staff provides information from printed sources if the object in question is easily identifiable. The Library does not assume responsibility for determining the final value of an object.

Ryerson University
Ryerson University Libraries
Toronto, Ontario, Canada

Appraisal of Books and Artifacts

Reference staff does not appraise the private property of patrons. Patrons are advised to consult a professional appraiser, but specific appraisers are not recommended.

University of Texas at Austin
University of Texas Libraries
Austin, Texas

Appraisal of Books and Artifacts

Staff members do not appraise items. Users are advised to consult appropriate reference materials or a professional appraiser, but specific appraisers are not recommended.

9.8 Other Appraisals

Ryerson University, Ryerson University Library
Toronto, Ontario, Canada

Appraisal of Books and Artifacts

Reference staff does not appraise the private property of patrons. Patrons are advised to consult a professional appraiser, but specific appraisers are not recommended.

HISTORY AND GENEALOGY

9.9 Genealogy Searches

Memorial Hall Library
Andover, Massachusetts

Staff members will provide general assistance in genealogical research, and guidance in locating items in our Andover Room Collection. Patrons may accompany staff to the Andover Room to choose resources but may not remain in the room. Identification and signing of the guest book is required for the use of materials from the Andover Room. Staff members will not engage in actual genealogical research for patrons. Help in locating materials may be requested from the Andover Room Librarian. Patrons calling long distance will be requested to mail or email their request to the Andover Room Librarian. Limited research will be done and referrals to the Andover Historical Society given.

Shiawassee District Library
Owosso, Michigan

Genealogical questions will not be taken over the phone, but may be researched if requested in writing from people outside Shiawassee County. Shiawassee County residents will generally be expected to come into the library to do their own research. Research done by staff is limited to in-house materials. The library will not provide staff to look at census microfilm, as this is available to local public libraries through a rental program.

Ryerson University
Ryerson University Libraries
Toronto, Ontario, Canada

Genealogical Questions

Genealogical searches are not undertaken by reference staff. Catalogue assistance and help locating standard reference sources are offered. Genealogical questions generally are referred to the Public Archives of Ontario and the Toronto Reference Library.

University of Texas at Austin
University of Texas Libraries
Austin, Texas

Genealogical Questions

Genealogical searches are referred to the Texas State Library and Center for American History, as appropriate. Staff members offer help in locating standard genealogical sources in the University of Texas Libraries and through the Libraries web site.

9.10 Obituary Requests

Rockford Public Library
Rockford, Illinois

Obituary requests will be searched as a reference question or an interlibrary loan request when the source is indexed or available to search online, or when a date of the obituary is provided. Otherwise, obituary searches will be part of the fee-based genealogy research service.

Santa Monica Public Library
Santa Monica, California

Library staff will search for obituaries in the local newspaper, the Evening Outlook, if a death date is provided. Because the obituaries are not indexed the exact date of death is required. Staff time is limited so we can search only the local newspaper microfilm, the Evening Outlook, for obituaries.

San Jose Public Library and San Jose State University Library
San Jose, California

Statement of Policy & Text

An obituary search may be requested in person, by phone or mail, or through Ask A Librarian, the reference email service.

The Library conducts obituary searches only for people who have died in Santa Clara County.

Standard obituary searches are free of charge.

All search requests are forwarded to the Reference Librarian who is the designated liaison with the System Reference Center (SRC) of the Silicon Valley Library System, the group that conducts all obituary searches for the King Library.

When a search is complete, SRC sends the results to the designated Reference Librarian who then forwards this information to the requestor.

Need for the Policy

Since the King Library receives requests for obituary notices from researchers all over the country, this is a high demand need for our customers.

Requirements & Guidelines

Customers must provide the following information for an obituary search: ·

Their name, as requestor, with their address, phone number and/or email address

The full name of the deceased

The date of death

If date is unknown, the online California Death Index will be checked.

Response time to searches may vary depending upon demand.

Depending on the search load in SRC.

Rush requests are not handled by the Library. This type of request would require a service fee and is referred to InfoEdge (a fee-based service available from the SRC).

Customers who request searches outside the local area will be referred to those area libraries for this information by the liaison.

Local customers are encouraged to come to the library to search the microfilm themselves (with staff assistance, as necessary).

9.11 Local History Searches

Rockford Public Library
Rockford, Illinois

Local History questions: Instruction in the use of local history materials will be provided to customers. Quick look-ups of information for phone questions will be treated as other telephone reference requests.

Schiller Park Public Library
Schiller Park, Illinois

Local History

Questions related to local history are welcome. When the information in our collection is insufficient, patrons will be referred to the Schiller Park Historical Society, whose offices are located in the lower level of the Library. Patrons must arrange visits with the Schiller Park Historical Society directly. Library staff are not permitted to access the Schiller Park Historical Society Collection.

University of Wisconsin–River Falls
Chalmer Davee Library
River Falls, Wisconsin

Genealogy and Local History.

Questions related to genealogy, local, and campus history are referred to the University Archives and Area Research Center.

TECHNICAL AND MATHEMATICAL QUERIES

9.12 Patent Searches

Glenview Public Library
Glenview, Illinois

Patent Searches

The library can supply some information concerning patents but cannot perform complete patent searches that would be required by an inventor and usually supplied by a lawyer. Patrons must visit the Chicago Public Library, the Illinois State Library, or consult a lawyer. Copies of identified patents can be requested through the Suburban Library System's System Reference Service.

Boerne Public Library
Boerne, Texas

Patent/Copyright–Patrons are directed to web sites and books on copyright and patent procedures. Patent searches are not provided. Patrons requesting patent searches are referred to service providers in this subject area.

9.13 Mathematical Calculations

Morton Grove Public Library
Morton Grove, Illinois

Mathematical calculations should be provided only if a person on the staff with appropriate expertise is available. Otherwise patrons should be referred to sources containing the formulas or tables necessary for them to complete their calculations.

Washington County Public Library
Abingdon, Virginia

Mathematical Calculations

Staff members should not perform mathematical calculations for patrons. Information from table and formulas may be consulted, or an electronic calculator may be provided, but patrons should do their own calculations.

9.14 Translations

Morton Grove Public Library
Morton Grove, Illinois

Translations should be provided only if a person on the staff with appropriate expertise is available. Otherwise, staff should contact System Reference Service or other appropriate resources to obtain information regarding translators.

St. Joseph County Public Library
South Bend, Indiana

Foreign language translation is limited to words and phrases found in current reference sources. Staff does not translate documents for the public due to foreign language proficiency problems, time constraints, and far-ranging legal ramifications that could result. Staff will refer requests for translations beyond this scope to appropriate community resources, including foreign language departments of local colleges and universities and the Library's Community Connection database which lists current ethnic clubs and organizations.

REFERRALS

9.15 Referrals to Outside Agencies

Dorchester County Public Library
Cambridge, Maryland

Referral

The Information and Referral file is updated and maintained by the Eastern Shore Regional Library.

Referral to other agencies may be made for informational questions after using community information files and other directories to determine the proper agency for handling the subject. Information provided should include a contact person, phone number, address, hours of service, and how to get there. When directly contacting an agency on behalf of a patron, the library staff member will first obtain the patron's permission to identify the patron and his question to the agency. If permission is not given, then the patron should not be identified.

If there is any doubt about the appropriate agency for referral, the library staff member should phone the agency if possible. The patron should be asked to get back in touch with the Information Desk if he does not get the information or service he needs from the agency to which he was referred.

9.16 Referrals to Professional Researchers

University of New England
Dixson Library
Australia

As appropriate, library staff shall reach beyond reference collections to tap the resources of the Library as a whole. To provide the information their users need, they shall also reach beyond in-house collections and in-house expertise by drawing on the resources of other organizations that collect and provide information, by consulting individual experts, by tapping external information sources regardless of their medium, and by accessing the world of information accessible via the Internet.

9.17 Referrals to Other Libraries

Morton Grove Public Library
Morton Grove, Illinois

If the staff member feels that it is appropriate to refer the patron to another library, it is required that the staff member verify that the material needed is actually there. If it is necessary to refer a patron to a corporate, university, or other special library, the staff member should make prior arrangements with the other library before sending a patron to that library.

University of Wisconsin–River Falls
Chalmer Davee Library
River Falls, Wisconsin

When another library is likely to have information of relevance to a user's need beyond that available at the Chalmer Davee Library, a reference librarian will refer the user to that library. Users are often referred to the River Falls Public Library to access a more popular level of information.

North Florida Community College
North Florida Community College Library
Madison, Florida

Referrals

Referrals to other libraries, agencies and organizations are made when informational needs cannot be located in the library or when the informational need is better served by an outside agency. Personal referrals to individuals such as doctors and lawyers should be avoided.

9.18 Referrals within the Library

University of Texas at Austin
University of Texas Libraries
Austin, Texas

Referrals

Staff members should recognize their own limitations and ask colleagues within the unit for advice and assistance as necessary. They also refer users to others who are better qualified to serve particular needs. Staff members confirm that other units, libraries, or special collections can be of assistance before referring users to them. Staff members do not recommend specific fee-based information services. They refer users to standard directories. Referrals to other libraries or agencies off campus are made whenever appropriate.

CONSUMER QUERIES

9.19 Car Repair and Price Information

Boerne Public Library
Boerne, Texas

Vehicle Price Information—Values on used vehicles are never given over the telephone. Patrons are instead directed to printed or electronic resources listing this information. Patrons seeking this information by telephone or correspondence will be asked to come to the library.

9.20 Consumer Evaluations

Memorial Hall Library
Andover, Massachusetts

The staff will help patrons locate objective consumer product information by showing him/her how to consult the indexes to Consumer Reports and related magazines, buying guides, and/or general periodical indexes. Short published consumer ratings will be read over the phone; however, in depth consumer information must be read at the library. The staff does not offer personal opinions recommending one product over another.

Morton Grove Public Library
Morton Grove, Illinois

The staff should help patrons locate objective consumer product information by showing them how to consult the indexes to Consumer Reports and related magazines, buying guides, and/or general indexes which may lead to product evaluations in other periodicals. Short published consumer ratings will be read over the telephone; however, in depth consumer information must be read at the library. The staff does not offer personal opinions recommending one product over another.

9.21. Stock Quotations

Glenview Public Library
Glenview, Illinois

Stock Quotations

Librarians will accept requests for stock quotations via the telephone and refer them to the magazine department on a call-back basis.

Schiller Park Public Library
Schiller Park, Illinois

A maximum of (3) three stock or car price quotations are provided from hard copy sources, by telephone, fax, e-mail or in person.

MISCELLANEOUS QUERIES

9.22 Contest Questions

The Logan Library
Logan, Utah

Contest questions are answered for a person over the phone only if the reference librarian can find the answer immediately.

Memorial Hall Library
Andover, Massachusetts

Contest questions will be approached with the same guidelines and time limits as any other type of reference question. However, contest questions are often designed to be interpreted in more than one way and have more than one answer that seems to be correct. The staff will not interpret contest rules.

Monroe Township Public Library
Monroe Township, New Jersey

TRIVIA AND CONTEST QUESTIONS

Staff provides answers to trivia, game and contest questions which require simple factual information from a standard source. However, those users who require lengthy searches because of the number or nature of their questions are offered guidance in locating likely sources for their answers. Staff takes no responsibility to guarantee correct answers.

Ryerson University, Ryerson University Library
Toronto, Ontario, Canada

Answering Quizzes, etc.

No searching is done for answers to puzzles, quizzes, TV contests, etc. Assistance is limited to advising individuals about where they might locate such information.

Weber State University
Stewart Library
Ogden, Utah

Trivial Requests

Assistance with questions related to contests, radio quizzes, etc. for purposes of the patron's personal monetary gain should be given lowest priority. The librarian should knowingly help in his case only if all serious informational needs of other patrons have been met. Patrons should be asked to come to the library where reference sources will be pointed out for them to use in actually doing the searching themselves.

University of Texas at Austin
University of Texas Libraries
Austin, Texas

Contests, Puzzles, and Scavenger Hunts

Staff members, when they have evidence that a contest is behind a question, suggest appropriate sources but do not locate the information.

9.23 Criss-Cross and City Directories

Bridgewater Public Library
Bridgewater, Massachusetts

Directories/Street List: Information will be given over the telephone as printed, with source cited. Nearbys will not be given. Such information will be limited to the ready reference time limit. Criss-cross information is not offered.

Schiller Park Public Library
Schiller Park, Illinois

Criss-Cross and City Directory Information

Information from the SBC Ameritech: The Street Address/Telephone Directory, NearWest Suburban will be provided by phone, mail, fax, e-mail and in person.

Braswell Memorial Library
Rocky Mount, North Carolina

City Directory

It is not the responsibility of the staff to function as adjunct bill collectors for non-residents of Nash and Edgecombe counties. Reference staff will provide one crisscross reference over the telephone. Those wanting more than one or who hang up and call back should put their request in writing. No "nearbys" will be given. Old editions of the city directory are part of the reference collection and do not circulate, as they are a valuable genealogical resource.

Chelmsford Public Library
Chelmsford, Massachusetts

The Chelmsford Public Library will provide any information from the City Directory and crisscross telephone directories EXCEPT the identity of "nearby"—persons living near an individual.

Schiller Park Public Library
Schiller Park, Illinois

Information from the SBC Ameritech: The Street Address/Telephone Directory, Near West Suburban will be provided by phone, mail, fax, e-mail and in person.

9.24 Periodicals and Newspapers

Bridgewater Public Library
Bridgewater, Massachusetts

Periodicals: The Library subscribes to approximately 170 periodical titles. These are general interest periodicals on a wide range of subjects and are chosen to reflect a balance of viewpoints. Access to a more extensive selection of periodical titles via IAC Searchbank, SIRS Researcher, Newsbank, Boston Globe archives on-line, and through the Boston Public Library and other library consortiums is also provided.

Santa Monica Public Library
Santa Monica, California

Library users have access to a wide variety of magazines and newspapers in the Library and by remote access through Library online databases such as InfoTrac OneFile and Newsbank. The Library also provides local newspapers such as Santa Monica Daily Press, Los Angeles Sentinel, Santa Monica Mirror, and Daily News and major national newspapers such as the Los Angeles Times, New York Times, Wall Street Journal, and Washington Post. Current year issues of most of the Library's magazines are available for check out. Newspapers and the current issue of all magazines are for use in the Library only.

Riverside Regional Public Library
Jackson, Missouri

PURPOSE:

To supplement and complement the materials in the adult collection. This collection is intended to be more timely and more frequently updated than the adult collection. Most materials circulate; exceptions are the most recent copies of all titles, special editions and issues, bound magazines, newspaper, catalogues, and microforms.

SPECIFIC CRITERIA:

    a. Offers ease of information retrieval, such as, but not limited to, inclusion in a standard periodical index or abstracting journal;

    b. Contributes to a balance and range of information;

    c. Provides lasting value;

    d. Has high quality of writing and/or design;

    e. Is within both budget and space constraints for the collection.

Chapter 10

REFERENCE RESOURCES POLICIES

ASSISTANCE OFFERED FOR SPECIFIC MATERIALS

10.1 Map Collection

Southern Connecticut State University
Hilton C. Buley Library
New Haven, Connecticut

Map Collection – The goal of the SCSU Map Collection is to acquire, house, organize, and maintain maps and related materials needed to support the teaching and research programs of the University. All maps are kept in map cabinets against the far back wall of the Reference book stacks. US topographic maps, US Geological Survey Maps, all state series and park series maps as well as maps from the US Defense Mapping.

Agency belongs in this collection. Access to specific maps is provided via continually updated index grid sheets. Other maps which can be acquired free of charge are also in this collection.

A representative collection of general and specialized atlases are available. The latest editions of most major atlases are purchased. Gazetteers, other atlases and globes are in the Reference Collection. Atlas display tables are located on the main floor near the Reference area.

San Jose Public Library and San Jose State University Library
San Jose, California

Statement of Policy & Text

The map reference collection of the King Library is operated jointly by SJSU Library staff and SJPL staff. Responsibility for collecting, developing, and maintaining the map collection is divided between these two staffs, based on their existing collection strengths.

Need for the Policy

The reference map collection represents the collection development philosophies of each institution, which differ based on the needs of the University community vs. those of the civic community at large. Consolidation of the map collection in the King Library should logically focus on the strengths of both organizations and their collections.

Coordination of the reference map collection between these two staffs is necessary to ensure the timely acquisition of needed map materials and eliminate duplication of effort.

Requirements & Guidelines

University and public librarians shall be responsible for the following map formats, not including media disk or electronically stored formats, unless so instructed by administrative decision:

> SJSU
>
> Classroom hanging maps
>
> Relief / raised maps
>
> Flat maps, like the USGS topographical sheets
>
> Nautical and astronomical charts.
>
> SJPL
>
> California cities, towns, and counties folded street maps
>
> California city road maps
>
> FEMA: flood insurance, real estate, and earthquake maps

10.2 Pamphlet File, Art Print, and Portrait File

Carbondale Public Library
Carbondale, Illinois

Due to the fact that some art prints are not returned to the library after the loan period is over, beginning April 1, 2004, Carbondale Public Library will require all patrons to pay a $20 deposit before art prints can be checked out.

The deposit will be refunded provided the art print is returned within 42 days from the date of original checkout. The deposit is forfeited if the print is returned after the item has been declared "LOST." Items go into LOST status when they are over 21 days overdue. Forfeiture of deposit does not substitute for an overdue fine. Overdue fines will be levied and collected, per library policy.

- Circulation period - 12 weeks. No renewals
- Borrower must have a valid Carbondale Public Library card. Art prints do not circulate on Shawnee Library System (unless the patron has a Carbondale address) or other library cards.
- The form used to check out art prints must be signed by the person whose library card is being used to borrow the print.
- Art prints are not available for interlibrary loan.
- Overdue fines - $1.00 per day up to a maximum of $30.

- There is a limit of one art print per card.
- Patron is responsible for any loss or damage to the art print or transport bag while checked out on their card.
- Click here to see our available art prints.

Southern Connecticut State University
Hilton C. Buley Library
New Haven, Connecticut

Pamphlet File – The Pamphlet File is located in gray file cabinets against the far back wall of the Reference stack area facing the encyclopedias. The file contains ephemeral material, miscellaneous information as well as information on Connecticut. As a rule, items which are judged to be of supplemental value to the general library collection are included. Usually nothing over fifty pages is kept in the vertical files. This collection is not cataloged—a printed list of subject headings for these materials is filed in the beginning of the "A" drawer of the pamphlet collection and serves as a point of reference for the kinds of materials available here.

Portrait File - A small collection of portraits (81/2" x 11") is filed in the cabinets right next to the Pamphlet File. These portraits are arranged in alphabetical order by the person's last name.

10.3 Ready Reference Collection

Southern Connecticut State University
Hilton C. Buley Library
New Haven, Connecticut

Ready Reference Collection - The ready reference collection is located at the Reference Desk. Materials in this collection include those reference sources that are used frequently to answer reference/information questions. Most of these materials are basic reference books such as almanacs, desk reference sources, dictionaries, directories, statistical sources, style guides, resume/job sources, thesaurus, etc. This section also has some frequently consulted books pertaining to information on Connecticut in the areas of Budget, Business, Census, Crime, Economy, Education, Geography, Government, Health, Social Services and Statistics. Connecticut telephone books and the Library of Congress Subject Heading volumes are also part of this collection.

Patrons are requested to return these materials to the Reference Desk after use.

Northern Michigan University
Lydia M. Olson Library

The reference collection is located on the main floor of the library.

A separate Ready Reference Collection is maintained at the information desk consisting of materials used frequently for quick reference by librarians, material used often by a great number of library users, materials of timely/topical/seasonal nature, and material that serves as a key to the collection. The ready Reference Collection is evaluated frequently.

10.4 Print Reference Collection

Southern Connecticut State University
Hilton C. Buley Library
New Haven, Connecticut

Print Reference Collection – Reference books are located on the first floor. Reference books have "Ref" before the call number and are arranged according to the Library of Congress call number.

Materials in this collection are limited to almanacs, dictionaries, (English language, foreign language and subject dictionaries), general encyclopedias, specific subject encyclopedias, handbooks, guidebooks, bibliographies(standard bibliographies, general bibliographies and specialized subject bibliographies), basic texts with high reference value, statistical/table compilations, biographical sources, manuals, yearbooks, atlases, loose leaf services, indexes and guides to research.

The library's special strengths in the Reference section include American Government, Area Studies, Art, Black Studies, Business, Current Issues, Law, Library Science, Literature (English and American), Medicine, Music, Nursing, Sports/Athletics and Women's Studies.

The newspaper and periodical indexes and abstracts are arranged in alphabetical order by the title in the index/abstract section following the Reference collection.

The Reference Collection is a non-circulating collection.

Spokane Public Library
Spokane, Washington

Basic print reference resources are maintained at all Spokane Public Library branches. The Downtown library maintains in-depth resources in the areas of business, government, fundraising, careers, education, consumer, and motor vehicle repair. A juvenile reference collection is maintained at the Downtown

Library in the Children's department. Reference materials are selected according to current Spokane Public Library service responses.

10.5 Microfilm Collection

Santa Monica Public Library
Santa Monica, California

The Library Collection includes the microfilm for the local newspaper, the Evening Outlook, from 1875 to March 13, 1998, when the newspaper ceased publication. The Evening Outlook changed titles several times during its publication. Those titles include: Santa Monica Evening Outlook, Outlook, Santa Monica Bay Outlook, Daily Outlook, Santa Monica Evening Outlook and Telegram, and The Outlook. However, for most of its life it was called the Evening Outlook. When The Outlook ceased publication, the Library microfilmed and indexed the Los Angeles Times Our Times section that covered the Westside from March 26, 1998, to September 14, 2000. When Our Times ceased publication in September 2000, the Library retrospectively indexed and microfilmed the

Santa Monica Mirror, which began publication with the June 24-30 issue in 1999. The *Santa Monica Mirror* is online at www.smmirror.com.

Indexing for all three newspapers, done by Library staff, is available online at the Santa Monica Index. The Library began indexing the Outlook in the early 1950s for Santa Monica topics of possible historical interest. Articles of interest from many other periodicals, such as the Life magazine article on the gambling ships in Santa Monica Bay, are also included in the Santa Monica Index.

The Library also maintains microfilm of the Los Angeles Times (1969-), New York Times (1896-), Wall Street Journal (1968-), and Washington Post (1984-). Print indexes are available for the Los Angeles Times from 1972 and for the New York Times from 1894. InfoTrac OneFile, a Library online database, provides indexing for the New York Times, Washington Post, and Wall Street Journal from 1980 to the present.

Norfolk Public Library
Norfolk, Virginia

Microfilm of Virginia and North Carolina court records are purchased selectively. Federal Census films are purchased for Virginia, West Virginia, North Carolina, South Carolina, Kentucky, Maryland and the District of Columbia. Print indexes to early census records are available and Soundex indexes to the microfilm collection are purchased as space and budgets permit. Internment cards for some of Norfolk's local cemeteries are also available on microfilm.

Eastern Washington University
Cheney, Washington

Microform collections which are of a reference nature will be acquired on the same basis as reference material in paper format. Comprehensive microform collections of retrospective materials will be purchased only when justified by frequency of request. Purchase of such collections will be coordinated with the regional library consortia, for example, the six state universities in Washington.

10.6 Electronic Collection CD-ROM

Southern Connecticut State University
Hilton C. Buley Library
New Haven, Connecticut

Electronic Reference Collection - Electronic Products include on-line databases and a few CD-ROM products. We have the following CD-ROMs:
- American Library Directory
- Encyclopedia of Banking and Finance
- Great Literature Plus
- Macmillan Digital World Atlas
- USA Trade
- Virginia Woolf Bibliography

The list of databases is subject to change as products are added or deleted. Any member of the Southern community may recommend the acquisition of new electronic products. All requests, however, will be evaluated by the reference librarians before purchase.

Patrons are requested to restrict their searches to 30 minutes if others are waiting.

On-line searching is available to non-affiliated users but at busy times, it may be necessary to give priority to affiliated users.

Guides on searching specific databases can be found on the library home page under "User Guides". Print copies of some guides are available on the "Info to Go" rack near the Reference Desk. User manuals are located at the Reference desk.

Tempe Public Library
Tempe, Arizona

Computer-Based Resources: This category includes computer-based information resources available via the Internet or on a locally installed CD-ROM. In some instances, this material may be available to registered library users at remote locations via the Library's Web page.

This collection includes, but is not limited to, citation or full-text databases and instructional multimedia programs. The following criteria should be considered when considering computer-based resources for the collection: compatibility with available equipment and/or existing operating systems; ease of use by library users, including enhanced searching capabilities; price of print format versus electronic; authority; accuracy; frequency of updating; anticipated demand by library users; impact upon staff for ongoing maintenance and updating of database; training requirements for staff and the public; remote access capability; and licensing fees and usage restrictions.

Spokane Public Library
Spokane, Washington

The library selects a limited number of CD-ROM titles that support educational, reference and instructional topics for children and adults. Business or office applications, utilities, clip-art and games which have no educational value will not be purchased. In the selection of titles primary consideration is given to the appropriateness of the material to the format. CD-ROMs are an addition and enhancement to the Library's collection of books, periodicals and AV materials and are not duplication or a substitution for other formats.

Chapter 11

REFERENCE ASSISTANCE POLICIES

GENERAL GUIDELINES

11.1 Managing Comments, Suggestions, and Complaints

Newark Public Library
Newark, New Jersey

While the Library shall strive to provide the best possible service for all patrons at all times, it is recognized that, given the volume and diversity of questions handled, problems may arise concerning the public's satisfaction with service received. In such situations patrons are encouraged to express their concerns to the individual Library staff involved or to that individual's immediate supervisor in order to effect an amicable resolution of the problem in the most direct manner. Complaints that cannot be resolved at the division head's level shall be referred to the appropriate department head for further attention.

Tempe Public Library
Tempe, Arizona

Reconsideration of Library Materials

In order to represent the diversity of thought within the Tempe community, it is very important that the public library's collection contain materials representing differing points of view on public issues of a controversial nature. The Tempe Public Library does not endorse particular beliefs or views, nor does the selection of an item express or imply an endorsement of the viewpoint expressed by the author. Library materials will not be marked or identified to show approval or disapproval of the contents, nor will items be sequestered, except for the purpose of protecting them from theft or damage.

There may be occasions when a Tempe resident may be concerned about a particular item in the Library's collection. If the resident wishes the Library to reconsider material that is in the collection, a Request for Reconsideration form is available at all public services desks. This form must be completed in its entirety and returned to a Library staff member who will forward it to the Deputy Community Services Manager-Library. Once the form is received, the Deputy Community Services Manager-Library will form a committee of professional librarians who will meet to review the Statement, as well as the criteria used in selecting the item, its place in the collection, and reasons for including the item in the collection. A written response from the Deputy Community Services Manager-Library will be sent within four weeks.

In the event that the Tempe resident who initiated the Request for Reconsideration is not satisfied with the response of the Deputy Community Services Manager-Library, she or he may arrange to meet to discuss the matter with the Community Services Manager. This must be done within fourteen days of receiving the written response. If the resident is not satisfied at this level, he or she will be invited to attend the next regularly scheduled meeting of the Library Advisory Board.

The Board, after hearing the complaint, may either wish to appoint a special review committee or recommend a policy regarding the item in question. In either case, a letter will be sent to the resident informing him or her of the Board's decision. A copy of this letter will be forwarded to the City Manager. If the resident seeks further consideration, final authority rests with the City Council.

University of Texas at Austin
University of Texas Libraries
Austin, Texas

Complaints

If possible users with complaints are conducted to a private room for discussion. Complaints concerning library policies are referred to the appropriate department head.

11.2 Positive Approaches to Problem Patrons

University of Texas at Austin
University of Texas Libraries
Austin, Texas

Dealing with the "Problem Patron"

Every staff member who deals directly with the public knows that library users exhibit a wide range of behavior and that not all of it is placid or pleasant. While cases of violent or physically threatening behavior are relatively rare on this campus, an encounter with a "problem patron" is always possible. This term is applied to a variety of individuals including irate complainants, suspicious characters prowling the stacks, and people whose bizarre words or actions are caused by mental disturbances.

Four categories of problem patrons and suggestions for dealing with them were reported in Reference and Selection News, no.14, January 28, 1982, issued by the Library, University of California, Berkeley. They are adapted for the University of Texas Libraries below:

The Verbally Abusive Patron

Acknowledge the patron's problem. (He/she could be correct; the Library may have made an error.)

214

REFERENCE ASSISTANCE POLICIES

Explain the steps which can be taken to solve the problem; perhaps an alternative solution is available.

A nearby colleague may have additional pertinent information; at the least, this additional effort may defuse the patron's anger.

The patron may accept your offer to investigate the situation and report back to him or her as soon as possible.

If the patron remains obdurate, and you feel unable to resolve the situation satisfactorily, refer the patron to your supervisor.

The Demanding or Difficult Patron (Who feels entitled to take exception to Library rules)

Explain or clarify rules pertinent to the situation. Circumstances such as budget or staff shortages may make rules necessary. If it is readily available, hand out the pertinent written policy.

Volunteer any available alternative service.

If the patron remains unsatisfied, refer her or him to your supervisor.

Staff members should be aware that, while supervisors have the prerogative of making exceptions to rules due to special circumstances, non-supervisory staff should not feel apologetic about refusing to make such exceptions themselves.

The Disturbed or Bizarre Patron

Ask the patron directly if you can be of assistance.

If the patron's behavior is annoying to others or otherwise disruptive of normal library service, state this fact to the patron, with the request that he or she stop that behavior.

If the annoying or disruptive behavior continues, ask the patron to leave the unit.

If the patron remains unruly and refuses to leave the unit, call for help.

Non-threatening situations or routine disturbances:

Call the guard station

Call University Police

Serious or threatening situations:

Press the emergency button (available in every library unit).

Call University Police at 911.

The Suspicious Character

The person whose appearance or behavior seems unusual, or any person in an unauthorized area, should be regarded as a potentially "suspicious character."

Ask such a person directly if he or she needs assistance.

Pay obvious attention to this person.

If continued suspicion seems justified, call Library guard stations or the University Police at the numbers given above.

During past presentations to library staff, University Police have stated that the police much prefer to investigate several instances of suspicious circumstances in which the "suspect" proves to be innocent, if by doing so they could prevent violence or theft or apprehend a perpetrator. University Police officers can and do quickly and quietly investigate such incidents without undue embarrassment to the "suspect," staff members, or other patrons.

Public service supervisors have given the following general suggestions for dealing with unsatisfied, upset, or angry patrons.

Make a concerted effort to understand the real problem or issue involved.

Respond in a calm, relaxed voice; do not escalate the confrontation by using angry or excited words or tones of voice in reply.

If possible, conduct the patron to a less public space or room, if the situation is or threatens to become disturbing to others.

Avoid the physical appearance of pontifical authority; if the situation allows, ask the patron to sit down. The staff member should place herself or himself so as to be at approximately the same height as the patron.

Use other body language to avoid the appearance of hostility, rejection or put down of the patron.

Do not hesitate to call in a backup, preferably the supervisor, if the situation seems to be getting out of hand.

Remember that it is not necessary to accept verbal abuse or the threat of physical abuse.

We cannot satisfy every patron; we can make it apparent, however, that we have done our best.

The Logan Library
Logan, Utah

If patron behavior interferes with the use of the library or disrupts the normal flow of library operations but does not require external intervention immediately, the library employee with the assistance of another employee will follow these steps:

Inform the patron that the behavior is inappropriate and if it is not stopped, they will be asked to leave.

Ask the patron to leave if the inappropriate behavior does not stop.

Call the police (911) if the patron refuses to leave or becomes threatening in any way.

File an incident report with the director of the library.

Muskego Public Library
Muskego, Wisconsin

Handling Problem Behavior:

General comments:

Keeping the library a peaceful and secure place is the responsibility of every staff member. Every library worker is expected to be aware of the provisions of this policy, and is expected to play a part in keeping the library as pleasant an environment for the public as possible. Your responsibility applies to the library, as well as to the remainder of the building. Any illegal or dangerous activities observed should be immediately reported to the police department. See "illegal behavior," below.

Know who is in charge and available in the building on any given day.

Take the time to evaluate the situation before you react. Assess the seriousness of the situation, then take immediate action. Ignoring a problem does not make it go away. On the contrary, it may escalate.

Conduct yourself in a manner that is designed to reduce rather than increase tension. Maintain a calm, non-judgmental manner. Remember that the problem behavior is not directed at you personally. Staying calm will often help defuse an unpleasant situation and will allow you to exercise better judgment.

Explain your position in clear, firm language. It is important that the problem causers see you taking charge. Don't be hesitant or appear unsure of yourself. Avoid a loud tone of voice or phrases that might be considered moralizing or condescending. Do not lose your temper or let yourself get drawn into an argument. Simply repeat your position firmly, if necessary.

Present suitable alternatives, if possible.

Give sanctions. Let the person causing the problem know clearly what will happen if the behavior persists. Example: "You will have to leave the library." Never touch a patron, such as taking his/her arm to escort him/her from the library.

Be supportive of your co-workers. No one should feel alone on the front lines. When any staff member becomes involved in a difficult situation, others in the vicinity should stop what they are doing and lend support, even if it is in a non-verbal way. Do not hesitate to call another staff member to back you up. Go to the aid of another staff member when necessary. Support and teamwork are especially important if you have any suspicion that the patron may become violent.

Call outside help if necessary. If you have warned a patron with no result, call the librarian on duty and relate the situation to her/him. Generally, this staff member will be the one to call the police. However, in the case of an obvious emergency, no staff member should hesitate to call the police. Safety is more important than protocol.

File an incident report. Whenever a problem arises, make a written report of the circumstances to the library director.

Examples of problem behavior:

PROBLEM BEHAVIOR

CHATTY PATRONS: Lonely people and people with mental disabilities, whose need for attention is often great, are attracted to public libraries. We must be patient with these patrons, while not allowing them to take up large amounts of our time.

Politely and firmly discourage long, irrelevant conversations. If a person persists, remind them politely that you have to return to work or help another patron.

DISRUPTIVE CONDUCT: Disruptive conduct is any behavior which impedes the normal functioning of the library. This would include, but not be limited to, loud talking and laughing, fighting, throwing objects and boisterousness.

Loud talking and laughing: Since it is difficult to maintain a consistent noise or quiet level, and sensitivity to noise varies from one person to another, the focus will be on whether one person or group is heard above the general noise level in the library at a particular time. People conversing in louder tones than the general noise level should be requested to lower their voices. ONE WARNING AND OUT.

Use of cellular phones, pagers, and similar devices: These devices should be silenced upon entering the library. Courtesy for other library users who may be trying to read, study, or concentrate requires that conversations be held outside the library. People conversing in louder tones than the general noise level should be requested to lower their voices or leave the library. ONE WARNING AND OUT.

Fighting: Whether real or pretend: NO WARNING—OUT.

Throwing objects: This would include wadded up paper, paper airplanes, and other small objects. ONE WARNING AND OUT. With larger objects, or anything that could cause injury: NO WARNING—OUT.

Possession of weapons: No person shall possess or use a weapon, facsimile weapon or firearm in the library, on library premises, at any library-sponsored function or event, or while under the supervision of library personnel. NO WARNING—OUT.

Exhibiting any tool or other item in a threatening manner is not allowed. NO WARNING—OUT.

Definitions:

WEAPON: Any object which, by the manner in which it is used or intended to be used, is capable of inflicting bodily harm or could pretend to be capable of inflicting bodily harm or endangering the health and safety of library users or staff.

FACSIMILE WEAPON: May be a toy gun, water gun, non-working replica of a weapon, cap gun, popper, war souvenir or any other object which could reasonably be mistaken for an actual weapon regardless of whether it is manufactured for that purpose.

FIREARM: Any weapon which will, or is designed to, or may readily be converted to expel a projectile by the action of an explosive; the frame, or receiver of any such weapon; any firearm muffler or firearm silencer; any destructive device (including any explosives or chemical weapons).

Weapon(s) or look-alike weapon(s) confiscated from a library user shall be reported to parent(s)/guardian(s) and to law enforcement authorities. Disciplinary measures may include immediate expulsion from the library.

Anyone who possesses a firearm while at the library, or under the supervision of a library authority, shall be expelled from the library for not less than one year. This expulsion may be modified on a case-by-case basis.

Policy exceptions include:

Weapons under the control of law enforcement personnel

Weapons properly registered and handled during the community use of library facilities.

Theatrical props used in appropriate settings

Items pre-approved by the library director or her/his designee as part of a presentation under staff supervision. (Firearms and ammunition together will never be approved as part of a presentation.) The weapon shall be kept in the possession of the librarian-in-charge, except during the actual demonstration or presentation.

Employees violating this policy shall be disciplined in accordance with employee policies and bargaining agreements and shall be referred to law enforcement officials for prosecution.

Any other person violating this policy shall be referred to law enforcement officials for prosecution.

Appeal: Any person permanently banned from the library by action of the staff may request a hearing on the propriety of that ban before the Library Board at its next regularly scheduled meeting.

Boisterous behavior: This would include running, horseplay, and annoying other patrons. ONE WARNING AND OUT.

Using obscene language: This is difficult, because "obscene" is defined as anything "grossly repugnant to the generally accepted notions of what is appropriate." A word may be obscene to one staff member and not another. For the purpose of this policy, obscenity may be defined as language or gestures which convey a sexually explicit message or describe intimate bodily functions in a coarse or crude manner. NO WARNING—OUT.

No staff member should be subjected to verbal abuse, whether obscenity is involved or not. Interrupt the patron and say, "Your language and behavior are inappropriate. You must either stop or come back when you are calmer." If the person persists, notify the librarian in charge, who will ask the person to leave the library.

SOLICITATION: This includes selling anything, such as raffle tickets or candy, for personal gain or for a charitable cause, and begging, surveying, panhandling, circulating petitions or political campaigning. Activities sponsored by the library are not included in this prohibition. ONE WARNING AND OUT.

EATING AND DRINKING: Eating and drinking of food and beverages is not allowed in the library. If patrons violate this rule, it may be they are unaware of it. Remind them of the policy, and if they do not comply, ask them to leave. ONE WARNING AND OUT.

SMOKING: No smoking or otherwise using tobacco or other substances in the form of cigarettes, cigars, pipes, snuff, etc., is permitted in the library. ONE WARNING AND OUT.

SLEEPING: Sleeping is not allowed in the library. However, a patron may become drowsy and doze off momentarily while reading. This regulation pertains to those who are noisy, sprawled on the floor or furniture, or generally disturbing other patrons. Awaken them by speaking to them. Do not touch or shake them. They should be asked if they are ill, and told to stay awake. ONE WARNING AND OUT.

LOITERING: Loitering is defined as remaining or wandering in a public place without any apparent legitimate reason. Anyone who mills about or sits doing nothing for 10 to 15 minutes should be considered loitering. ONE WARNING AND OUT.

MOVING FURNITURE: Chairs, tables and other furniture are not to be moved without the permission of a staff member. ONE WARNING AND OUT.

RUNNING AND PLAYING This is distracting to other patrons, and dangerous, as it can lead to accidents. The degree to which this can be tolerated will depend on the age of the patron. Small children may need to be guided into more appropriate use of the library. If their behavior is creating a problem, parents should be told. Older children who seem to view the library as a playground should be reminded that running and playing are not allowed. ONE WARNING AND OUT.

SKATES, SKATEBOARDS, SCOOTERS, AND SIMILAR NON-MOTORIZED DEVICES Concern for the safety of pedestrians, drivers, and skaters means that use of skates, skateboards, scooters, and similar non-motorized devices is prohibited on library property during library operation hours. The library parking lot is posted to that effect, and violations will be prosecuted.

PETS: Animals are not allowed in the library. The only exceptions are service animals, such as seeing eye or hearing assistance, or seizure disorder detection dogs. Anyone entering the library with a pet should be asked to leave. NO WARNING—OUT. If the patron returns without the pet, s/he should, of course, be allowed to use the library.

NO SHOES OR SHIRT: Patrons are not permitted in the building without shoes or shirt. Remind the patron of the rule. If they have no shoes or shirt with them, they will have to leave at once. ONE WARNING AND OUT.

FEET ON TABLES OR CHAIRS: Placing feet, whether bare or shod, on tables or chairs, is prohibited. A staff member should remind the patron of this rule. ONE WARNING AND OUT.

LEAVING CHILDREN UNATTENDED: The younger the child, the more difficult the problem. Staff are far too busy to function as baby sitters. This situation could be potentially dangerous, as the child may be injured, become ill, or leave the building. Any unattended child should be brought to the attention of the librarian in charge, who will attempt to locate the parents within the library. If they are located, explain firmly that the library cannot be responsible for their child, and cannot care for him/her.

If parents cannot be located, the staff member in charge should call the police. A staff member should remain with the child until authorities arrive. Under no circumstances should a staff member drive a child home.

ILLEGAL BEHAVIOR: Some behavior is not merely disruptive, but is also against the law, and should be handled in a different manner. If you witness illegal behavior, report it to the librarian in charge. This staff member will generally notify the police. In the case of an obvious emergency, any staff member may call the police. Examples of illegal behavior include:

BATTERY (ASSAULT) Whoever causes bodily harm to another by an act done with intent to cause bodily harm to that person so harmed.

SANCTIONS:

Repeated disregard or violation of these problem behavior guidelines must be taken seriously and acted upon to prevent the behavior escalating to the point where library operations are severely disrupted and staff and the public exposed to behaviors that diminish their ability to accomplish their work or use the library in a comfortable, undisrupted and unthreatened manner.

In order to provide a means by which the response to repeated violation of the code is escalated and the seriousness of the continued activity driven home to the individual(s) involved, the following staged procedure is to be used. If an incident is deemed extremely serious and/or dangerous by the librarian in charge, some or all of the penalty stages may be skipped.

Accurate and complete record keeping is absolutely necessary to make this escalation procedure successful. An incident form should be filed at each stage of the escalation. Be aware that any written reports may be considered public records under Chapter 19 of the Wisconsin Statutes.

Sanctions:

Stage 1   The Stage 1 penalties involve a verbal warning and, in the event of repeated behavior, possible removal from the library for the week.

If, for any reason, a customer is told to leave the library as a result of their violation of a regulation, it is mandatory that an incident report be completed and filed as soon as possible.

In the case of a minor child, when practicable, a copy of the incident report should be mailed to the parent or guardian.

Stage 2   Should a customer involved in a Stage 1 incident repeat their previous behavior or engage in other problem behavior violations, the customer's behavior is to be escalated to Stage 2. Stage 2 results in the customer being denied entry to the Library for a period of three weeks.

Again, it is mandatory that an incident report be completed and filed as soon as possible. It should be noted on the form that this is a Stage 2 violation.

The Library Director, in consultation with the involved staff and library managers, must approve the Stage 2 discipline.

If the discipline is approved, the customer will, when practicable, be given a written notice detailing the violation history along with the start and end dates of the period during which they are denied entry.

In the case of a minor child, when practicable, a copy of the incident report should be mailed to the parent or guardian.

Stage 3   Should a customer involved in a Stage 2 incident repeat their previous behavior or engage in other problem behavior violations, the customer's behavior is to be escalated to Stage 3. Stage 3 results in the customer being denied entry to the Library for a period of six months.

Again, it is mandatory that an incident report be completed and filed as soon as possible. It should be noted on the form that this is a Stage 3 violation.

The Library Director, in consultation with the involved staff and library managers, must approve the Stage 3 discipline.

If the discipline is approved, the customer will, when practicable, be given a written notice detailing the violation history along with the start and end dates of the period during which they are denied entry.

In the case of a minor child, when practicable, a copy of the incident report should be mailed to the parent or guardian.

Stage 4   Should a customer involved in a Stage 3 incident repeat their previous behavior or engage in other problem behavior violations, the customer's behavior is to be escalated to Stage 4, the final stage. Stage 4 may result in the customer being permanently denied entry to the Library.

Again, it is mandatory that an incident report be completed and filed as soon as possible. It should be noted on the form that this is a Stage 4 violation.

The Library Director, in consultation with the involved staff and department manager, must approve the Stage 4 discipline.

If the discipline is approved, the customer will, when practicable, be given a written notice detailing the violation history along with the start date after which they are denied entry.

In the case of a minor child, when practicable, a copy of the incident report should be mailed to the parent or guardian.

Appeal:

Any person permanently banned from the library by action of the staff may request a hearing on the propriety of that ban before the Library Board at its next regularly scheduled meeting.

11.3 Taking Requests for Materials Purchase

Culver-Union Township Public Library
Culver, Indiana

Requests for Purchase: Items published within the last year, or other items that will add to our collection, may be purchased upon request. The patron making the request will be placed on hold for the item if we decide to purchase unless they indicate otherwise. When the item arrives and is processed, we will notify the patron. The item will be held for a minimum of three days. If the item is not picked up after three days, the item may be returned to shelf or, if there are other holds on the item, the next person on hold may be notified and given an opportunity to pick up the item.

Las Positas College
Livermore, California

Students, college staff, and administrators are also encouraged to make recommendations for book and media purchases to the Library faculty. Requests for purchase of library materials, from all sources, will be considered in light of this document and in relation to the overall instructional and educational purposes of the college. After a request meeting these criteria has been made by faculty, staff or students, an order will be placed for the materials if funds are available, or the request will be placed in a future-orders file for such time when funds will allow it to be reconsidered for purchase.

11.4 Offering Internet and Equipment Assistance

Oakland University
Kresge Library
Rochester, Michigan

Microforms Equipment Assistance

Circulation staff will instruct and assist with the use of the microforms readers and printers. For assistance in finding microforms materials, ask at the Reference Desk.

New College of Florida
Sarasota, Florida

MICROFORM READER/PRINTERS. The library maintains coin and card-operated microfilm and microfiche reader/printers for use in copying from fiche and film. The Reference staff can assist you in the use of these machines.

University of South Florida Sarasota-Manatee
Cook Library
Sarasota, Florida

INTERNET ACCESS is available through this web-site. The Cook Library homepage provides answers to your questions about library personnel, services, and collections. It also furnishes links to a great many Internet resources to assist you with your scholarship and research. Public-use computers are available in the library and the Reference staff will be happy to get you started with "surfing the net" if you are a first time user.

Manhattan Public Library
Manhattan, Kansas

Availability of Staff Assistance

Library staff will offer searching suggestions and answer questions, but cannot provide individual training concerning Internet use or computer skills. Interested customers are encouraged to use manuals and guides available in the library, to attend library-sponsored programs about Internet use, or schedule time with a member of the reference staff or the Assistive Technology Center for individual help.

Huntsville Public Library
Huntsville, Ontario, Canada

Staff Assistance

Time permitting, staff will be glad to assist you with start-up procedures. Patrons who need extensive assistance can ask for an appointment for one-on-one assistance with a volunteer Computer Tutor.

11.5 Offering Faculty Liaison Service

Jacksonville State University
Jacksonville, Alabama

An important component of the subject specialists' role is that as Faculty Liaison. This component includes direct contact with the specialist respective academic departments, and individual faculty to promote awareness of library programs, collections, and services. Among the most important areas are cooperative planning and development of collections, formal and informal library instruction, and reference services.

Austin College
Abell Library
Sherman, Texas

A librarian acts as a liaison with each academic department. This librarian should meet regularly with the faculty members (or the faculty liaison) of each department to exchange information about curriculum developments, library needs. The librarian should keep the faculty member informed of developments in the library, such as new services, policies, and collection development activities. Each academic area's liaison is the contact person for any questions or issues relating to the library and will make every effort to respond to requests or queries as quickly as possible. This librarian liaison will expedite the flow of information between faculty and library staff, thus enabling the library to provide better service to the academic community.

11.6 Requesting In-Process, Pre-Order, and Order Materials

Jacksonville State University
Jacksonville, Alabama

Inquiries for In-Process, Pre-Order, or On Order Materials:

Materials that have the status "In Process" can be located and made ready for circulation at the request of a patron. Patrons should discuss these requests with the Reference Librarian to ascertain if the item is unique. The reference librarian can contact the Cataloging Department on behalf of the patron to determine the processing status of the item. Those items in the last stages of processing may be rushed on demand. To obtain items in the early stages of processing will require that the patron complete and submit the In Process Material Request Form available on the library's Web site. Requested material will be available for pick up by 10:00 a.m. on the weekday following the request. It will be held for the patron at the Circulation Desk in the lobby for up to seven (7) days.

University of Texas at Austin
University of Texas Libraries
Austin, Texas

In-Process Materials

Users are not referred to Technical Services departments.

Staff members may use the online acquisitions database to check order and receipt status for books, serials, and other library materials. For more information about in-process materials, staff members contact the appropriate Technical Services section. When these areas are closed, questions are deferred until the next working day. Users are contacted as soon as the information is located.

11.7 Establishing Disclaimers and Liability

Apache Junction Public Library
Apache Junction, Arizona

GENERAL DISCLAIMER

Library staff tries to provide the best service possible; however, materials in the library may not be accurate, complete, or current. Apache Junction Public Library disclaims any warranty of the accuracy, authoritativeness, timeliness, or usefulness of the information obtained from its reference services. Apache Junction Public Library shall have no liability for any direct, indirect, or consequential damages related to the use of the information contained in, or obtained through its reference services.

LIMITATION OF LIABILITY

The Apache Junction Public Library is not responsible for damage to any personal storage media, computer or equipment, or any loss of data or damage that might occur from a library user's utilization of the Library's electronic information resources and/or equipment.

The Apache Junction Public Library disclaims any warranty of the accuracy, authoritativeness, timeliness, or usefulness of the information obtained from its electronic information systems. The Apache Junction Public Library shall have no liability for any direct, indirect, or consequential damages related to the use of the information contained in, or obtained through, its electronic information systems.

As is the case with printed materials, materials accessed through electronic information systems may not be accurate, complete, or current. The library encourages users to evaluate electronic materials just as they do printed materials.

Santa Fe Community College
Lawrence W. Tyree Library
Gainesville, Florida

The Lawrence W. Tyree Library does not guarantee the accuracy of information contained in any materials owned or obtained by the Library; neither is the Library liable for any consequences or damages the user of materials owned or obtained by the Library may suffer based on actions taken or decisions made using information from the Library. Further, the Library does not guarantee that the source of any information to which a Library employee may direct a user seeking reference or informational assistance is the best possible available source of that information either in materials which the Library owns or is able to obtain from other sources.

11.8 Use of Quiet Study Areas

University of Wisconsin–River Falls
Chalmer Davee Library
River Falls, Wisconsin

QUIET STUDY

The reference area is not intended to be a quiet study area, and consultation in a normal voice between librarians and library users is necessary for effective reference service. Library users requiring quiet study are directed to designated quiet study areas.

Weber State University
Stewart Library
Ogden, Utah

It is library policy that a quiet environment be maintained in the public study areas of the library. Persons acting against library policies or a conducive study atmosphere should be approached diplomatically, tactfully, and cordially in the spirit of soliciting their cooperation. Related policies and regulations should be courteously explained and the rationale behind them, if necessary. Any continued opposition should be referred to proper authority. Every effort should be made to avoid confrontation or embarrassment.

11.9 Answering Patron Requests for Office Supplies

University of Wisconsin–River Falls
Chalmer Davee Library
River Falls, Wisconsin

SUPPLIES

Generally, reference staff will provide small amounts of supplies to patrons. Scrap cards and pencils are routinely supplied at public workstations. Small amounts of paper clips, rubber bands, white-out, etc. are provided. A stapler, scissors, and three hole punch are provided for public use at the Reference Desk. A typewriter for public use is available in the Reference Area.

11.10 Offering Service to Patrons with Disabilities

University of Texas at Austin
University of Texas Libraries
Austin, Texas

Services to Students with Disabilities

Users with disabilities may need assistance in using library resources such as using reference tools. For those tools that are available on computer, a simple accommodation, like setting the display to large print, may be the solution. Other disabilities may require more extensive help. Whenever possible, such users are helped in the course of normal desk work. If a user with a disability requires more help than can be provided at the time, the staff member should attempt to locate another staff member who can help provide the service. If the person's need goes beyond one instance, as in the case of an extended project, he/she is referred to the Office of the Dean of Students, Services for Students with Disabilities Office. They may provide training in the adaptive equipment, volunteer readers, or an interpreter for the deaf.

University of Tennessee
University Libraries
Knoxville, Tennessee

The University of Tennessee Libraries is committed to providing access to library materials and services for all users and will make every effort to accomodate reasonable requests from library users with disabilities. If you need assistance or have questions/comments, please contact [name].

Retrieving Materials and Photocopying.

Students registered through the Office of Disability Services are eligible for special library services including the retrieval of materials from the stacks and assistance with photocopying.

How do I request these services?

Library Express provides paging and photocopying services for students with disabilities. Requests can be made by:

Using the online form in ILLiad.

Bringing a list of items to be pulled and/or photocopied to the Circulation Desk at the Melrose entrance on the 2nd floor of Hodges Library.

Telephoning Library Express at [telephone number].

Sending e-mail to Library Express

Call numbers must be provided for all items. If you need help determining call numbers, contact the Reference Department through the Ask Us Now service.

How long does it take?

Requests will be filled within 24 hours, Monday through Friday.

What about weekends and evenings?

Request assistance at the main Circulation desk on the 2nd floor. Circulation personnel will retrieve materials and assist with photocopying for walk-in users as staffing allows. All telephone requests and lengthy lists will be referred to Library Express for completion during weekday operating hours.

Is there a charge?

The only costs you will incur are the standard self-service photocopying rates of six cents per sheet.

Can materials be delivered?

Undergraduates must pick up materials at the Circulation Desk located on the second floor of Hodges Library. Faculty and graduate students may have materials delivered to campus offices as stated in the Library Express policy or electronically through ILLiad.

227

As always, staff in other departments and branch libraries will provide point of use assistance in their respective locations whenever possible.

Research Assistance.

Reference librarians are available to answer your questions and to provide instruction in the use of information resources. You may contact us:

In person: Visit the reference desk on the first floor of Hodges Library or ask for assistance at any of the branch libraries.

By phone: Call for Hodges Reference, or call any branch library.

Via chat or e-mail: Ask questions through the AskUsNow service.

For in-depth research assistance, users are encouraged to make an appointment with a subject librarian or the Libraries' Disabilities Services Coordinator.

Physical Access.
  • Hodges Library.
  • Agriculture-Veterinary Medicine Library.
  • Music Library.

Adaptive Equipment and Software.

The following equipment and software are available in the Reference Department on the first floor of Hodges Library:
  • TDD. A campus phone is also available in the Starbucks area.
  • Adjustable workstation with trackball mouse.
  • CCTV.
  • Workstation with JAWS 5.0, Kurzweil 1000, and Zoomtext 8.1.

Denver Public Library
Denver, Colorado

The Denver Public Library is committed to providing equal access for all people who wish to use the library and its collection. In order to provide this service there are various adaptive technologies available at the Central Library and many of our branches to assist customers who might need different modes of access to print and electronic resources. If you need any additional information please contact any of the listed libraries.

Visual Access Workstation Equipment

Chroma CCD Magnifier

This equipment allows the user to enlarge everyday printed reading materials. Simply place the book, newspaper, or any printed material on a platform and the image appears enlarged on a screen above. It magnifies up to 60 times, minimizes glare, and eliminates hot spots. The monitor is placed directly in front of the user for comfortable reading. (Only available at the Central Library – 1st floor General Reference and 5th floor Western History Departments).

ZoomText Extra Level I

This software enlarges items on the computer screen for individuals with low vision. Using ZoomText, an individual can increase the size of the icons, text, and other graphics on the screen. It can magnify up to 16 times, though most people typically use between 2 times to 8 times.

Jaws for Windows Screen Reader

This software assists the person who is blind by speaking what is on the computer screen. This screen-reading software works in conjunction with a speech synthesizer to enable the computer to talk about what is currently on the computer's screen. Jaws for Windows can also be used to browse the Internet.

IBM Home Page Reader (HPR)

This product is a World Wide Web browser for persons who are blind or visually impaired. HPR accesses Web pages and reads them using computer speech. You use the numeric keypad on your computer's keyboard to move around Web pages.

Open Book Ruby

This product is designed for individuals who are blind. It is a scanner/reader that converts typewritten or typeset material into clearly spoken computer speech. Text can be read immediately by the computer, stored on computer disk, or prepared for Braille production. Ruby uses a scanner to read the text in a book or on a printed page.

Braille Printer

This product prints text documents in Braille format so that persons who are able to read Braille can read them. (Only available at the Central Library, 1st floor General Reference Department)

Braille Display

This device attaches to the computer and converts the text on the computer's screen into Braille. (Only available at the Central Library, 1st floor General Reference Department).

The equipment listed above is available at the following libraries (unless otherwise indicated) [list of libraries].

Physical Access Workstation Equipment

Keyguards

Keyguards are plastic, metal, or fiberglass keyboard overlays that snap or lock over a keyboard and prevent unintentional keystrokes. Keyguards are useful for individuals with physical disabilities who often need to rest or support a hand on the keyboard surface between keystrokes. The keyguard covers the entire keyboard but has holes over the individual keys.

Intellikeys Keyboard

This special keyboard can facilitate the use of a personal computer for persons who have difficulty typing on a standard keyboard. The Intellikeys keyboard functions just like a regular keyboard but with special options so that an individual with a physical disability can run all the software programs on the computer. The Intellikeys uses overlays, which allow for different keyboard layouts with features such as large letters and numbers, high contrast colors, and alphabetical as well as QWERTY (standard keyboard) arrangement of keys.

Tracker

This device is a substitute for the traditional mouse. It uses an optical sensor that tracks a tiny disposable dot that is placed on the user's forehead or glasses. The mouse is then moved when the individual moves his or her head while looking at different locations on the computer's screen. This mouse emulation can be used with an on-screen keyboard such as Screen Doors (see below).

ScreenDoors

This software is simply a computer keyboard that appears on the computer screen. Individuals who cannot use the standard keyboard may be able to access the onscreen keyboard by using the Tracker or the standard computer mouse.

Dragon Dictate Voice Recognition Software

Voice recognition technology allows users to speak directly to their computers and is helpful for people who have significant difficulty using the traditional mouse and/or keyboard. Dragon Dictate offers the capability of using the computer completely hands-free.

The equipment listed above is available at the following libraries (unless otherwise indicated). For further information please call or visit: [telephone number and address].

Children's Related Equipment

Touch Monitor

With this device, the child's eyes do not need to leave the monitor. Items such as icons or buttons can be selected on the computer screen by directly touching them. This is helpful for children who find it difficult to use a conventional mouse.

Intellikeys Keyboard

This keyboard is unique in that its function can be totally changed by replacing a thin overlay on its surface. It comes with many different overlays included, and custom overlays can easily be developed for specific purposes. The Denver Public Library has developed two custom overlays that are designed to work with the Kids Catalog and Kids Web pages.

Little Fingers Keyboard

Conventional computer keyboards are built for adult size hands. When children or persons with small hands use these keyboards, extra work is required. This smaller keyboard is just right for these small hands, is more comfortable, and will reduce the risk of a keyboarding related injury.

MicrosoftTM Kidball

Many kids find this device makes "mouse" use easier. The extra large surface is easier to grip, and the unit does not need to be moved around like a conventional mouse. The user can rest his/her hand on the top, and gently spin the ball to move the cursor on the computer screen.

The equipment listed above is available in the Children's Department (Central Library only). For further information please call or visit: [telephone number and address].

11.11 Collecting Statistics

University of Wisconsin–River Falls
Chalmer Davee Library
River Falls, Wisconsin

A daily record is maintained of all questions answered by reference staff at the Reference Desk. Three types of questions are recorded: reference, ready reference, and directional.

Santa Fe Community College
Lawrence W. Tyree Library
Gainesville, Florida

Recording statistics

Statistics on reference transactions will be gathered on and analyzed at periodic times throughout the semester. Statistical information on library tours, BI sessions, programs, and other services is also maintained.

The Logan Library
Logan, Utah

Reference Statistics and Requests

Reference staff is responsible for recording the number of questions received at the reference desk. Unfulfilled requests and needs will also be reported on the form. Telephone statistics will also be recorded.

A directional transaction is defined as an information contact that facilitates the use of the library and does not involve the knowledge, use, recommendations, or instruction in the use of any information sources other than those which describe the library.

A reference transaction is defined as an information contact that involves the knowledge, use, recommendation, or instruction in the use of information sources by the reference librarians.

Mansfield Public Library
Mansfield, Connecticut

Reference transactions are tallied for statistical purposes and are defined as:
- Requests for help with the online catalog or use of the library
- Questions of fact or requests for help in finding facts
- Literature searches or reader's advisory services
- Requests for information and referral
- Requests for help with resources, all formats

11.12 Forms: Requests to Purchase Forms

Wichita Falls Public Library
Wichita Falls, Texas

Are We Missing Something? Library users play a very important role in our collection development process. Let us know if there is a specific title and/or subject that you are unable to locate in our library. Please be aware that if we are unable to obtain the items you suggest, or if we decide that the items do not meet the Library's needs, you may wish to borrow through Interlibrary Loan. We generally will not purchase items that are more than 2 years old, that are available only as mass market paperbacks, or that cannot be obtained through normal library book vendors.

Contact Information: Tell us about yourself. We're sorry, but we will only order books that are suggested by Wichita Falls Public Library patrons with valid cards.

Type in your name:_____

Your e-mail address:_____

Library card barcode number:_____

Would you like to be notified if and when the Library obtains the suggested title?
Yes_____ No_____

Would you like to be added to the hold list for this title if we order it?
Yes_____ No_____

Format Requested (click to see list — choose one) (None Selected) Book
Book (Large Type) Audiocassette Videocassette DVD Magazine Other

What We Need: Write your request in the following spaces. Please give as much information as you have. If you have more than one request, please use a new form for each request.

Title:_____

Author:_____

ISBN:_____

Publisher:_____

Subject Area:_____

_____

Different browsers read our pages differently. If you have any trouble using our form, please submit your question by email to acq@wfpl.net We value your input! Thanks for your suggestion!

Request for Purchase E-mail Form

City of Palo Alto Library
Palo Alto, California

Purchase Request Form

Use the form below to suggest a book, CD, DVD, audiobook, or other item you think the library should purchase. The library endeavors to purchase items suggested by customers if the funds exist to do so, and if the requested materials are currently in print and meet the library's selection criteria.

You can also request to be notified by e-mail if the library purchases the item you suggested.

Once the item is "On Order" in the library catalog, you can reserve it free of charge. New items are added daily to the catalog, so check the web catalog frequently.

TELL US ABOUT THE ITEM:

Author/Composer/Artist/Actor/Director*

Title*

If known:

Publisher/Label/Studio Year of publication

ISBN

Please indicate the format of the item*

COMMENTS OR ADDITIONAL INFORMATION: If you heard or read a review of this item, please tell us where—the name and date of the broadcast, the name and date of the newspaper or magazine, the URL of the Web site, etc.

EMAIL NOTIFICATION: To be notified by email if the library purchases the item you suggested, please enter your email address.

Input your email address

Confirm email address (type it again)

* indicates required fields

11.13 Form: E-mail Request for Individual Appointment

Merrimack College
McQuade Library
North Andover, Massachusetts

Research Advisory Request Form

The Research Advisory Service offers students the opportunity to meet one-on-one with a librarian to get help with library research. The librarian will talk with you about your assignment and the type of information you need, and then guide you to appropriate databases, indexes and other library resources that will be most relevant for your search, and show you how to use them. The librarian can also help you obtain hard-to-find materials, give you ideas for locating primary sources, and show you how to evaluate information on the Web. Keep in mind that the librarian cannot write the paper for you, but can help you to complete the research process effectively and efficiently.

Use the form below to request a consultation session with a librarian to help with your assignment. You will be notified of the date and time of your appointment by e-mail.

Your name:
Phone number:
E-Mail:
What is your research topic?
What course is it for?
When is it due?
What kind of assignment is it? (e.g. paper, project, presentation)
How long does the assignment need to be? (e.g. 15 pages, 20 minutes)
How many sources are required?

What sources has your professor suggested you use? (Check all that apply)
      Books
      Newspapers or popular magazines
      Primary Sources
      Scholarly Journals
      Other (list)

Are there sources your professor has asked you NOT to use? (list)

Where have you been searching? (Check all that apply.)
      Haven't started yet
      EBSCO (list databases)
      InfoTrac (list databases)
      LexisNexis Academic
      World Wide Web (list best URLs)
      Other (list sources)

Have you encountered any problems? (Check all that apply.)
     Found too much information
     Found too little information
     Need more scholarly resources
     Materials not in our library
     Other (Explain)
     What days and times are best for you to meet with a librarian?

Part VI
Reference Services:
In-Person
Patron Assistance

Chapter 12

FACE-TO-FACE REFERENCE DESK SERVICE POLICIES

GENERAL GUIDELINES

12.1 Establishing Patron Priorities

Glenview Public Library
Glenview, Illinois

Service Priorities

Service to the public has priority over all other tasks. Simultaneous requests will be managed at the librarian's discretion with regard to urgency, complexity and availability of staff resources. In-person, telephone, e-mail, and Internet reference requests will be handled in the order they are received. If the librarian cannot answer a request immediately, he or she will obtain contact information from the patron and see that the patron receives a response within twenty-four hours. If it becomes necessary for a librarian to leave a desk, he or she will make suitable arrangements for coverage.

Washington County Public Library
Abingdon , Virginia

Priorities

Service to the public receives priority over any other duties. Clerical tasks, conversations with co-workers and other professional assignments are secondary. In-person and telephone request for service should be handled in order of their arrival. Confidentiality of user requests must be respected at all times.

University of Texas at Arlington
University of Texas at Arlington Libraries
Arlington, Texas

Service Priorities:

Information Services staff adheres to the Reference and Adult Services Division's "Guidelines for Behavioral Performance of Reference and Information Services Professionals"

In-Person Services:

In-person inquiries are on a first-come, first-served basis

During peak times, the Information Services staff will try our best to give assistance to each individual in order to accommodate all users

Reference Desk hours differ from the Libraries' hours

Telephone Services:

Telephone reference service is available during service desk hours

Priority is given to in-person inquiries

The Information Services staff may not be able to conduct in-depth research for phone callers. An in-person visit is suggested for more in-depth assistance

Sometimes Information Services may not be able to answer the telephone but voice mail is available, and staff will respond to voice mail as quickly as possible

E-mail Services:

E-mail services are intended to answer factual inquiries; we will try our best to offer research assistance via e-mail

Information Services staff will respond to e-mail requests as soon as possible during regular Reference Desk hours

12.2 Offering Reader's Advisory

Brampton Public Library
Brampton, Ontario, Canada

Reader's Advisory – Staff will assist customers by helping them identify their reading preferences and making recommendations for selection based on criteria the customer and staff have established.

12.3 Furnishing Individual Service and Appointments

St. Joseph County Public Library
South Bend, Indiana

Reference Service by Appointment

A. Services offered by appointment

Librarians have the option of scheduling reference appointments:

1. For research interviews before an online search (see Section VIII, Online Reference Services)
2. For extended instruction sessions (for example, Census CD-ROM or Internet instruction)
3. For questions that require considerable interaction with the customer in the development of strategies to find the best answer in the most cost effective way.

B. Priorities

Priority is given to on-site ready and intermediate reference questions and telephone inquiries.

C. Time limits/Scope of service

1. Appointments should generally last no longer than 30 minutes.
2. Appointments will vary according to the staff time available; limits may be set to ensure that other customers will be able to obtain service. (See Section L, Limitations of Reference Service.)

D. Parameters of conduct

Staff should adhere to the Customer Service at Information Desks Guidelines. (See Appendix B)

E. Confidentiality

Information services staff subscribe to the American Library Association's "Code of Ethics, 1995." (See Appendix A)

F. Fees

For users within the library's service area there is no charge. For users outside the library's service area there is a charge of $25.00 per half hour of staff time, to be paid at the time of service. Other fees may be applicable.

Indiana University–Purdue University Fort Wayne
Walter E. Helmke Library
Fort Wayne, Indiana

Rationale

There are two types of reference appointments available at Helmke Library, walk-in and scheduled. Both types of appointments are available at the library's reference consulting areas - general reference on the first floor and Science Information Center on the fourth floor. The library maintains statistics on reference appointments and its performance is judged on such indicators, so it is important to make and record appointments accurately. This document outlines the policies and procedures governing the provision of reference and information services on a walk-in and scheduled basis.

Policies

The library's basic and in-depth reference and information services and two-tiered instructional services are described in detail on the library's homepage under Reference & Instruction. Any librarian, library staff member, or student worker may respond to a patron's request for information by scheduling a reference appointment with a librarian.

Appointments are recorded by library staff in separate appointment books kept at the Service Desk. The Science Information Center's appointment book will be transferred to the fourth floor during the Center's normal hours of operation (2-4 p.m., Monday-Thursday, during fall and spring semesters), and it will be returned to the Service Desk when the Center is closed.

The Science Information Center schedule provides eight (8) hours in addition to the regular general reference schedule's 60 hours, for a total of 68 hours of reference appointments per week. Extra Saturday hours are also added during the peak mid-semester schedule to accommodate demand.

It is important for library staff to convey the message to patrons that a librarian is available to assist them. Patrons who seek assistance on a walk-in basis should be assigned to the next available librarian working in (1) the first-floor general reference area, followed by (2) the fourth-floor Science Information Center, according to the procedures below.

Procedures for Recording Walk-in Appointments

When an appointment is for the next available time, and the patron does not ask to meet with a particular librarian, write "walk-in," "student," or "patron" in the appointment book next to the initials of the librarian on duty.

Schedule all walk-in appointments for the general reference consulting area first, then assign patrons to the next available Science Information Center librarian (whether the question is science related or not).

Procedures for Recording Scheduled Appointments

When the patron asks to meet with a particular liaison librarian or subject specialist (e.g., "the education librarian," "psychology librarian," etc.), write the patron's full name in the appointment book next to the librarian's initials. See the posted list of Library Fund Managers by Subject or Department to identify the appropriate librarian.

When scheduling an appointment hours or days in advance, also record the patron's name, even if the patron does not request the librarian by name.

Procedures for Making Referrals to Librarians

Staff should encourage patrons to meet with the next available librarian, who will help them begin their search and perhaps make a referral to a subject specialist for further help. When a patron clearly needs specialized assistance, make an effort to schedule an appointment with the appropriate librarian.

If the librarian's hours listed on the reference appointment schedule do not suit patrons' schedules, encourage them to contact the librarian by phone or e-mail to arrange a more convenient appointment time. Do not convey the message that a librarian is not available if he or she does not have a regular shift listed on the schedule. Make every effort to offer the librarian's business card and allow the patron to use a library telephone to reach the librarian or to leave a message with their name, brief reference question, phone number, and/or e-mail address.

Librarians are responsible for keeping their business cards stocked at the Service Desk, the first-floor reference consulting area, the Science Information Center, and the Electronic Information Training Center (EITC).

Librarians who are called to respond to a patron's immediate need should negotiate a convenient time to meet if they are busy with other obligations.

Please direct questions about reference and information services policy or reference-appointment procedures to Head of Reference & Information Services.

San Jose Public Library and San Jose State University Library
San Jose, California

Statement of Policy & Text

This policy establishes Reference by Appointment as the means for acquiring in-depth research consultation with a librarian with appropriate expertise at the new King Library.

This policy, which has been traditionally used for the academic community of San Jose State University, will now also extend to the community currently served by the San Jose Public Library.

Need for the Policy

The SJSU academic community often requires in-depth consultation with a subject specialist to satisfactorily meet the demands of their research.

Historically, SJSU has provided Reference by Appointment to its academic community, but SJPL has not previously provided Reference by Appointment in a formal manner.

This policy must apply to both communities served at the King Library.

Requirements & Guidelines

Referrals to a subject specialist are made when:
- The librarian on either the Reference Desk or the Reference Connection determines the patron has an in-depth research question and would greatly benefit from an appointment with a subject specialist
- A Faculty member, student or community member requests a consultation with a subject specialist

All Librarians are expected to:
- Provide appropriate specialized instruction, if possible
- Perform these consultations at times other than assigned Reference desk times
- Conduct consultations by:
Phone
Email
In-person.
Virtual reference software once they are trained in its use

To implement this policy, SJPL subject specialties need to be determined. To do this, a survey of SJPL Main Librarians will be conducted in early 2003.

Benedictine University
Benedictine University Library
Lisle, Illinois

RESEARCH CONSULTATIONS

Research consultations are available at the Benedictine Library to faculty, staff, and students of Benedictine University. Research consultations are scheduled in advance to insure uninterrupted

243

time for the researcher to consult with a librarians about appropriate resources and strategies for a project.

12.4 Conducting Extensive Patron Research

Morton Grove Public Library
Morton Grove, Illinois

Requests for and/or completion of lengthy research is not considered a traditional role of the public reference librarian. Research and reference differ in terms of time required, sources employed, and ease of determination of search strategies; research is the more involved of the two. Patrons needing extensive compilations (bibliographies, lists, statistics, etc.) or research should be directed to the appropriate resources and offered as much assistance as staff time allows.

12.5 Evaluating Service for Using Fee-Based Services

Glenview Public Library
Glenview, Illinois

Fee-Based Searching

Librarians will use professional judgment to determine when a fee-based electronic database would be the best means of answering a question. The librarians will complete online searches within three working days of the request, and the library will subsidize these searches up to the level of twenty dollars apiece for three searches per year for Glenview cardholders.

Stillwater Public Library
Stillwater, Oklahoma

REFERENCE RESEARCH POLICY

Due to staffing and time constraints, the Stillwater Public Library Reference Department's primary focuses are reader's advisory, answering ready reference questions, and assisting in locating materials to answer more complex questions.

In general, any questions requiring more than fifteen minutes of Reference staff research in which a patron does not assist; compound questions; and questions involving microform research fall under this research policy.

Fees for research are $20.00 per hour with a $5.00 minimum. This fee includes first class postage. Photocopies are .10 per page and microfilmed copies are .15 per page.

The total charged time includes time used for the preparation of mailing.

The Reference staff will have discretion over deciding which questions in the above list fall under the Research Policy. Considerations include, time involved, complexity of the question, number of questions asked, sources used, and ease of determination of search strategies.

The Library reserves the right to refuse to contract for additional services, if it would interfere with primary services given to other patrons.

The Reference staff will make every attempt to find the answer or information to a question or request. However, staff may not be able to find certain information. Nonetheless, fees will be assessed for the research.

Patrons must specify a maximum fee at which the Reference staff must cease researching until an agreement for additional research is negotiated.

Research is performed only as time permits and other reference duties take precedence over research. The Reference staff and patron may negotiate a date by which the research should be completed. However, intervening reference duties may delay research completion. In such an event, the staff will contact the patron and renegotiate a later completion date.

Prior to beginning research, the Reference staff will contact the patron for fee authorization. This authorization must be given before any work is done.

Rutgers University Library
Rutgers University Libraries
Newark, New Jersey

General Statement

The Rutgers Online Automated Retrieval Service (ROARS) is a librarian-mediated online information retrieval service offered by the Rutgers University Libraries. ROARS searches are performed on a fee-for-service basis and are partially subsidized by the University Libraries. Electronic resources used for ROARS include licensed databases available without charge on the university network or databases available on a "pay as you go" basis. The Libraries participating in ROARS are Alcohol Studies, Alexander, Chang Science, Dana, Kilmer, Douglass, Mathematical Sciences, Library of Science and Medicine, and Paul Robeson.

Eligibility

The purpose of the ROARS service is to support the academic research and teaching endeavors of Rutgers students, faculty, administrators, and staff and university affiliates.

The primary community to be served by ROARS consists of individuals who are currently part of the university community by virtue of enrollment or employment, formal agreements with other institutions, and certain affiliated persons considered on a case-by-case basis.

ROARS is not available to:

- Alumni of either Rutgers or affiliated institutions
- Corporate borrowers
- Former university students (not alumni)
- Unaffiliated scholars or researchers
- Students and faculty attending short-term institutes at Rutgers.

These individuals will be referred to the contract library for searching services in the appropriate New Jersey Library Network region.

If it becomes known prior to the search that a search request is not in support of an eligible individual's own research or teaching and is being requested for an ineligible outside individual or company, the search request will be denied and a referral made to an outside search service.

Searches for library faculty in support of professional research are treated as other faculty searches, that is, performed on a cost-recovery basis.

Costs related to system maintenance, searcher updates on news, etc., should be accounted for by ROARS coordinators.

Extensive searches for administrative, job related, or committee work should be authorized, in brief written form, by the appropriate library director, chairperson, or associate university librarian and noted in monthly statistics reports.

Database Coverage

Generally, each Rutgers library will handle search requests that fall within the scope of its collections. Regardless of where the original search request is made, referrals should be made among libraries, taking into account the availability of expertise in a database at a particular library and the proximity of a requester's office or place of residence.

Search Responsibility

Librarians at Rutgers University who have expertise in database searching will perform ROARS searches using licensed databases available on the university network or databases available on a "pay as you go" basis.

Search Charges

The University Libraries absorb the costs for general overhead and searcher's time devoted to search strategy and conducting searches.

All direct costs of a ROARS search using databases available on a "pay as you go" basis will be passed on to the search requester. Results may be printed, downloaded to a disk, or sent to the requester via e-mail. The search requester must supply the disk or, if available, purchase it from the library at normal library charges. A service charge of $3.00/search is added to the cost of each search and passed on to the search requester.

A flat fee of $10 will be charged for a librarian-mediated search using licensed databases available on the university network. Results will not be printed but will be downloaded to a disk or sent to the requester via e-mail. There is no additional charge for the disk.

Searches can be paid for by cash (not at Paul Robeson), personal check, through grant or departmental account funds, or blanket account funds. Billing options are available. Uniform accounting procedures are established system wide.

The estimated costs of a search should be shared with the search requester when the search is conducted.

In the case of long overdue and unpaid balances for ROARS searches, the ROARS library coordinator will first make personal contact with the individual who made the search request to discuss payments. Procedures for cessation of borrowing privileges will be initiated if payment is not forthcoming following this contact.

Beyond the initial level of contact, the coordinator will judge what succeeding levels of contact should be made, by the unit librarian or by the university librarian. The library coordinator in conjunction with the library director will decide when contacting the individual's departmental chairperson is warranted.

Search Request Procedures

ROARS search requests can be made in person, by e-mail, by phone, or by mail. A search request form is completed for every ROARS search performed. Forms are available at the reference desk of each library.

For every search, an interview is conducted with the person making the request. The interview appointment is made with the search requester in person or via the phone. The search, however, can be conducted with the requester present or not. The requester should be allowed to make this choice, although the final decision is left to the discretion of the searcher.

Coordinating ROARS

The Public Services Council monitors the system wide coordination of ROARS, recommending policies and procedures for the service.

A coordinator for database searching is appointed at each library to oversee the day-to-day operations of ROARS.

Statistics

The coordinators maintain all records for ROARS accounting at each library. Statistics maintained are: date of search, searcher, database(s) used, cost, service charge, date paid.

Ready Reference Searching

An online ready reference search is a short search of one or more databases for the purpose of providing a quick answer to a reference question at no cost to the library patron. The librarian who conducts the search determines if the question is an appropriate one for such service. Online ready reference searches should be considered when the librarian has determined that other references (i.e. RLIN, OCLC, printed tools, etc.) will not satisfy the patron's needs or when a significant amount of the reference librarian's time can be saved.

The preferred tools for ready reference searching are the licensed databases available on the university network. Ready reference searching using databases available on a "pay as you go" basis is limited by time spent, cost, and result. Suggested limits are =ten minutes, =$10, =five online citations.

ROARS coordinators maintain statistics locally for ready reference searching.

Weber State University
Stewart Library
Ogden, Utah

Commercial Database Searching

A. Reference staff responsibilities

It is the proactive responsibility of the reference staff person, when other library reference materials are proving inadequate or inappropriate, to refer the user to the appropriate bibliographer or the R&IS Librarian, to schedule the online search.

B. When the University Library will subsidize commercial database searching

The University Library will subsidize searches that support the instructional and research needs of WSU faculty, staff and students.

Please Note: In instances where a faculty person, staff person or student has obtained a grant and/or contract to offset the expense of research, and the grant and/or contract includes commercial database expenses, all search expenses will be billed to the grant/contract.

C. Non WSU Faculty, Staff or Students

Commercial database searches are done for non-WSU faculty, staff or students by appointment. Non-WSU faculty, staff or students are expected to pay all expenses incurred during the search.

D. Searches for Classes

Searches for class assignments or classroom demonstrations are scheduled with the subject bibliographer at least a week in advance.

E. Other Online Services

Other vendors offer online services. Although the University Library does not currently subscribe to many of these services, we will work with faculty in developing services that fill their need.

12.6 Time Limits

Falmouth Public Library
Falmouth, Massachusetts

Accurate answers to ready-reference questions within a 3 to 5 minute time frame.

Accurate answers to questions by fax and e-mail within a two-hour time frame. If a question cannot be answered in the above time frame the patron will be contacted to provide an estimated time for researching and responding to the question or staff will provide referral as appropriate.

Glen Ellyn Public Library
Glen Ellyn, Illinois

Prompt Service

In order to provide effective service to all patrons in an equitable manner, certain priorities and limits have been established. Answering patron questions takes precedence over all other staff duties. In general, in-person questions will take precedence over questions received by telephone, mail or other means, but all questions will receive a response within 24 hours. If a question from a Glen Ellyn cardholder cannot be answered with sources available in the Library, it will be referred to a supplementary reference service. The time that can be spent on an individual question depends on whether other patrons or questions are waiting. To insure that patrons do not have to wait too long for service, generally no more than 10 minutes will be spent with a patron while others are waiting. If the question cannot be answered within that time, the staff member will offer to continue the search and contact the patron with the answer later.

Memorial Hall Library
Andover, Massachusetts

Time Limits

No two reference questions are alike; therefore, no special time limits can be placed on an actual question. The amount of time devoted to a question is at the discretion of the reference librarian. When questions from member libraries cannot be answered in-house within a day's time, they will be referred to another source.

St. Joseph County Public Library
South Bend, Indiana

Questions requiring more than 20 minutes of assistance should generally be handled on an appointment basis.

Washington State University
Washington State University Libraries
Pullman, Washington

The amount of service that can be given at any particular time will vary, depending on such factors as:

How busy it is in the library.
The number of patrons waiting for assistance.
The number of personnel available to help patrons.
The nature of the request.
The patron's prior knowledge of library resources and use.

If possible, do not leave other patrons waiting for lengthy time periods. If help is not available, get patrons started on their projects and then return to them as time permits.

If the inquirer is beginning his or her search and is unfamiliar with the relevant sources, you may suggest setting an appointment with you or another librarian for an instructional tour/consultation on how to make use of resources in that field. If you are unfamiliar with what sources might be available and wish to investigate when you have more time, offer to call the patron.

12.7 Incomplete Transactions

Memorial Hall Library
Andover, Massachusetts

Incomplete Reference Transactions

Although every effort is made to complete questions immediately, some can remain at the end of a shift or day. Unfinished questions are turned over to incoming staff. A patron will be advised if more than one day is needed to complete the question or if the question has been referred to another source. If a question is waiting for a reply from another source, or if a patron has been notified that a printout is waiting for them, the Reference Pending Form will be filled out and materials will be attached to it in the Reference Question Pending notebook. Staff members will consult with colleagues if they need assistance with a puzzling or difficult question. The Regional Reference Librarian checks the Reference Pending Notebook each day for completed questions and performs any follow up.

Morton Grove Public Library
Morton Grove, Illinois

Although every effort is made to complete questions immediately, some can remain at the end of a shift or day. Unfinished questions will be turned over to incoming staff if the patron is in immediate need of the requested information. The patron will be given an agreed-upon time frame in which the reference question will be answered. Staff members are encouraged to consult with colleagues if they need assistance with a puzzling or difficult question.

Washington County Public Library
Abingdon, Virginia

Incomplete Reference Transactions

Staff members are encouraged to consult with colleagues if they need help with a puzzling or difficult question. If the requested information cannot be provided within two (2) working days, the patron should be notified of the status of the request.

12.8 Directing Versus Accompanying Patron to the Shelf

Bridgewater Public Library
Bridgewater, Massachusetts

Whenever possible and/or practical, staff should go with patrons to locate materials. When this is not possible, staff should encourage patrons to return to the reference desk for additional assistance if they are unable to find the required materials. In the event that the librarian is not able to immediately accompany the patron to the shelf, she/he should follow up as soon as possible in order to assure that the patron has located the required information or materials.

Rockford Public Library
Rockford, Illinois

Whenever possible, staff accompany customers to the catalog, computer workstation, or to the stacks where needed resources are located. If customers are directed to the shelves, they are encouraged to return to the service desk for additional help with a nutshell statement such as "Let us know if you don't find what you are looking for."

12.9 Creating Bibliographies

Rockford Public Library
Rockford, Illinois

Staff creates print and electronic materials lists and bibliographies to promote awareness of collections, to provide finding aids and search instruction and to increase efficiency in answering requests. Lists of bestsellers and new books are provided to customers. Individual and organization requests for bibliographies are honored within the established time guidelines.

Sarasota County Libraries
Sarasota, Florida

Patrons desiring bibliographies will be given brief information of appropriate resources and invited to come in to develop extensive bibliographies. Requests for bibliographies to support an area of study or interest from community organizations will be considered individually. Decisions will be based on available staff and resources and on the impact on the community.

Ryerson University
Ryerson University Library
Toronto, Ontario, Canada

Bibliographies

The reference staff does not normally compile or check bibliographies. Staff do assist patrons in the use of bibliographical tools.

Weber State University
Stewart Library
Ogden, Utah

Bibliographies

Bibliographies of materials housed in the Stewart Library collections may be compiled on request of campus faculty and administration. These may be used as class handouts or for workshops, discussion groups, seminars, etc.

Bibliographies may be annotated or not annotated depending on the given need and the amount of time available for completion. Costs of photocopying or printing will be charged to the department or the faculty member originating the request.

Bibliographies needed for projects funded by outside agencies may also be produced on request, provided appropriate funding for "library research" is allocated to the Stewart Library. Arrangements, for such projects are to be made through the Director of Information Services. Two copies of all bibliographies will be placed in the University Archives and twenty copies will be sent to the State Library Depository System for distribution to other institutions and agencies. The library, however, does not compile bibliographies to fulfill personal needs but in this case assists patrons in the use of the necessary bibliographical tools. Bibliographies produced to patron specifications may be printed from the DYNIX online catalog (see full description of this feature under Circulation, sec. VI.E.6).

ASSISTANCE OFFERED

12.10 Answering Extended Questions

University of Texas at Austin
University of Texas Libraries
Austin, Texas

Extended Reference Questions

When it becomes apparent that a question will require extensive searching, staff members on desk duty may offer to search further and make arrangements for reporting results. Reference staff members work on extended reference questions as time permits and consult other staff in their own or other units as necessary.

12.11 Answering with Ready Reference Resources

Bridgewater Public Library
Bridgewater, Massachusetts

Ready Reference: This service provides for brief factual answers and requires a search of not more than five minutes.

St. Joseph County Public Library
South Bend, Indiana

Ready reference – a search, which requires little, if any interaction with the customer in determining the nature of the inquiry and search strategy which would best provide the answer. Ready reference questions are those in which answers can be found and read in 10 minutes or less.

Within this time limit, no more than 5 questions should be answered.

Boerne Public Library
Boerne, Texas

Ready Reference - Ready reference questions (phone numbers, addresses, names, etc.) are answered during all open library hours.

Answers are given as quickly as possible. Patrons at Public Services desks take precedence over patrons who phone in. Staff will avoid reading lengthy passages from materials over the telephone in response to phoned-in questions. In the interest of protecting individuals' privacy rights, directory information about individuals, such as a telephone number or address, will not be given out over the telephone. Instead, patrons will be referred to online telephone directories and telephone companies' directory services.

12.12 Answering with Print Collection Resources

Glenview Public Library
Glenview, Illinois

Compilations and Literature Searches

Librarians cannot prepare extensive compilations (bibliographies, lists, statistics, etc.) for patrons, nor can they undertake exhaustive literature searches. If patrons ask librarians to search the library's holdings on a topic and to have materials ready for them to pick up, librarians should do a quick search in library databases and/or scan periodical citations and retrieve some relevant books. Librarians will hold retrieved materials for patrons at a service desk. Librarians should offer to assist patrons in their research.

12.13 Answering with Internet and Electronic Resources

Morton Grove Public Library
Morton Grove, Illinois

When all in-house print and online resources fail to answer the patron's reference needs, the Reference Librarian can, at his/her discretion, fill out an online reference request to the North Suburban Library System's Night Owl Reference Service.

St. Joseph County Public Library
South Bend, Indiana

Online Services Offered
  1. Quick online information searches
    a. Quick online reference searches are conducted to locate needed information as efficiently as possible, and are without cost to the customer.
    b. Quick online searches may be conducted as part of a reference transaction to:
      1. verify or locate information in the most efficient and cost effective manner.
      2. verify or locate a citation that will guide the customer to materials.
      3. locate information too current to be included in print materials.
      4. find information not available in other SJCPL resources.
      5. make a brief preliminary online search of a database to determine whether an extended search would be warranted or beneficial.
    c. Quick online information searches are conducted at the discretion of the staff. As a general guideline, quick searches are $15 or less in database, telecommunications, and print fees.

2. Extended Online Searches

    a. The purpose of an extended online search is to provide users with access to a wide range of information and bibliographic sources on a topic.

    b. Extended searches are conducted:

        1. by appointment.

        2. on demand, if trained staff are on duty and there is sufficient time to conduct the search.

    c. Staffing

Online searches are performed by Adult Reference and Information Services staff. Most staff are trained to perform quick online searches of selected databases. A limited number of staff are trained to perform extended online searches.

Wilmington Public Library District
Wilmington, Illinois

Internet Database Searches

The Internet provides a world of resources and organizations beyond the walls of Wilmington Public Library District. The library makes no guarantees, implied or otherwise, regarding the reliability or accuracy of information obtained from the Internet using the library's connection.

The library provides Internet access for public use. The library does not have sufficient staff to provide individualized instruction or assist in formulating search strategies. Patrons may do their own Internet searching if they have signed a User Agreement. There is a charge for all printouts from the Internet.

Customers who do not choose to personally use the Internet may request Reference Staff assistance. Staff will provide the answer while the customer waits if the material can be located within 10 minutes.

If staff is not aware of a site that will answer the patron's question and more time is needed for searching, staff will complete a Reference Request Form and search for an answer at a later time.

Patrons will be notified when their material is ready to be picked up. Material will be held at the circulation desk with the name and date clearly noted for three days.

University of Texas at Austin
University of Texas Libraries
Austin, Texas

ELECTRONIC REFERENCE SERVICE

Electronic reference service, which utilizes electronic mail for both inquiry and response, is comparable to telephone reference and correspondence.

Priorities

Electronic reference service is available to current UT Austin students, faculty, and staff. Students enrolled in UT Austin distance education programs are also eligible to use this service. Other users should expect an answer only about unique resources of the University of Texas Libraries.

Priority is always given to persons who come to the library for service.

Types of Questions Answered

Questions requiring short, factual answers or requests for information about UT Austin library holdings or information about UT Austin are appropriate for this service.

Assistance is provided in the use of electronic resources accessible from the Libraries web site, including brief explanations about search techniques and connection questions. Users may be directed to online search help or to appropriate offices for more specialized technical assistance.

Types of Questions Not Answered

Users with long or complex research questions, including term paper research, receive brief guidance in the selection of resources and are invited to visit the library or a library near them for more in-depth assistance.

Users requesting URLs for non-UT Web sites may be referred to search engines.

Electronic reference service is not appropriate for general Internet instruction. Local users should be encouraged to attend University of Texas Libraries electronic information classes.

Response

All responses are made by e-mail, usually within 48 hours during the regular work week. Non-UT affiliates receive a standard reply restating the service policy, along with brief suggestions for finding the needed information using online resources.

Electronic Information Sources

Staff are familiar with and honor license agreements regarding use of online databases when providing electronic reference service to non-UT Austin affiliates.

12.14 Offering Internet and Database Assistance

Glenview Public Library
Glenview, Illinois

Instruction and Orientation Services

Instruction and orientation in library use may range from basic individual and class instruction on how to use catalogs, reference tools, and the Internet to more formal assistance which can be scheduled by appointment.

Memorial Hall Library
Andover, Massachusetts

Basic Assistance: Reference staff members will assist patrons at every level of the Reference transaction, if the patron so desires. This may require accompanying the patron to the computer catalog to explain its use, or physically locating the materials for the patron. In the event that the staff member is unable to accompany the patron to the stacks area, it is important to remind the patron to check back with the reference desk if the material cannot be located.

Rockford Public Library
Rockford, Illinois

Brief individual instruction in use of the catalog and other library tools is given. Customers are referred to classes offered for more extensive instruction in computer resources. Classes are offered to give customers sufficient instruction to use library-provided electronic resources.

Assistance with Internet resources: Staff provides instruction and assistance in the use of the Internet. Staff may not take actions for customers that involve giving customers' personal information, registration, or payment. Staff will refer customers to classes on setting up email, filling in forms and office applications when customers need lengthy assistance. Staff may not fill out tax forms or other forms for customers.

Wilmington County Public Library
Abingdon, Virginia

Basic Assistance: Never assume that a patron knows how to locate library materials. Assistance should be offered whenever a patron appears to need it. This may require accompanying the patron to a service area or electronic resource. Whenever patrons are sent to the stacks on their own, remind them to report back to the reference desk if they are unsuccessful in finding what they need.

Shiawassee District Library
Owosso, Michigan

Staff at public service desks will assist library users in getting started on the Internet. However, the Library cannot guarantee that Internet-trained staff will be available to assist users at all times the Library is open. Regrettably, staff is not able to offer extensive explanations about the Internet or personal computer use or provide in-depth training. Time permitting, staff will try to answer specific questions about the Internet and offer suggestions for effective searching. Staff mediated assistance is limited to the guidelines presented in policy VI—Reference Services. Staff can also provide information about Internet training opportunities and Internet books and manuals. More extensive instruction is available through the Internet Training Center.

12.15 Offering Instruction in Use of Resources or Equipment

Dorchester County Public Library
Cambridge, Maryland

An important component of the duties of the staff member working at the Information Desk is that of familiarizing the patron with all library services and giving instruction in the use of the card catalog, Maryland Room, microfilm reader, computers, and other equipment (the library staff member does not provide anything beyond basic instruction on software programs and the Internet. For Internet tutorial information see Adult Services/Programs section). In working with students and researchers, the library staff member may help by giving advice on the scope of a research topic, suggesting appropriate sources for the research and giving assistance in the use of library tools. The level of assistance and level of materials (all formats) should be centered around the goal of answering all reference and information questions efficiently, accurately and completely.

Library orientation programs for groups or individuals are available upon request.

12.16 Offering Bibliographic Instruction

University of Texas at Austin
University of Texas at Austin Libraries
Austin, Texas

LIBRARY INSTRUCTION

Library instruction activities are intended to enhance the ability of University of Texas Libraries patrons to understand and use information sources whether they are accessed within the libraries or from remote locations.

Administration of Library Instruction Programs

Library staff members contribute to library instruction activities by preparing materials and giving presentations, as well as contributing to the overall instructional mission of the University of Texas Libraries.

Unit and department heads are responsible for overseeing and reporting on library instruction activities in their units, as well as participating directly when appropriate. The Administrative Assistant in the Library Office will collect the instruction statistics from each unit at the end of each semester.

The Publications Coordinator will provide assistance with the technical aspects of preparing and producing printed materials in support of library instruction throughout the University of Texas Libraries.

The Head of Library Instruction Services is responsible for the coordination of library use activities, which includes promoting communication among library staff and instructors, soliciting suggestions from staff on instruction needs and methods, and reviewing ideas for major new ventures.

Referral of Requests

Requests for library instruction classes, tours, and presentations should be referred to the appropriate bibliographer. Bibliographer directories and lists are available from the Collection and information Resources web site. Occasionally the subject bibliographer does not participate in instructional activities and another staff member will take on this role. Requests which do not clearly fall to a specific bibliographer may be directed to the Head of Library Instruction Services. The Head of Library Instruction Services will seek out an appropriate staff member to instruct the class.

Problematic Class Assignments

Some assignments designed by instructors cause enormous problems for staff members assisting students. These assignments may require large numbers of students to look for one piece of information, work with incomplete or incorrect information, use materials the library does not own, or hunt for answers to obscure questions. It is the responsibility of the appropriate library staff member to contact the instructor and discuss possible alternatives to the assignment.

Additional information about "Designing Effective Library Assignments" is available from the Digital Information Literacy Program web site.

Services Offered

The University of Texas Libraries offers a variety of services designed to support library instruction. All instruction programs endeavor to increase user awareness of the library as a primary source of information and as an agency to which users may turn for assistance with their information needs. Orientation activities are intended to make users familiar with facilities, printed materials, electronic resources, service points, and procedures of the University of Texas Libraries. Library instruction classes, or "bibliographic instruction," is designed to enhance user ability to make effective use of information sources, regardless of format, and to suggest strategies and methods for organizing research.

Orientation Tours

The University of Texas Libraries provides scheduled general orientation tours as well as course-related tours when requested by instructors or other University personnel.

The University of Texas Libraries does not generally provide tours for groups outside of the University. Some pre-visit preparation is highly desirable. A staff member may meet with the group leader prior to a visit to identify appropriate library resources and to explain library services and policies. As an option, library handouts containing similar information may be mailed to the group leader. In addition, the leader can be directed to University of Texas Libraries information found on the Libraries web site.

Library Instruction Classes

General instruction presentations, such as the Electronic Information Classes, are provided by University of Texas Libraries staff at scheduled times each semester. A UT ID card is required to attend hands-on classes; all other classes are open to everyone.

Course-related bibliographic instruction presentations are provided by library staff either in response to requests for such classes or other indications of the need. Class presentations may be held in library lecture rooms, hands-on training rooms, or classrooms located within specific colleges and departments. Staff may prepare appropriate instructional materials such as handouts, slide shows, computer presentations, or Web "pathfinders."

Self-Paced Instructional Materials, Guides, and Bibliographies

General instructional materials for use by individual library patrons, such as point-of-use guides or online tutorials, are designed and produced by library staff as needed, within budgetary limitations. Efforts should be made to share materials between libraries.

User aids such as the Library Directory, a campus map with library locations and phone numbers, A Guide to the University of Texas Libraries, unit brochures and bookmarks are available to assist users in locating resources in the University of Texas Libraries.

The University of Texas Libraries provides bibliographies covering a wide range of subject areas through the "Selected Reference Sources" and other series. Each series is maintained by the appropriate staff member. These are distributed at appropriate University of Texas Libraries service points and electronically from the Training and Publications web site.

Signs, Graphics, and Exhibits

Clearly-worded signs and graphics are used in all units to aid users in locating information sources. The unit or department head is responsible for assessing the needs for and initiating requests for signage.

Exhibits of library or library-related materials are designed to increase users' awareness of the services, resources, and unique features of the University of Texas Libraries. Exhibits are handled by the Exhibits Committee.

North Florida Community College
North Florida Community College Library
Madison, Florida

General and Directed Bibliographic Instruction

a. Bibliographic Instruction - a mandatory one-credit class, Library and Information Skills (LIS 1001), is taught by professional library staff, and is designed to introduce the resources of the library to all NFCC students. Students are instructed in the use of the online catalog and other electronic resources, and are taught basic research techniques using a variety of reference tools. Students are encouraged to take this course early in their college career.

b. Course-specific bibliographic instruction – Faculty members are encouraged to bring their classes to the library for course-related bibliographic instruction, in order to introduce students to the specific resources available to them for a given assignment. Instruction is tailored to the needs of a particular class in that library tools are identified and described which are applicable to the class (i.e. statistical sources, biographical sources, and/or subject encyclopedias.

c. One-on-One Instruction – Patrons are provided with personal assistance at any time during library operating hours on a needs basis. Extra assistance is usually requested by patrons in the use of the online catalog, the Internet, and the online databases, as well as in the use of the microform reader/printer and copy machine.

All librarians are expected to conduct bibliographic instruction classes. Librarians are scheduled to teach the for-credit bibliographic instruction classes, and faculty-requested BI sessions are conduced by the librarian on duty at the time. Faculty are encouraged to schedule course-specific bibliographic instruction sessions in advance, so that sufficient staff may be available to assist their classes. Any staff member currently scheduled at the reference/circulation desk handles one-on-one instruction.

Santa Fe Community College
Lawrence W. Tyree Library
Gainesville, Florida

The Lawrence W. Tyree Library offers bibliographic instruction to the students of Santa Fe Community College. This instruction takes the form of either instructional non-credit sessions for classes at SFCC or credit courses taught by Library staff.

A. Non-credit instruction – SFCC faculty may request a bibliographic instruction session for their class by either filling out the online form or calling the Bibliographic Instruction Coordinator. Each session is taught by a librarian and is tailored to the individual needs of that course. Instructors must accompany their class to each session or send a substitute if unable to attend.

B. Credit-instruction – The Lawrence W. Tyree Library offers two 1-credit library science courses held at predetermined times throughout the semester. These courses are taught by Librarians.

The Reference Staff periodically evaluates and updates these courses as needed to ensure currency and accuracy of the information.

University of Wisconsin–River Falls
Chalmer Davee Library
River Falls, Wisconsin

Library Instruction. Library instruction staff schedule formal library instruction classes when a library assignment is a component of a class. Faculty must schedule sessions directly with the librarian who will meet with the class. Generally, classes will be scheduled with a one week minimum lead time. Instructors must be present during a library instruction session. A master schedule of sessions is maintained at the Reference Desk.

The library endorses the Information Literacy Competencies and Criteria for Academic Libraries in Wisconsin (Adopted by the Wisconsin Association of Academic Librarians October 9, 1998). Librarians design instructional sessions with faculty in order to integrate these criteria into the University's curriculum.

Reference staff work with staff from Student Services to orient new freshmen to the library at the start of each new academic year.

High school groups and other groups not affiliated with the University are welcome to schedule a formal instruction session if need dictates.

Boston Public Library
Boston, Massachusetts
Bibliographic Instruction/Training Classes

Research Library

Public service staff offers bibliographic and subject-related orientation and instruction classes to patrons and staff from the Boston Regional Library System and other libraries across the state. Orientation workshops are created by subject and format departments in response to special request by groups, schools and organizations.

General Library and Branches

Bibliographic instruction and orientation tours are done for patrons, schools and organizations in the General Library and Branches. Internet Workshops are offered to provide patrons with a starting point in accessing electronic resources. Children's and Young Adult librarians offer orientation tours designed to introduce the Library's resources to elementary and secondary students. In addition, neighborhood school visits are scheduled throughout the year to create awareness of Branch collections.

12.17 Offering Private Research

Weber State University
Stewart Library
Ogden, Utah

Private Requests

Requests for extended research service coming from patrons outside the priority groups stated in section 2 above cannot be honored on library time by Stewart Library personnel. However, the Stewart Library has no policy prohibiting any library employee from privately contracting with patrons to do research or prepare custom bibliographies for a fee so long as that employee pursues the work on his/her own time. However, in this case the Stewart Library assumes no responsibility for the quality of the results.

12.18 Offering Special Services for Faculty Members

Weber State University
Stewart Library
Ogden, Utah

Special Services

Special services are unusual services in the sense that they go beyond the normal, required services provided the request for this type of special treatment usually comes from the faculty. An example of this is a request for the library to photocopy the tables of contents each month from selected journals in a certain discipline for distribution to a specific academic department on campus. Each request for special service shall be reviewed on a case-by-case basis by the library committee most affected. Since any decision has the potential of impacting the library image at large, the appropriate committee, after studying the request and the library's ability to meet it, shall offer a recommendation to the body of the library faculty who will make the final decision on the request. Primary considerations in each decision are the human, financial, and information resources available and the real or potential return benefits to be realized.

University of Wisconsin–River Falls
Chalmer Davee Library
River Falls, Wisconsin

Faculty Consultations. Consultation with faculty members who give their classes library assignments is occasionally necessary. Such faculty members are contacted when students or librarians have difficulty interpreting an assignment. Any information provided is made available to all staff working at the Reference Desk.

12.19 Offering Service to Nonaffiliated Patrons

North Florida Community College
North Florida Community College Library
Madison, Florida

The North Florida Community Colleges serves a diverse clientele. Primary users are NFCC students, faculty, administrations and staff. Over 3,3000 students were enrolled at NFCC during the 2002-2003 school year. The college serves a diverse student population and offers the AA, AS and AAS degrees. Certificate programs are available as well as community education and adult education programs. The college serves dual enrollment students from the six county service area. The college offers a four-year degree through FAMU and St. Leo. The college is home to the CISCO Networking Academy.

The library also serves community patrons in the surrounding six-county area. The six country services are includes the rural counties of Madison, Hamilton, Jefferson, Lafayette, Suwannee and Taylor. Based on the 2000 Census, this services area represents a total population of 102,365 people (Florida Estimates of Population 2002). The population is predominately rural. The largest town (Perry) has a population of 6,800 (U.S. Census Bureau, Census 2000).

Many area high school students depend upon the NFCC Library for much of their information needs. The college library collection services as a supplemental resource center to the collections at high school and public libraries for these students. NFCC offers a dual enrollment program that allows high school students to earn college credit while in high school. Dual enrollment students are accorded the same library privileges, as are registered NFCC students. High school students who are not in the dual enrollment program are extended checkout privileges through their parents, who are assigned community patron status.

Ryerson University
Ryerson University Library
Toronto, Ontario, Canada

Access to library buildings and hard-copy collections will be available to all that require it, whether or not they are members of the University community. Electronic resources will be available according to the individual terms of product licensing agreements, and thus access may vary. Non-Ryerson patrons may be eligible for library cards that allow them to borrow material (except Reserves), for a fee. Interested patrons are referred to Access Services regarding external borrower cards.

No distinction is made between University and non-University patrons when giving routine reference service, but priority will be given to Ryerson patrons if funding, space or staffing is inadequate to meet demands for reference service either at any given time or over a prolonged time.

As a general rule, patrons with time-consuming inquiries who are not affiliated with the University may be referred to public libraries or their own organizations, if appropriate. In cases where the

Ryerson Library has special resources in staff or materials and the needs of the user seem to warrant it, assistance beyond the routine may be given.

12.20 Offering Service to Alumni

Kent State University
Kent State University Libraries and Media Service
Kent, Ohio

Borrowing privileges: KSU Alumni Association members can borrow up to 20 items at a time from the Libraries' collection, including a maximum of 5 items from other OhioLINK libraries. To take advantage of this benefit, the member needs to show a valid Alumni Association membership card and a photo identification. All other community borrowers pay $30/year.

Interlibrary loan services: Alumni with library borrowing privileges can borrow materials (e.g., journal articles, books not available through KSU or OhioLINK) through the Libraries' Interlibrary Loan service. There is a charge of $10 for each filled request in addition to any charges assessed by the lending library.

Access to Research Databases: Licensing agreements with publishers limit off-campus access to research databases to current students, faculty, and staff. These databases are available to all onsite visitors to the Libraries.

Use of the Information Commons: The 1st and 2nd floors of the Main Library provide a variety of access to specialized resources and information technology applications. The in-person user has access to all OhioLINK resources—research databases, electronic books and journals, as well as to express multimedia workstations equipped with scanners and imaging software.

Attendance at 60-Minute+ Seminars: Alumni are welcome to attend any of the 60-Minute+ Seminars offered by Libraries and Media Services. These highlight new information resources and how to use various information technologies. The complete listing is found at http://www.library.kent.edu/60min

Librarian Assistance: Personalized assistance is available in person or by phone. Alumni with borrowing privileges and who identify themselves may also ask a question by e-mail (library@kent.edu).

Media Services: In addition to these benefits, alumni can take advantage of specialized, fee-based services offered by Libraries and Media Services. These include: video production services and video, DVD and CD duplication.

Indiana University – Purdue University Fort Wayne
Walter E. Helmke Library
Fort Wayne, Indiana

Library Privileges for Alumni

IPFW graduates are welcome to continue using the Helmke Library. The University Services Card may be used as a library card after graduation, or an Indiana University Libraries card can be created. Either card may be used at any IU library. At the Helmke Library, graduates may check out two items per subject area. The loan period for most material is six weeks, the same as for undergraduates.

Members of the Alumni Associations

Members of the IPFW Alumni Association or the Indiana University or Purdue University Alumni Associations who present current membership cards may check out up to four items on a subject, rather than the usual limit of two items per subject for non-students. In addition, the library will obtain books and other returnables from IU and Purdue libraries for Alumni Association members.

Brandeis University
Brandeis University Libraries
Waltham, Massachusetts

Policies for Alumni

The primary mission of the Brandeis University Libraries is to serve the students, faculty and staff of the University. However, we do offer limited library service to graduates of Brandeis who are members of the Alumni Association. This service allows eligible alumni to borrow materials, but does not include access to Boston Library Consortium cards, Interlibrary Loan, or recall/hold privileges. Licensing requirements imposed by vendors limit off-campus use of electronic resources to current students, faculty and staff.

In order to borrow books from the Brandeis University Libraries, alumni must present a valid alumni card to the Circulation Staff. No other form of ID may be substituted for this card. The Brandeis University Libraries do not distribute alumni cards. For information on how you can obtain an alumni card see: [name, contact information].

Alumni borrowers have a 10-book limit.

Books circulate monthly with one additional renewal.

Books can be renewed either in person or by emailing circulation@brandeis.edu.

Material cannot be renewed over the phone.

Cards must be renewed yearly at the Alumni Office (located in Bernstein-Marcus).

Borrowing privileges apply to the cardholder only.

AVAILABLE PLATFORMS FOR RECEIVING QUESTIONS

12.21 Telephone

Apache Junction Public Library
Apache Junction, Arizona

Telephone patron requests are welcomed; however, when the library staff determines that the quantity of information requested is sufficient to warrant it, the staff member may ask the patron to come into the library to examine the material held on the subject. The staff will not read long passages from various sources, nor is it their place to synthesize or interpret information for the patron.

Because the library has a limited number of telephone lines, under most circumstances the caller will be asked to give a name and telephone number where he or she can be reached with the answer to the query posed, rather than being asked to hold. This is to insure the opportunity for other patrons to complete calls to the library, rather than being discouraged by a busy signal.

Austin Public Library
Austin, Texas

Telephone Reference

Providing information by telephone is an integral part of library service. Austin Public Library's Telephone Reference service gives customers the opportunity to ask questions without coming to the Library. Telephone staff can briefly answer questions on any subject, search the catalog for holdings, assist with the Library's electronic databases, and provide customer account information.

The Telephone Reference staff can answer three short fact questions or search for five minutes, whichever comes first. When a telephone reference request requires more than five minutes of staff time, a callback will be arranged. Librarians will spend up to 20 minutes searching for an answer to a clear specific question. The response time is 24 hours for callbacks. Users requiring more answers or extended searching will be encouraged to come to the library. In all instances, the source and date of information will be cited.

Telephone reference calls are accepted Monday through Friday from 10 a.m. to 5 p.m.

Restrictions due to limited staffing:

- No more than three Items may be requested by phone per day. Titles can be held at the Faulk Library or transferred to a branch.
- No more than two interlibrary loan requests will be taken per call.
- Reserve cards for items with volumes may be taken over the phone.
- No telephone renewals of checked out items.

The Logan Library
Logan, Utah

Telephone reference is a service of the library. The reference staff verifies answers, cites sources that are used and gives the date of the source when relevant. The reference staff responds to telephone requests as received in turn. The questions are answered with quick, specific answers. For questions that take longer to find the answer, the reference staff calls the patron back within twenty-four hours.

Long passages are not read over the telephone. A photocopy of lengthy material may be mailed to the patron or the patron may come to the library to pick it up.

Patrons are encouraged to come to the library to do their own research.

Memorial Hall Library
Andover, Massachusetts

Telephone reference will be handled in the same sequence and manner as in-person inquiries. Book checks will be done to confirm that titles are on the shelf and will be held at the circulation desk. If the desk is busy or if multiple titles are requested, staff will offer to call the patron back to let him/her know we have found and are holding the titles. If the answer to the question seems too involved to relate easily over the telephone, this will be explained to the patron and the suggestion made that the patron come to the Library. Information may be faxed to a patron who has a dedicated fax machine. A maximum of thirty pages is suggested; however, it is up to the discretion of the librarian.

For calls from out of state, the callers will be asked to call back at a prearranged time or the librarian will return the call if that is more convenient. Genealogy questions should be mailed or emailed to the attention of the Andover Room Librarian. Genealogy searches will not be done over the telephone.

When a staff member must transfer a call to another department, the caller will be told where the call is being transferred and why.

Morton Grove Public Library
Morton Grove, Illinois

Telephone reference should be used for short, factual information questions which do not require extensive reading or interpretation on the part of staff members. If the answer to a telephone question seems too involved to relate easily over the telephone, this should be explained to the patron and the suggestion made that the patron come to the Library.

Staff will answer the telephone with a department name, such as Reference Services or Children's. If callers must wait, they should be given the option to remain on hold or to have their calls returned. If the patron prefers to be called back, the staff member should take the patron's phone number and call the patron back as soon as possible. For calls from out-of-state, the callers should be asked to call back at a prearranged time.

When a staff member must transfer a call to another department, the caller should be told where the call is being transferred and why. When a reference staff member transfers a call to another department, the staff member should briefly convey to the other department the patron's question and what sources have been checked. When receiving a transfer call, however, always consult with the patron directly in order to fully understand the question being asked.

Washington County Public Library
Abingdon, Virginia

Telephone reference should be used for short, factual information questions that do not require extensive reading or interpretation on the part of staff members. Only factual information dates, names and addresses, specific citations, or catalog checks shall be given out over the telephone. Brief information may be read verbatim without interpretation. The source shall be given for all information provided.

If the answer to a telephone or mail requests is too involved to relate easily over the telephone, this should be explained to the patron and an invitation made for the patron to come to the library. Questions received through the mail or email shall be answered with full citations for the source.

Monroe Township Public Library
Monroe Township, New Jersey

LONG DISTANCE AND TOLL CALLS

The Reference Department does not give priority to long distance and toll calls.

Return long distance and toll calls are made collect.

St. Joseph County Public Library
South Bend, Indiana

Reference Service via Electronic Correspondence

A. Services offered via electronic correspondence
  1. Ready reference
  2. Intermediate reference

B. Priorities
  Priority is given to on-site and telephone inquiries over electronic inquiries.

C. Time limits/Scope of service
  1. A reply will be made to electronic inquiries normally within 2 business days, Monday through Friday.
  2. Users are limited to 1 inquiry in 24 hours.
  3. Electronic reference service is offered to SJCPL cardholders only. The exception will be questions concerning local information which can only be answered by sources unique to our collection.
  4. The service will be provided by the Adult Reference Department; inquiries will be forwarded to another department or branch if appropriate.

D. Parameters of conduct
  The response should reflect the library favorably in form, content, and grammar.

E. Confidentiality
  1. Information services staff subscribe to the American Library Association's "Code of Ethics, 1995." (See Appendix A)
  2. Inquiries and their responses will be kept for 30 days to assure the customer's receipt of response, then the request will be saved and archived with the customer's identification removed.

12.22 Fax Only

Braswell Memorial Library
Rocky Mount, North Carolina

Faxing Materials

The library reserves the right to limit the number of pages which may be faxed to a patron, business, school, agency, or library. Five pages are the maximum staff is required to fax to individual patrons. Schools and libraries should limit their requests for faxed materials to ten pages or three separate articles totaling no more than ten pages.

The Logan Library
Logan, Utah

Library personnel answer fax requests within twenty-four hours, except on holidays and weekends. In order to comply with copyright law, these requests must be on the appropriate request form and signed by the person wanting the material.

Athens Regional Library System
Athens, Georgia

FAX Transmission

Branch staff may request that materials at the main library be faxed to them. The telephone reference staff person on duty when such a request is made will be responsible for copying and transmitting the material to the branch. Material should be faxed within the hour, if at all possible, so that the patron at the branch will not need to make a return trip to the branch to pick up the materials. A charge per page will be assessed for this service based on the Fines/Fees Schedule. Payment will be collected at the local branch.

Materials may be faxed directly to offices of the Athens-Clarke County Unified Government at no charge.

Other library cardholders who have access to a FAX machine at their homes or offices may request the transmission of library materials to their FAX number. A charge per page will be assessed for this service based on the Fines/Fees Schedule. Telephone reference staff will obtain the name, library card bar code number, and FAX number of any patron requesting telefacsimile service. After verifying that the patron has a current library card, the staff member may photocopy and FAX the requested materials. The FAX charge will be added to the patron's library account, via the Dynix terminal. Telephone reference staff shall take responsibility for seeing that this charge is recorded in the system.

St. Joseph County Public Library
South Bend, Indiana

a. Every attempt will be made to fill requests within 24 hours. However, in person and telephone requests for information take precedence over Fax service. Due to these changeable factors, the Library will guarantee a maximum turnaround time of two business working days, Monday–Friday.

b. Only SJCPL cardholders are eligible for Fax document delivery service. All SJCPL cardholders requesting Fax service must be in good standing.

c. Quality of transmission cannot be guaranteed. It is the customer's responsibility to notify the Library immediately of any problem. The Library will try one additional time to transmit via Fax. If still unusable, the photocopied material will be sent to the customer via the U.S. Postal Service with charges for Fax.

d. Limit: 10 pages per customer request. There is no charge for the transmission sheet. The Library staff reserves the right to make exceptions regarding maximum number of pages requested.

e. All photocopies faxed to patrons will be accompanied with a Fax Transmission Form & Invoice citing bibliographic sources and any other relevant information.

f. Information will be faxed to the customer with copyright notification stamped on the first page.

12.23 Fax, E-Mail, and Telephone Policies Combined

Morton Grove Public Library
Morton Grove, Illinois

FAX, Mail, Electronic Mail Requests

It is the Library's practice to respond to all reasonable reference inquiries received by mail, FAX, or electronic mail. Fax, mail, and electronic mail requests are defined as short, factual informational questions which do not require extensive reading or interpretation on the part of staff members. If the question becomes too involved or time-consuming, the staff member should explain the limitations on such service and suggest that the patron visit the Library for further assistance.

The patron may request that the response to the question be made by FAX, mail, electronic mail, or telephone. The nature of the question may determine the form of response. Any area outside the Chicago metropolitan area will be considered long distance, and the Library will respond to long distance fax or telephone requests through the mail.

In the event that a photocopy is requested by out-of-area patrons, the Library will provide no more than 10 (ten) photocopied pages to a patron at no charge to the patron. Standard copyright guidelines/notice will be attached to any pages faxed to a patron. Additional copying for out-of-area patrons must be done on a cost recovery basis, with prepayment required.

12.24 Mail Questions

University of Texas at Austin
University of Texas Libraries
Austin, Texas

CORRESPONDENCE REFERENCE SERVICE

Correspondence is an integral part of reference and information services and every effort is made to answer written requests for information within a week of receipt.

Routing Incoming Correspondence

All units of the University of Texas Libraries route letters to the appropriate library unit for reply.

The unit head is responsible for correspondence reference service. The responsibility for answering letters may be delegated.

Referral form letters may be used when sending an inquiry to another unit on campus for the information requested. One copy of the form letter is sent to the inquirer; one copy of the form letter and the original letter requesting information are sent to the unit receiving the referral and one copy of the form letter is retained as a record of the referral.

Types of Questions Answered

Letters requesting bibliographic information about University of Texas at Austin theses and dissertations are answered in detail. If the number of titles concerned is large, e.g., theses concerning Mexican-Americans in Texas, a printout from the library catalog or photocopies of the thesis catalog cards involved should be made.

Letters requesting information about publications written by UT Austin faculty or staff members, sponsored by UT Austin departments or institutes, or published by campus bureaus are answered as completely as possible.

Letters requesting broad subject information require only a brief indication of sources with an invitation to visit the University of Texas Libraries for personal assistance or with a referral to a library near the correspondent.

The Perry-Castañeda Library uses form letters to refer requests for genealogical searches to appropriate libraries. Requests for information about Texas residents are referred to the Center for American History and the Texas State Library.

Photocopying

A maximum of eight pages is photocopied from hard copy without charge when a letter is being answered. If photocopying exceeds eight pages, the citations are sent to the inquirer with instructions to request the items through their local public library from our Inter-Library Service.

Telefacsimile

Telefacsimile may be used when time is of utmost importance, particularly when information is for another state agency. A maximum of eight pages may be sent by telefacsimile without charge.

Reply

Most replies are by mail. However, an electronic response is appropriate if the requestor includes an e-mail address.

Record of Correspondence

Each letter received and copies of the reply are retained in the unit for one year.

St. Joseph County Public Library
South Bend, Indiana

Reference Service via Written Correspondence
    A. Services offered via written correspondence
       A reply will be made to correspondence received by SJCPL.

B. Priorities

Priority is given to on-site and telephone inquiries over written inquiries.

C. Time limits/Scope of service

1. A reply will be made to reference correspondence normally within 7 days of receipt of letter.

2. Letter writers who reside within the Library's service area may be answered via telephone, if appropriate.

3. Letter writers from outside the SJCPL service area will be sent a form letter referring them to their local library for general information.

4. Letters containing questions concerning local information and/or answered in sources unique to our collection may be answered in detail.

5. Staff will limit their search to 30 minutes before referring the letter writer to another source.

D. Parameters of conduct

The response should reflect the library favorably in form, content, and grammar. The response should be on official stationery or cardstock; a computer or typewriter should be used.

E. Confidentiality

a. Information services staff subscribe to the American Library Association's "Code of Ethics, 1995." (See Appendix A)

b. Letters and their responses will be kept for 30 days to assure the customer's receipt of response, then the request will be destroyed.

F. Fees

There will be a $1.00 minimum for photocopies up to ten pages, and $.10 per page thereafter.

Wilmington Public Library District
Wilmington, Illinois

Written correspondence will be handled the same as all other requests. When patrons are unable to come to the library due to disability or unusual circumstances, the librarian may copy and mail information back to the patron.

Washington State University
Washington State University Libraries
Pullman, Washington

Inquiries by correspondence—-All requests for information by mail should be referred to the Information Services Coordinator who will, if necessary, refer them to an appropriate subject specialist or to ILL. An attempt should be made to answer the question unless the amount of information requested is unreasonable. All inquiries requiring extensive bibliographic research and checking should be tactfully turned down, with the suggestion that s/he try to come to the library in person or find another library within a reasonable distance of their residence. When the information could have been obtained from their local library, suggest this when responding.

12.25 Document Delivery

University of California–Irvine
University of California Irvine Libraries
Irvine, California

DOCUMENT DELIVERY SERVICE

Eligible UC Irvine faculty, graduate students and administrators may place online requests for materials from the UC Irvine Libraries. Eligibility is based on departmental participation and must be authenticated before requests are placed. Requests for materials owned by UC Irvine may be placed using Request on the CDL/Melvyl Web, and ANTPAC Web. Requests are processed within 48 hours from the time the requests are received by DDS. Library materials not owned by UC Irvine or unavailable at UC Irvine will be processed by Interlibrary Loan. A valid UC Irvine library card is required.

DELIVERY

DDS delivers to UC Irvine campus department offices only. An authorized departmental signature is required for ALL deliveries signifying receipt of material and responsibility until returned. Deliveries are made between 1:00 p.m. and 4:00 p.m., Monday through Friday. Book delivery is offered at no charge.

PICK UP

DDS will pick up library materials at no charge. Retrievals MUST be scheduled in order for DDS to pick up the materials. This can be done by phone (x44364), e-mail (dds@uci.edu), or on the web. Same day pickups must be scheduled by noon. In the case of recalled books, call prior to the due date to avoid overdue recall fines. Unscheduled pickups may be refused. A receipt for items picked up may be obtained from the DDS courier at the time of pick up.

CHARGES

DDS charges for photocopy services. A recharge account number must be provided at the time the request is placed. There is a charge of $3.50 per article up to 20 pages with an additional .20 cents per page beyond 20 pages, for web delivery or photocopies. There is a charge of $3.50 per article up to 10 pages with an additional charge of .50 cents per page beyond 10 pages for microform materials. DDS photocopy services are processed within the guidelines of Copyright Law (Title 17, United States Code).

12.26 Interlibrary Loan Document Delivery

Cal Poly Pomona University
Cal Poly Pomona University Library
Pomona, California

Document Delivery/Interlibrary Loan

Documentation of requests is retained as necessary for the Library to comply with auditing, copyright or other regulations. Because of the software the Library uses this documentation will include names of borrowers. Personal information provided in order to request ILL service might be forwarded on to other library lenders. In some cases, information about requests may be shared with other library staff for collection development and fine collection purposes; however, it remains confidential within the library.

Part VII
Reference Services:
Virtual Reference

Chapter 13

CHAT POLICIES

GENERAL GUIDELINES

13.1 Guidelines for Patrons

Pennsylvania State University
Pennsylvania State University Libraries
University Park, Pennsylvania

All users must comply with the University Policy on Computer and Network Use and Security (AD20)

Virtual Reference Chat Netiquette:

Be patient. Network traffic may degrade response time. A Virtual Reference librarian will respond to your question as soon as possible. If you can't wait, you may submit your question by email.

Communicate in short sentences.

If you need to communicate at length, break your message into chunks.

Do not type in all capital letters. All caps is equivalent to SHOUTING.

Harassment and misconduct of any type will not be tolerated. Common courtesies are expected and appreciated.

North Harris College
North Harris College Library
Houston, Texas

Guidelines for Users

Library users who are present in person at the reference desk will receive help before users requesting online help.

Initiate a chat by clicking on the "Live Reseach Help Chat with a Librarian" link from the library home page. If the service is unavailable, or if a Librarian fails to answer your chat request, you can leave an email message which will be answered the next working day. Alternatively, call 281-618-5707 and speak with a Librarian.

Be patient. Wait for the Librarian to respond. Sometimes, Internet traffic will slow down the connection and it may seem as though the Librarian is not responding. Wait at least a minute before you decide to close the session. Another reason may be that the Librarian could be already chatting with another patron and may need to finish one chat before starting another.

Be precise in stating your information request. For example: instead of saying "I cannot connect to this database from home" say, "I cannot connect to Academic Search Premier from the home access to databases link."

Wait for a response before typing another question unless you have useful information to add to your previous statement.

Close the chat window when done.

13.2 General Service Statements

Houston Public Library
Houston, Texas

InfoLive! is a chat reference service with real-time online assistance by Houston Public Library staff. The Basic Chat module supports all browser versions and operating systems and no downloads are required. You can communicate live with a librarian from home, school, or work. We can provide brief answers to factual questions or suggest sources to answer your query through chat and e-mail services. Houston Public Library professionals use a wide range of resources including the Internet and online databases to deliver answers efficiently and effectively. We can also offer assistance with search strategies. At the conclusion of your chat session, you will receive a transcript by e-mail for your future use.

University of Pittsburgh
Pitt Digital Library
Pittsburgh, Pennsylvania

About Ask-A-Librarian Live

Ask-a-Librarian Live is the interactive Digital Reference Service offered by the University Library System at the University of Pittsburgh. Ask-a-Librarian Live offers online, real time research assistance to University of Pittsburgh students, faculty, and staff. This service complements other reference service points throughout the ULS (consultation, email, and telephone reference services) that have been traditionally available.

13.3 Defining Provider of Assistance

Boise Public Library
Boise, Idaho

Who provides this service?

Experienced reference staff from participating libraries, cooperative library staff, and vendor library staff, who are trained in Internet searching and in using the vendor software will be on duty to assist online patrons/students 24/7.

Columbia University
Columbia University Library
New York, New York

Who answers my reference questions?

A. A librarian from Columbia, Barnard or Teachers College will answer your reference questions. If you have a subject-specific question, you may be referred to a subject specialist in the libraries.

Pennsylvania State University
Pennsylvania State University Libraries
University Park, Pennsylvania

The Virtual Reference Service is staffed by Penn State librarians at campuses throughout the Penn State system. The librarian answering your question may or may not be at your campus. If your question requires information that is only available locally, you will be referred to your campus library staff.

University of Scranton
Weinberg Memorial Library
Scranton, Pennsylvania

Who answers the questions?

Reference staff of the Weinberg Libraries at the University of Scranton will answer all phone and e-mail reference questions. Virtual live chat will be monitored by the librarians of the American Jesuit Colleges and Universities (AJCU) and Tutor.com librarians to provide 24/7 virtual chat reference.

To chat specifically with a University of Scranton Librarian, login during the following hours: Monday and Wednesday 4–5 and 8–10 PM, Tuesday 8–10 PM, Thursday 3–5 and 8–10 PM.

13.4 Providing Time Schedules for Assistance

Queens Borough Public Library
Jamaica, New York

When is InfoLine Chat available?

Currently this service is available Mondays-Fridays from 1:00 p.m. to 8:45 p.m., and Saturdays from 10:00 a.m. to 4:00 p.m. Visit the Queens Library InfoLine Ask a Librarian section of the website during these hours to ask a question and to see how the service works.

University of Maine–Fort Kent
Blake Library
Fort Kent, Maine

Live Mode: Available hours are typically the same during the fall and spring semester. Hours may change according to need. Service will not be available during holidays, school closings, or other circumstances the library staff determines necessary. Evening hours will be available during fall and spring semesters only. Refer to the Ask-the-Librarian page for a current schedule.

Pennsylvania State University
Pennsylvania State University Libraries
University Park, Pennsylvania

During Fall 2005 and Spring 2006, service hours are: Monday – Thursday, 12:00pm – 12:00am; Sundays, 6:00pm – 9:00pm. E-mail reference service is available when the Virtual Reference Service is closed.

Houston Public Library
Houston, Texas

Live chat with InfoLive! librarians is available Monday through Friday, 9:00 a.m. to 6:00 p.m.

13.5 Clarifying Eligible Users

Boise Public Library
Boise, Idaho

Who can use this service?

The primary clientele of this project will be residents of SW Idaho and BSU students. However anyone who submits a question will be served. Zip code information will be requested, but will not be used to limit our service area until demand requires it. Promotional efforts will be focused on students from Jr. High through Adult.

Pennsylvania State University
Pennsylvania State University Libraries
University Park, Pennsylvania

The Penn State Virtual Reference Service uses QuestionPoint software to provide online research assistance to Penn State students, faculty, and staff. Use of the vast electronic and print resources of the Penn State Libraries will be emphasized, and authoritative sites on the World Wide Web will be recommended when appropriate. Virtual Reference Service is open to non-Penn State researchers on a limited basis. Only authorized users will be given access to licensed databases.

University of Scranton
Weinberg Memorial Library
Scranton, Pennsylvania

Who can use Electronic Reference?

PLEASE NOTE: Chat is only available to students, faculty, and staff currently affiliated with the University of Scranton. Following a chat session, users will receive a transcript of their online discussion via e-mail. An e-mail address is required for using the chat reference service.

E-mail reference services are available to the community at large. The e-mail reference service availability will be determined by the University of Scranton academic calendar.

13.6 Verifying Users

Boise Public Library
Boise, Idaho

At some point in the virtual reference transaction, it may become necessary to verify our patron/student's home library, location, and/or card holder status in order to more efficiently answer their questions. Entrance into proprietary databases may be dependent upon the patron having the required login/password or number. Patrons may only go into proprietary databases escorted if they do not have the required login, etc., but all databases will be available.

Washington Research Library Consortium
Upper Marlboro, Maryland

Who can use the service? The primarily clientele of this service are WRLC faculty, staff and students. The IP address and /or Aladin Patron Validation will authenticate a patron as a WRLC faculty, staff or student.

13.7 Terminating Incomplete Transactions

Boise Public Library
Boise, Idaho

Incomplete transactions

Referral, continued online sessions, email are methods staff will use to complete transactions. Until demand requires a change, librarians will make every effort to successfully conclude virtual reference sessions online.

Long-distance phone calls, faxing, and other responses that are not covered in the grant will be at each library's discretion.

Washington Research Library Consortium
Upper Marlboro, Maryland

System-wide message scripts. While there will be common scripts loaded on to each log-in, the use of these messages will not be required. However, it is recommended that we use them as needed to uphold our standard of service in respect to speed, courtesy and consistency. It is especially important to send quick messages to keep the customer informed about searching progress. Scripted responses are very useful for this purpose.

13.8 Determining Appropriate Questions

University of Maine–Fort Kent
Blake Library
Fort Kent, Maine

Rules pertaining to submitted questions
   A. Reference staff may refuse to answer questions.
   B. Reference staff may refuse services to a patron if they determine the patron is not using the service in the way in which it was meant to be used. Including, but not limited to, questions that are: illegal, harassing, libelous, threatening, harmful, obscene or objectionable, or that violates any applicable local, state, national, or international law or regulations.

13.9 Using Proprietary Databases

Washington Research Library Consortium
Upper Marlboro, Maryland

Proprietary Databases. In answering a question, the librarian may use any database available to the patron through their campus library's affiliation only during the virtual reference session. Librarians will never authenticate a patron. The patron will always authenticate themselves to their set of databases.

13.10 Types of Questions Answered

Queens Borough Public Library
Jamaica , New York

What are the guidelines for using InfoLine Chat?

The InfoLine Chat service is intended to answer brief, factual questions. Please be specific about what information you need when stating your question. If you have asked a question with a broader scope, you may get suggestions for further independent research.

Columbia University
Columbia University Library
New York, New York

What types of questions will you answer?

A. We will identify an appropriate database for your research; help you use CLIO or show you how to find e-journals and e-books; provide guidance on researching a topic; suggest print and electronic sources you might find helpful; and help solve problems you may be having connecting to a library service or database. We will not provide legal, medical or financial advice.

13.11 Scripted Messages

Boise Public Library
Boise, Idaho

Scripted messages

While there will be common scripted messages available, the use of these messages will not be required. However it is recommended that we use them as needed to expedite speed, courtesy and consistency. It is important to send quick messages to keep the patron/student informed about the searching process.

Chapter 14

E-MAIL POLICIES

GENERAL GUIDELINES

14.1 Guidelines for Patrons

Enoch Pratt Free Library
Baltimore, Maryland

Reference Questions

When asking a question, please use the following guidelines:

Be specific. Providing as much information as helps the librarians to answer your questions better.

Answers to questions. Questions are answered by librarians, usually within 2 business days. If additional time is needed by the librarians, you will be notified.

Complex questions. If a question requires extensive research, the librarians may only be able to point you to sources inside and outside of the library where you may start your search.

Long distance calls. The librarians will call collect if the phone number provided is long distance.

Mailing or faxing copies. Photocopies or print outs of information can be mailed or faxed to you for a fee. Include your address or fax number with your question. A bill with the total amount of the charges will be returned with your information. Payment should be returned to the library using this bill. The prices are as follows:

Mailing: $2 minimum (which includes postage and approximately 7 pages), plus $.20 for each additional page.

Faxing: Up to 5 pages will be faxed free of charge. Additional pages can be faxed at a cost of $1 per page. A maximum of 20 pages may be faxed.

Peoria Public Library
Peoria, Illinois

To make this service most effective, and to help us answer your question correctly, please be as specific as possible in your request. Try to provide as many details as you can. It is helpful to know the purpose of your request (assignment for high school, work, etc.) The more you tell us, the better our answer will be. If you have a deadline, please include that information as well. You should receive a response to your query within 48 hours except for on weekends and holidays.

14.2 General Service Statement

University of Pittsburgh
Pitt Digital Library
Pittsburgh, Pennsylvania

About Ask-A-Librarian

Ask-a-Librarian is the email version of the Digital Reference Service offered by the University Library System at the University of Pittsburgh. This service is open to anyone with a question concerning the research and teaching mission of the University of Pittsburgh. In responding to these requests, priority will be given to University of Pittsburgh affiliated students, faculty and staff. You must have a valid email address to receive a response. If you are a University of Pittsburgh student, faculty or staff you can also receive reference assistance using the Ask-a-Librarian Live service, in person at any ULS library reference desk, by telephone, or through reference consultation.

14.3 Clarifying Eligible Users

Western Kentucky University
Western Kentucky University Libraries
Bowling Green, Kentucky

Who can use the service?

WILLS is open to all. We will attempt to assist all who ask questions; however, due to contractual arrangements and legal provisions, we are unable to provide access to WKU-licensed databases for anyone other than our own faculty, staff, and students. You may be referred to your local library if we find we are unable to answer your question.

Peoria Public Library
Peoria, Illinois

Email reference service provides brief answers to factual questions and/or gives referrals to resources (online, print, and to other agencies). This service is provided to patrons in Peoria and Illinois only, unless you are asking about local information which can only be answered by resources unique to our collection. We cannot answer queries from out of state residents which could be answered by a library in your local area.

14.4 Determining Service Limitations

Monroe County Library System
Rochester, New York

Are there limits to this service?

Certain kinds of questions, such as genealogical, medical, legal, and tax inquiries, may not be suitable or appropriate for e-mail reference. Staff may request that you come to the library yourself to use materials on these subjects.

Submitting lists of questions is not appropriate for this service. Typical limits for multiple questions would be up to three addresses and phone numbers, or four stock quotes.

In general, we cannot devote more than one-half hour search time to your question. Should the information you requested require more time than that to answer, we will advise you as to whether the library has the necessary materials for you to come in and use, or direct you to other sources of information.

A subject division reserves the right to decide what is a reasonable amount of time that can be spent on a question that has been referred to it.

14.5 Who Can Use the Service?

University of Texas–Pan American
University of Texas–Pan American Library
Edinburg, Texas

Who may use this service ?

While this service is intended for use by the faculty, students and staff of the University of Texas-Pan American, it is available to anyone. However, if you are not affiliated with UTPA, we regret we can only reply to your questions or comments if they concern the university or resources unique to its library.

Emory University
Emory University General Libraries
Atlanta, Georgia

Answers may be determined by the affiliation of the correspondent. Non-affiliates requesting e-mail assistance will be subject to the same restrictions applied to personal and telephone reference service. Site-licensing restrictions on databases and software limits their use to e-mail questions from currently enrolled students, faculty and staff.

If user affiliation prevents us from providing an answer, we will explain this in our response, and provide (if possible) suggestions for other resources and recourses which may be available to the questioner.

Humboldt State University
Humboldt State University Libraries
Arcata, California

General email reference service is available to the students, faculty, and staff of Humboldt State University with valid HSU email accounts.

14.6 Appropriate Questions

Western Kentucky University
Western Kentucky University Libraries
Bowling Green, Kentucky

What kind of questions we answer:

The types of questions best handled via WILLS or email are ready reference (quick research and answer) questions and instruction in the use of our online catalog, indexes, and databases. Use this service to ask questions that you might ask over the telephone or at the reference desk: What was the population of Kentucky in 1980? I have an incomplete citation, what year was volume 7 of Monthly Labor Review published? What is the best index to use to find periodical literature for my research on the effect of classroom size on student learning? In-depth questions or requests for long lists of citations are not appropriate for this service. For this kind of assistance please visit the reference desk during regular service hours.

If your reference question takes a longer time to research than we can provide during a WILS chat session, we will either send an answer through email, or ask you to come in. If you are outside the local area, we might suggest you go to your local library for help.

University of Texas–Pan American
University of Texas–Pan American Library
Edinburg, Texas

What questions can I ask via this service ?

This service is intended for questions that may be asked of our reference department either in person or over the telephone. Questions of this type might include, but are not limited to :

Does a library have a copy of a particular book/journal ?

Where might I begin to search for information on a particular topic ?

What department at UTPA may I contact if I need _____ ?

Questions or comments relating to specific departments or collections at the University Library.

Hartford Public Library
Hartford, Connecticut

What kinds of questions can I ask?

Ask the Librarian is a ready-reference service designed for specific questions with brief, factual answers. Use this form for the following types of inquiries:

Assistance with homework and/or class projects

Information about the library's holdings and services

Basic Internet navigation tips, search engines, and search strategies

Information on electronic database usage such as the Magazine Index or the Hartford Community Database

Requests for quick facts, statistical information, and citation identification and/or verification

If your answer cannot be answered with the resources available, you will be notified of that fact and we will make an effort to include referrals to other sources.

New Haven Free Public Library
New Haven, Connecticut

Types of questions we can answer:

Brief questions that have a documented factual answer, such as a historical date or fact or the source of a quotation.

Requests for suggestions about appropriate sources to research a topic. We are unable to do lengthy research, but we can suggest sources you might want to consult. List any resources that you have already consulted so we do not duplicate your attempts.

Humboldt State University
Humboldt State University Libraries
Arcata, California

The email reference service is provided to help users become self-sufficient in their research endeavors.

The Library provides advice on how to begin a research with suggestions of possible print or electronic resources, search strategies, and other non-HSU libraries/resources, etc.

Whenever possible, users will be referred to electronic resources that may provide them with the information requested.

You may ask questions you would normally ask at our reference desk, such as:

- Where would I begin to look for information on a topic?
- I have looked in all the usual places, but where else might I look?
- Does the Library have a subject librarian who could help me with this topic?
- Specific ready reference questions; e.g., quick factual information (When did the Challenger space shuttle explode?), do we have a particular book or journal? (check the Library catalog, Catalyst, first), etc.
- Verification of references
- Assistance with the Library's online catalog and other online services
- Questions about library services and facilities

Citations to the source of information will be given whenever possible.

Interpretations of information will not be given.

The Library does NOT perform information searches for users, create or check lists (e.g., bibliographies), or answer questions about medical or legal advice, citation form, statistics or class assignments.

Houston Public Library
Houston, Texas

Types of questions we can answer by email

- Brief, factual questions, such as the source of a quotation, a company or organization address, a historical fact or date, etc.
- Requests for suggestions about appropriate sources to research a topic.
- Questions about the Library or the City of Houston, such as how to obtain an obituary from a Houston paper or how to contact the local chamber of commerce.
- Requests for shelf checks for items the library owns.

Specific examples:

Can you do a patent search for me?

We can provide material for you to learn more about patents. The Patent and Trademark Collection at Fondren Library at Rice University is the official patent depository library for this region. They have complete patents. We have only the patent abstracts.

Can you email me a stock or bond price for a particular day?

We can find prices for a variety of securities from the turn of the century to the present. Prices for municipal bonds are not available in our collection.

Can you email me a complete recipe?

If we find the recipe for you on the web we can forward it to you. If we find the recipe in a book, we will email you the title, author, and call number. If you tell us your local phone number, we can read the information to you over the phone. Extensive recipes from books can't be retyped into email.

Can you tell me about my medical condition?

We can provide citations of reading material about these conditions or a brief paragraph from a reference book or a web site. We cannot evaluate the outcome of your medical condition, or provide you with a plan for recovery.

What is the best doctor for my medical condition?

We have several physician directories, and can provide contact information for physicians by medical specialty. These directories don't tell you whether a physician is good or bad. We have a reference book called Best Doctors in America from Woodward/White Publishers, behind the desk at the Central Library which you may wish to consult. If you want to purchase a report about physicians registered in Texas, call the Texas State Board of Medical Examiners. The Library cannot provide recommendations for particular physicians or medical tests.

Can you check if an obituary was placed in the newspaper for someone who has died in Houston?

If a death date is known for the requested person, we will check the local newspapers for an obituary for three days following the date of death. If the death date is unknown, we may still be able to identify the person. We have an index that covers deaths in the Houston area for selected years.

For the cost of obtaining photocopies, please refer to the Photocopy Policy.

Can you do a reverse look-up for me if I give you a street address or telephone number?

Houston Public Library will only provide this service if you send a letter to us. However, if you have access to the Internet, there are some web sites that may be able to help you. The Ultimate White Pages (http://www.theultimates.com/white/) has several links to sites that allow you to search by telephone number, street address or by name.

Does the library have old telephone books and other directories?

The Texas & Local History department has telephone directories for Houston beginning in 1904 and Houston city directories from 1866 forward. Similar collections for other Texas cities are less complete. The staff will be glad to verify whether a particular directory of interest to you is available.

What about old high school yearbooks?

Thanks to donations from the public we have many yearbooks from Houston high schools and Texas colleges. Most date from years prior to 1980. If you are looking for a particular volume we can check the collection for you. If you would like to donate one not already in the collection we would be very grateful.

Are there aerial photos of Houston from years past?

Yes, indeed. Sets of aerial photography of the city go back to 1935; every decade since then is represented at least once in the collection. Using these photos to trace the development of a property or area over time can be fascinating.

Is there a way to find accounts of historic events in the old Houston newspapers?

If you know the date of an event you can go directly to the news coverage on microfilm in the Central Library. An extensive collection of clipping files and scrapbooks make it possible to locate some information by topic. The years before 1950 are covered lightly and those after 1950 more thoroughly. Printed indexes to the Houston Post begin in 1986; computer searching of the Houston Chronicle is possible beginning with 1987.

14.7 Inappropriate Questions

Western Kentucky University
Western Kentucky University Libraries
Bowling Green, Kentucky

What our E-Reference service does NOT provide:

We do not handle Interlibrary Loan or reserve materials from this service. We can answer questions about these services; otherwise, you can call Circulation at 270-745-3951 or Interlibrary Loan at 270-745-6118.

We do not renew materials for you from this service. For information on renewals, call Circulation at 270-745-3951.

We do not offer faxing, copying, or printing services from a distance. You must come into the library to obtain materials. However, if you are a WKU student taking classes on an extended campus, online, or through distance education, we will be happy to refer you to our Extended Campus Library Services office.

We will not answer or read information over the phone for questions involving medical or legal advice, appraisals, product evaluations, etc.; however, we will suggest a source for you to consult.

We do not give criss-cross or reverse telephone directory information.

California State University–Los Angeles
University Libraries
Los Angeles, California

Please note the following restrictions:

Interpretations of information will not be given.

The Library does NOT perform information searches for users, create or check lists (e.g., bibliographies), or answer questions about medical or legal matters, or give medical or legal advice. We also do not answer questions about citation forms, look up statistics, or do class assignments.

University of Texas–Pan American
University of Texas–Pan American Library
Edinburg, Texas

What types of questions are not appropriate for this service?

We will not answer any questions about matters of a legal or medical nature.

We will not offer any type of medical, legal or tax advice.

We cannot answer questions that require extensive research.

While we may suggest or recommend particular resources, we will not advise you as to which is best for you to use for the purposes of your research.

We will not be able to create bibliographies.

New Haven Free Public Library
New Haven, Connecticut

Types of questions we cannot answer:
- Requests which require lengthy research on a topic.
- Questions requiring legal or medical interpretation. We can recommend and provide sources of information you can consult, but the Library cannot offer guidance or opinion in regard to these questions.

- Essays and school assignments. We can point you to information sources on your topic, but you will need to do the work of interpreting the resources and answering the question your teacher has assigned you.

Houston Public Library
Houston, Texas

Types of questions we can NOT answer by email
- Requests for bibliographies on a topic.
- Questions requiring legal or medical interpretation.
- Requests for lengthy research on a topic.

14.8 Appropriate Use of Service

Western Kentucky University
Western Kentucky University Libraries
Bowling Green, Kentucky

Rules pertaining to the questions submitted to our services:
- We may refuse to answer questions.
- We may refuse services to you if we determine you are not using our services in the way in which they were meant to be used, including, but not limited to, questions that are: illegal, harassing, libelous, threatening, harmful, obscene or objectionable, or that violate any applicable local, state, national, or international law or regulations.
- You agree your question will enter the public domain, and you will retain no ownership rights to your question.

14.9 Establishing Turnaround Time

California State University, Los Angeles
University Libraries
Los Angeles, California

Turn-Around Time

Your question will be forwarded to the e-mail reference coordinator in the Library. Program-related and subject-related inquiries will be forwarded to the appropriate individual.

The Library will try to respond within two weekdays, but response time may vary depending upon the nature of the inquiry. Questions received during the weekend will be treated as received on Monday.

Monroe County Library System
Rochester, New York

How soon should I expect an answer?

Our goal is to answer all questions quickly, but we will only be able to work on your question and respond to it during the days and times the Central Library is open.

Humboldt State University
Humboldt State University Libraries
Arcata, California

Your question will be forwarded to the email reference coordinator in the Library. Program-related and subject-related inquiries will be forwarded to the appropriate individual, if necessary.

Requesters may expect a response by 5:00 PM the following weekday. However, response time may vary depending upon the nature of the inquiry.

14.10 Determining Mailing and Faxing Fees

New Haven Free Public Library
New Haven, Connecticut

Mailing and faxing policies:

If you request that we send your answer via mail or fax, include your address along with your question; the following fees will apply. Mailed photocopies cost 50 cents per page plus a $5.00 service charge for all residents. Mailed microform copies and all faxed material cost 50 cents per page plus a service charge of $5.00 for New Haven residents, $10.00 for Connecticut residents or $15.00 for out-of-state residents.

14.11 Establishing Ownership of Transactions

New York Public Library
New York, New York

You agree that your question will enter the public domain, and you will retain no ownership rights to your question. This means that anyone, including the Library, can reproduce, copy, modify or otherwise use your question without your permission. In addition, your question may be displayed, distributed, transmitted and broadcast without your permission. As part of its public service mission, The New York Public Library provides information for NON-COMMERCIAL, PERSONAL or RESEARCH USE ONLY. Pursuant to the fair use provisions of federal copyright law, the Library may also provide short excerpts from material that is subject to copyright protection. You should be aware that such material may be subject to restrictions, including but not limited to copyright, in favor of parties other than the Library. You are solely responsible for determining the existence of such rights and for obtaining any permissions, and paying any associated fees, which may be necessary for any proposed use. The Library may also provide links to other Web sites. The Library does not monitor or control information accessible through the Internet and is not responsible for its content, for changes in content of the sources to which the Library pages link, or for the content of sources accessed through secondary links.

14.12 Disclaimer

Monroe County Library System
Rochester, New York

Disclaimer: "Ask A Librarian" is provided as a public service. Please be aware that we do not control the content of resources used and cannot guarantee the accuracy, relevance, timeliness, or completeness of information provided. Our answers are not a substitute for professional, legal, medical or financial advice.

New York Public Library
New York, New York

Disclaimer

The following disclaimer must be noted:

WHILE EVERY EFFORT IS MADE TO PROVIDE ACCURATE INFORMATION, THE NEW YORK PUBLIC LIBRARY SPECIFICALLY DISCLAIMS ALL EXPRESS AND IMPLIED WARRANTIES WITH RESPECT TO THE INFORMATION AND MATERIALS PROVIDED HEREIN, INCLUDING ANY WARRANTY OF MERCHANTABILITY OR FITNESS FOR A PARTICULAR PURPOSE OR NON-INFRINGEMENT OF PROPRIETARY RIGHTS. THE LIBRARY, ITS TRUSTEES, OFFICERS, EMPLOYEES AND OTHER REPRESENTATIVES SHALL HAVE NO LIABILITY FOR ANY DAMAGES, INCLUDING, WITHOUT LIMITATION, DIRECT, INDIRECT, CONSEQUENTIAL, COMPENSATORY, SPECIAL, PUNITIVE OR INCIDENTAL DAMAGES ARISING OUT OF OR RELATING TO USE OF THIS WEB SITE OR THE INFORMATION AND MATERIALS PROVIDED HEREIN.

14.13 Privacy Guidelines for Protecting Patron Confidentiality

New York Public Library
New York, New York

Privacy Policy

As part of your participation in the New York Public Library's Ask Librarians Online, the Library would like to know your name, e-mail address, and current mailing location. This allows us to better serve you in answering your question. The Library will not publish this information or provide it to other organizations. The Library will compile this information for its own internal purposes, including determining the number of people asking questions.

University of Maine–Fort Kent
Blake Library
Fort Kent, Maine

All reference transactions are confidential. Please be assured this information will not be shared, sold, etc. outside Blake Library. For statistical purposes library staff will keep track of the questions and number of users but not specific information on the users. Transcripts will be kept for a period of time to help evaluate the service and help staff with collection development.

Columbia University
Columbia University Library
New York, New York

Who else sees the transcript of my session?

A. The chat software keeps a transcript of every session that is completed, which includes the complete conversation between you and the librarian as well as a list of all web sites visited during the session. Chat session transcripts may be reviewed by the librarians managing the Ask Us Now service at Columbia. Your name and e-mail address as entered in the chat form are stored in the system. However, this information is strictly confidential and will not be used for any other purpose. Refer to the Library Confidentiality Policy.

Washington Research Library Consortium
Upper Marlboro, Maryland

Customer Confidentiality Transcripts from sessions will be used for analysis only. In keeping with library policy, customer information is considered confidential and accessible only by library staff. A patron may choose to check the anonymous box on the virtual reference form, thereby ensuring their name and e-mail will be not appear on the virtual reference transcript.

Ball State University
Ball State University Libraries
Muncie, Indiana

Live Chat privacy policy

The privacy of our library users is very important to us! The Ball State University Libraries will take reasonable steps to ensure the confidentiality of our library users. In order to further this goal, the Ask a Librarian: Live Chat privacy guidelines will explain the following:
  • What information is collected by our Live Chat service
  • What that information is used for
  • Who has access to the information
  • With whom the information may be shared
  • What choices are available to library users regarding collection, use, and   distribution of the information

1. What information is collected by our Live Chat service?

In order to maintain service quality, the BSU Libraries keep internal records which include the following information about each Live Chat session:

    user's name

    user's e-mail address (if provided)

    user's IP adress

    user's BSU status (student, faculty, visitor, etc.)

    librarian's name

    date and time

    complete transcript

Transcripts of all chats are also recorded by the software we are using, LivePerson http://www.liveperson.com/. LivePerson has a strict privacy policy regarding the information that they collect and how it is used. This policy is available here: http://www.liveperson.com/help/privacy.asp .

2. What is the information used for?

At all times, the privacy and confidentiality of our Live Chat users will be maintained to the extent permitted by law. The information that the BSU Libraries collect will be used internally to help analyze the amount and types of questions we are being asked in order to provide better service. It will not be used for marketing or for commercial purposes, and will never be sold, rented, or traded to third parties.

3. Who has access to this information?

Librarians and staff associated with the Ask a Librarian: Live Chat service and LivePerson employees (they are the company which provides our software). See their privacy policy at: http://www.liveperson.com/help/privacy.asp.

4. Who does the library share the information with?

Live Chat transcripts and information about individual chats will not be voluntarily shared with anyone outside of the BSU Libraries staff. Statistics generated from chat logs and surveys, as well as brief excerpts of chats, may be used for reports or publications. All personally identifying information will be stripped from these items before their use. The BSU Libraries will not provide information about specific Live Chat users (such as IP addresses, E-mail addresses, names, phone numbers, etc.) to anyone except as noted in 4a below.

    4a. Law Enforcement exception

    As with any form of business record, law enforcement officials with a valid court order (such as a subpoena or warrant) may obtain access to our Live Chat records, including chat logs and transcripts.

    Additionally, the Live Chat logs and transcripts of library users engaging in disruptive or dangerous behavior (such as threatening or harassing library staff) will be shared with library administrators and/or law enforcement officials.

5. What security measures are taken to protect library user privacy?

During chat sessions, Ask a Librarian: Live Chat uses Secure Socket Layer (SSL) encryption to encode information as it goes between the librarian and the library user. To help prevent hacking, the BSU Libraries do not maintain copies of Live Chat logs or transcripts on a Web server, and LivePerson maintains its records on secure servers. Please note: if a library user requests that a copy of their chat transcript be e-mailed to them, that e-mail is not encrypted, and is as vulnerable to unwanted interception as any other e-mail.

6. What choices do users have about the collection, use, and distribution of their information?

Any library user who wants to have the Ball State University Libraries' record of their Live Chat deleted may e-mail Information Services librarian to request the deletion of their chat transcript from the Ball State University Libraries' chat transcript log. Users will need to know the date and time of their chat in order to make sure that it can be located and deleted.

LivePerson (our software vendor) does not typically erase chat transcripts from their servers upon request. If you have any questions about their storage or recording of personal information, please contact LivePerson at [contact information].

Remember, the privacy of our library users is very important to us! Anyone who has questions about these guidelines should contact [contact information].

14.14 Form: E-mail Ask

Houston Public Library
Houston, Texas

Email Reference Form

To help us answer your question more efficiently, please fill out the form completely. Items marked with an asterisk ("*") are required.

*Your Name:
*Your email address:
Your address:
Street or P.O. Box
City:
State or Province:
*Zip/Postal Code:
Country if not USA:
Your phone number:
If you are in our local calling area,
please include your phone number.

I would like an answer by (mm/dd/yy).
Please allow 36 to 48 hours, excluding weekends and holidays.   Do you have a HPL Library Card? Yes: No:
HPL Library Card Number:

*Your question: Type your question in the box below.

Please describe the question or problem to be researched as specifically as possible. For example, rather than "1988 Olympics" say, "How did Katarina Witt place in the 1988 Olympics?"

If there are limitations to your question, such as dates or context, please let us know. For example, "I have Consumer Price Index figures for Houston through [date]; is there any more recent data?"

If you want your answer limited to resources that you can find on the Internet, please let us know. For example, "Where on the Web can I find the Fortune 500?"

If you are a student using this information for school, please tell us what grade or level you are in; this may determine the sources we use to answer your question.

Part VIII
Reference Services:
Children

Chapter 15

CHILDREN'S REFERENCE POLICIES

OVERVIEW

15.1 Service Philosophy

Apache Junction Public Library
Apache Junction, Arizona

It is the desire of the Apache Junction Public Library to provide children in the infancy through early teen years a collection that can satisfy their informational, cultural and recreational reading needs. Primary emphasis is placed on the selection of a wide variety of print materials to help stimulate the child's intellectual, emotional and creative abilities and to help satisfy the child's natural curiosity about the world and his or her relationship to it. The library will add non-print materials for children as the budget allows.

Southern Ontario Library Service
Galway-Cavendish & Harvey Township Public Library
Buckhorn, Ontario Canada

A goal of the Galway-Cavendish & Harvey Township Public Library is to provide ready access to sources of information, knowledge and the creative imagination for all people of all ages.

The Galway-Cavendish & Harvey Township Public Library believes that the intellectual growth of children,* their cultural appreciation and recreational activities should be encouraged through quality library service, delivered with consideration and respect.

The Galway-Cavendish & Harvey Township Public Library believes that a children's collection in a small library is important because it encourages children to read and satisfies their curiosity and need for information about the world around them. For children, the library should be a place to explore, a place to return to time and again, a place where they will always be welcome.

The Galway-Cavendish & Harvey Township Public Library believes that children's services are as important a component of the library as any services offered to adults.

Public Library of Enid and Garfield County
Enid, Oklahoma

Services provided in the Children's and Young Adult Area of the library promote family literacy and life-long learning by providing access to a variety of age-appropriate materials to children and young adults. Children and Young Adult services also provides for the educational, informational, and recreational needs through programs both in the library and through a variety of out reach programs and services.

REFERENCE AND MATERIAL SELECTION

15.2 Reference

Southern Ontario Library Service
Galway-Cavendish & Harvey Township Public Library
Ontario, Canada

Reference service is a major responsibility of library staff working with children. Staff must be patient and receptive to the many questions asked by children. Library staff should conduct reference interviews to help understand what each child wants and needs. It is the responsibility of library staff to point out the variety of resources available in the library.

The Galway-Cavendish & Harvey Township Public Library will ensure that reference services and reader's advisory are available for children.

PROCEDURES
1. Reference service shall be a major responsibility of library staff working with children. Library staff should conduct reference interviews to help understand what each child wants and needs. It is the responsibility of Library staff to point out the variety of resources available in the library.
2. Readers' advisory service involves the process of connecting readers (and viewers) to materials they want or need — "the right book for the right child at the right time." It is providing and sharing knowledge of materials that make up the collection and taking the time to help each child find books he or she will enjoy reading. It requires a broad collection of material selected with children's interests in mind.
3. Reference service and readers' advisory for children shall take into account the policies and procedures in place in the Library for adults.

15.3 Selection

Carbondale Public Library
Carbondale, Illinois

Materials for Children and Youth

In general the Carbondale Public Library subscribes to a policy of free access to library materials for minors. However, the library's Internet access is filtered and minors must have a signed parental permission form on file in order to use this resource. Children under 10 must have a parent/guardian present when using the Internet. At the Carbondale Public Library, children and young people have access to all parts of the Library; however, collections in Children's Services serve children and young people from preschool through eighth grades and their parents and care givers.

Materials appropriate for the interests and needs of the ages served are chosen for this collection.

Collections in Children's Services include traditional picture books, beginning readers, junior non-fiction, junior fiction, junior high fiction, periodicals, nonbook materials, reference materials, and a collection on parenting. This last collection contains some duplication of materials on parenting found in the adult collection. A sampling of children's books in a variety of foreign languages is also selected for the Children's Services department. The junior high fiction collection is selected especially for the needs and interests of 7th and 8th graders. It contains some duplication of classic titles found in both the adult and junior fiction collections, but is also strongly stocked with those titles that deal with the contemporary scene as it concerns 12 to 14 year-olds. Young people in the 7th and 8th grades are expected to use non-fiction materials throughout the Library in preparing school assignments or for any other reason.

Southern Ontario Library Service
Galway-Cavendish & Harvey Township Public Library
Ontario, Canada

1. Materials for children shall be chosen in accordance with the library's overall collection development policy.
2. In addition to the collection development policy (relevant to children's material) there shall be an emphasis placed on collecting award-winning children's titles.

15.4 Periodicals

San Jose Public Library and San Jose State University Library
San Jose, California

Statement of Policy & Text

Young Adult and Children's periodicals at the King Library may be checked out for a one-week period by any patron who has a current SJSU or SJPL library card. This policy applies to even the most current issue of a periodical title.

Need for the Policy

The King Library houses a valuable periodicals collection that is a resource to citizens, students, and faculty. For this reason the Adult periodicals collection is a non-circulating collection.

Young Adult and Children's periodicals on the other hand, are an ephemeral collection, read mostly for entertainment. This policy allows these periodicals to be borrowed just as are other children's and young adult materials.

Requirements & Guidelines

- All Young Adult and Children's periodicals may be checked out for one week with one renewal allowed.
- Young Adult and Children's periodicals are not reservable.

TYPES OF ASSISTANCE OFFERED

15.5 Service to Teachers

Stillwater Public Library
Stillwater, Oklahoma

TEACHER CARD

The library staff will issue borrower's cards to teachers who are residents of Payne County for classroom use according to the following guidelines:

1. Teachers must provide proof of employment with a public/private school or daycare system by:
   a. Providing a current payroll stub from the school
   b. Providing a letter from the principal or the Board of Education stating that they are employed at the school
2. Verification of continued employment will be required to renew a teacher's card that has expired.
3. Teacher cards are valid from August through May of the current school year.
   A limit of 50 items for classroom use may be checked out for a period of 30 days. These items cannot be renewed.
   Items checked out on a teacher's card are not transferable to a personal borrower's card.
6. Items not available for checkout on a teacher card include: bestsellers and CD-ROMs.
7. Teachers are responsible for fines due to late, lost, or damaged books just as if they were checked out for personal use.

Wichita Falls Public Library
Wichita Falls, Texas

Teacher Collections

A TEACHER or ORGANIZATION COLLECTION may be set up to allow check out of up to 30 items.

TEACHER COLLECTION status must be set up through the Youth Services Department. A teacher must be currently employed by a public or private institution and have at least 5 students in his/her care to qualify for this status. The teacher will be issued a card on submission of a signed agreement accepting responsibility for any lost materials and/or fines and fees for each item checked out.

ORGANIZATION COLLECTION status must be set up through the Circulation Desk. ORGANIZATION cards are issued on submission of written request on official organizational stationary, signed by an official of the organization accepting responsibility for all lost materials and fines or fees and designating a contact person.

Additional limitations are as follows:

FIVE holiday books (Christmas, Halloween, etc.)

TEN audio items (Cassettes, with/without books, CD's)
TEN books in any ONE subject area
TEN VIDEOS per collection.

These limitations are placed so that each borrower has an equal opportunity to check out special materials which may be in short supply due to demand.

All items including videos will be checked out for a 4-week period with no renewal. The library takes no responsibility for the use of videos in the classroom. Please check to see if public performance rights are included before showing a video in the classroom.

FINES AND LOST BOOKS

Individual teachers and organizations will be assessed overdue fines when any items checked out to them are returned late. All materials are charged at the rate of 10 cents per day. The maximum fine is the replacement cost of the item. There is a 7-day "grace period" for all materials before fines begin to accrue. After the 7-day grace period, fines accrue from the original due date at ten cents a day per item (i.e. a book returned on the day following the grace period will generate an 70 cent fine).

Items returned damaged beyond repair are set to "lost" status, as are long overdue items. Lost items require payment of replacement cost, plus a non-refundable $15.00 processing fee ($5.00 for paperbacks). If any lost item is found within three months and returned in usable condition, the replacement cost may be refunded. A repair or rebinding cost may be charged at the discretion of the library for any damaged material that can be repaired.

STAFF SELECTION SERVICE

The library staff will pull books for teachers/organizations by title, author, subject, reading level, or from a list. Requests for this service must be received five days prior to the time needed. Requests may be made by:

telephone:
fax:
email:

Request forms are available at the Youth Desk.

Southern Ontario Library Service
Galway-Cavendish & Harvey Township Public Library
Ontario, Canada

1. The information needs of school-aged children are influenced to a large extent by their school studies. Although the school library holds the primary responsibility for the provision of curriculum-related support material, the public library shall endeavor to provide additional resources and assistance when called upon. Cooperation and communication should exist between the public library staff and school staff to ensure that the best interests of children are served.
2. The public library can best acquaint students, teachers and school librarians with its resources and services by inviting classes to the public library for orientation visits.

3. Where time and staffing permit, visits to schools by public library staff will reinforce the public library's informational and recreational relevance to students.
4. Public library staff should keep local schools informed of forthcoming child-oriented programs and events.

15.6 School Assignments

Monroe Township Public Library
Monroe Township, New Jersey

RESERVE COLLECTION FOR SCHOOL ASSIGNMENTS

When notified of assignments involving large numbers of students, the Reference Department reserves materials to support assignments from Monroe public and private schools. These materials are chosen and made temporary reference by the librarian in charge of this service and are set aside in the Department for the duration of the assignment. Materials in this collection must be used in the Library.

Wilmington Public Library District
Wilmington, Illinois

The reference staff will assist patrons requesting information to complete school assignments. Assistance will include locating the source, using the index, and indicating the section of material that answers the question. ILL requests will be placed for materials when necessary. The staff is unable to anticipate the instructor's purpose in assigning homework and does not interpret the instructor's questions for students. Homework telephone requests will be answered if the information can be located in 3-5 minutes.

15.7 Service to Parents and Childcare Providers

Monona Public Library
Monona, Wisconsin

Parents and Family

In addition to giving parents and caregivers essential and accurate parenting information, the Monona Public Library also provides a variety of library services which stress the importance of a parent or caregiver being a child's first teacher.

MATERIALS AND RESOURCES

The Monona Public Library has an extensive collection of books, magazines, video tapes, and handouts that provide information ranging in topics from parenting a newborn to parenting a teenager. There are parenting books just for mommies or just for daddies ...and a special selection of picture books on topics such as "going to the hospital" or " going to school." The Children's Room also provides parents and caregivers with free pamphlets, flyers, and booklists containing helpful information.

LITTLE FRIENDS OF THE LIBRARY

The library reaches out to new parents with our "Books for Babies" program through the Friends of the Monona Public Library to welcome a new baby into the Monona Community. Parents with a baby up to 12 months old receive a free board book. Stop into the library with your library card and birth certificate, or your baby, to pick up the book.

AGE APPROPRIATE PROGRAMS FOR CHILDREN AND PARENTS

These programs are designed to fit developmental steps and stages leading to preschool and kindergarten readiness.

Preschool and Toddler Storytime programs effectively supply important parenting information in a supportive environment that is designed to encourage one-on-one play between the parent and child while also giving the parent ample opportunity to network with other parents in the Monona Community. Programs consist of stories, books, rhymes, songs, and fingerplays. See the Events Calendar for themes, dates and times.

Family Fun Night programs are held each month. See the Events Calendar for details. Attending library programs with your children is one way that you can create time for valuable family togetherness and at the same time teach children a wide variety of lessons and skills that can strengthen your family. Programs vary from month to month and may include storytelling, music, dance, hobbies, animal programs, and more. We encourage parents to talk with their children about the programs and check out books to lead to further discussion. Participating in this type of activity can strengthen communications skills and increase the bond of the family.

Participation in the Summer Library Program:
1. Keeps children reading over the summer break.
2. Promotes the development of reading interests.
3. Helps children and teens develop the reading habit.
4. Helps children and teens retain more of their reading skills so that they are better prepared for school in the fall.
5. Helps children gain the educational benefits that voluntary reading provides.
6. Encourages children to develop the habit of using their public library.

Nashville Public Library
Nashville, Tennessee

The Children's Division of the Main Library has traditionally been a resource center for branch libraries, area schoolteachers and students, parents of children from birth to age 13, daycare programs, and other agencies focused on the development of a love of reading in children. Generations of Nashvillians have enjoyed its well-known marionette productions, its enchanting Tudor style story room, and a collection on all topics with a strong emphasis on supporting the core curriculum of public schools.

Special Services and Notable Collections:

- We provide access to children's literature and technology through informed reader's advisory service.
- Well over half of the collection consists of juvenile nonfiction titles.
- Some of the strongest areas of the collection are folklore, poetry, the sciences, and juvenile biographies. Many of the biographies are about unique individuals and are sometimes the only book available in the library system on a subject.
- The division's collection of picture books is a definitive one. These books offer children their first experience with the pleasure of stories, language, and the written word.
- Strong reference collection emphasizing professional materials, a variety of sources invaluable to homework assignments, and a collection of Newbery and Caldecott award winners.
- We are currently building toward the development of a definitive Juvenile Literature Collection.
- Programming designed to illuminate literature as it inspires independent learning and exploration of the world around us including marionette theater, storytime for the young child, other hands-on activities, outreach to schools and agencies who work with children, and special guest programming such as the Nashville Ballet and Nashville Jazz Society programs for youth.

Huntington Public Library
Huntington Station, New York

Youth & Parent's Services

Youth and Parent's Services provides information and reading services to patrons from birth through High School, as well as their parents and caregivers. Available materials include books, videos, CDs, and computer software. Librarians provide a variety of advisory services, from recommending a good book, assisting with a home work assignment, to personalized reference assistance.

Programs for children, young adults, parents, and caregivers are regularly offered throughout the year. Some examples are Mother Goose rhyme time, parent/child activity sessions, craft workshops, holiday and vacation shows. The Summer Reading Club is an annual favorite of all children. Please contact Children's Services for a list of their current and upcoming programs.

Young patrons have their own bank of computers in this department. Workstations are available for reference, word processing, and child-oriented software. Free Internet access is provided for children who have received parental permission to use the computers.

Patrons ages 12 and up (i.e., Young Adults) will find recreational reading materials in print and audio format, paperbacks, magazines, and a "school assignment" collection. Computers with Internet access and word processing programs are also available in a separate room catering specifically to the needs of this age group.

Young Adult non-fiction books are shelved in stacks located right outside the Young Adult Computer Room. Book discussions and other types of programs that appeal to young adults are scheduled each month. Ask for our Young Adult Librarian who specializes in serving this age group for help with information requests and research.

15.8 Service to Home-Schooling Families

Glen Ellyn Public Library
Glen Ellyn, Illinois

Homeschool Support Services

The Glen Ellyn Public Library welcomes home schooling families in the community. The Library supports these families through programs, materials and services. A valid Glen Ellyn Library card may be required.

Many of our services of interest to Homeschooling families are listed below. If you have a question or suggestion, please click here Contact: Glen Ellyn Public Library

Youth Services Programs

- story times for children six months through seven years of age
- an extensive Summer Reading program for ages 2 through eighth grade in Youth Services
- monthly book discussions
- special programs such as puppet shows, children's theatre, animal discovery and music
- yearly program for home schooling parents about the Library's resources

Youth Services Materials

- Parent and Teacher collection of materials to be used with children
- extensive collection of book lists to help in selecting age-appropriate books
- puzzles and puppets to check out for younger children
- public school textbooks, grades K-8, for use in the library
- foreign language materials
- educational computer programs available for check out
- computers with games and educational software to use in the library
- Internet access with a parent
- music cassettes and CDs
- educational videos available at no charge

Adult Services Programs and Materials

- separate Young Adult collection for middle school and high school students
- home school materials at call numbers 371.04 and 371.3
- computer introduction classes
- Home Education magazine in print
- Summer and Winter Reading programs for 9th grade to adults
- Internet access with a valid Glen Ellyn library card
- study rooms

Library Services

- inter-library loan and extensive search for materials
- classroom collections in which a Youth Services Librarian will assemble books on a particular subject for you to check out

- special tours and training to introduce students and parents to the library and resources
- Internet access to the library's catalog, magazines, newspapers and other reference databases from home or in the library
- personalized reading lists based upon a short survey completed by independent readers

Additional Information
- special group or family tours and training in using the catalog may be scheduled with a Youth Services librarian
- classroom collections may be requested online by e-mailing the Library or by calling the Youth Services department
- librarians are always available to assist in locating materials
- computers for word processing

Kennebunk Free Library
Kennebunk, Maine

Resources at KFL for Homeschooling Parents

Reference services available in person, by phone or via our email from our website.

The Library catalog available 24/7 online.

Topical Book selection—call us to select and hold materials on specific topics for your classes.

Items on hold—we will put aside these items and hold them for you for up to one week.

ILL—Interlibrary loan, at no charge, for the materials you need. Some restrictions apply.

Lengthened borrowing privileges—Homeschoolers are eligible for a one-month lending period for curriculum related materials, with an additional 2-week renewal if no one is waiting for the item

Free KFL library cards for residents of Kennebunk, Kennebunkport, Arundel and Wells

Over 40,000 items (books, magazines, videos, audios, DVD's) to select from

Booklists for subject research, genre suggestions and recommendations

Free use of KFL computers for Internet, word processing, spreadsheets, etc.

Volunteer opportunities for students

Use of Hank's Room (meeting room)

Make requests for KFL purchases

Computer Classes

MARVEL (formerly the Maine Databases) for your research needs at the library or from your home computer

Library tours

Telephone renewals

PROGRAMMING! Various children's and young adult programs, book discussion groups, summer reading programs, special events (i.e. Chewonki presentations)

Free library card at Portland Public Library (available to all York Co. residents)

Display space in the children's room for your students' projects

15.9 Form: Teacher Assignment

Wichita Falls Public Library
Wichita Falls, Texas

Teacher Assignment Form

Assignment Alert

This form is intended for use by teachers of Wichita Falls area schools.

Teachers -

Notify the Library of upcoming assignments so that we can be better prepared to assist your students with materials and Internet resources. We can also use this information for collection development purposes.

Please fill out the form below and press submit - OR- send us a copy of the assignment by mail, fax, or email to: [contact information].

Also, be sure to sign up for a Teacher Collection! It will enable you to check out extra materials for a longer period of time to be used in your classroom! Sign up at either the Youth or Information Desks. Call the Youth Desk for more information.

Length of assignment/dates: from to _____

School:_____

Phone or E-mail so we can contact you:_____

Teacher:_____

Name of Course:_____

Number of Students:_____ Grade: _____

Assignment (Please be as specific as possible. A copy of the assignment is helpful.)

Purpose of the assignment: (please Check)

_____Practice using library materials with only normal librarian assistance.

_____Information gathering with as much special attention as can be provided by the Library.

Type(s) of library materials students will probably seek to meet this assignment:

Reference_____

Nonfiction_____

Fiction_____

Periodicals_____   _____

AV Materials_____

Internet_____

Are you requiring a specific number of sources? If so, how many? _____

Please suggest titles for purchase relating to this assignment that we do not already own:

_____

_____

Additional information to aid the librarians (e.g., titles in our library where students would find needed information):_____

_____

_____

Thanks for your cooperation!

15.10 Form: Assignment Alert (E-mail)

Roselle Public Library
Roselle, Illinois

All alerts will be confirmed by telephone or email.

If you have any questions, please call one of the above numbers.

An asterisk (*) indicates required information.

*Name
*School
*Telephone
Fax
Email

Description of your homework assignment:

*Assignment Due Date

*Grade Level   Number of Students

Students may use (check all that apply)

Books Magazines Internet Resources* General Encyclopedias Specialized Encyclopedias

*Teachers please note: A Minors User Agreement must be on file for anyone under 18 years of age.

Will students be working in groups? Yes No

Would you like us to place materials relevant to this assignment on temporary reserve on the homework shelves at Roselle Public Library? Yes No

Do you have a web page with relevant related links? Yes   No

15.11 Form: Teacher Assignment (E-mail)

Comsewogue Public Library
Port Jefferson Station, New York

This form will be sent to the Children's and Youth Services Department.

By providing the Comsewogue Public Library's Children's and Youth Services Department, with advance notice of your class assignment, our librarians will try to provide your students with as many library resources as possible. Please give us one-week notice before you hand out the assignment.

Today's Date:
Teacher's Name:
Phone:
E-mail:
Fax:
School:
Name of Assignment:
Students:
(estimated number
given this assignment)
Date assignment begins:
Date assignment is due:
Assignment Description:
Length of Assignment:
(in pages)
Resources:
Any
Books
Magazines
Newspapers
Internet
Library Databases

CIRCULATION, ACCESS TO MATERIALS, INTERNET, AND PRIVACY POLICIES

15.12 Borrowing Privileges

Stillwater Public Library
Stillwater, Oklahoma

CHILDREN'S LIBRARY CARDS

To obtain a library card for children under 18 years of age, both the parent/legal guardian/responsible adult and the applicant must be present at the time of application. Parent/legal guardian's signature is also required on the library card. Additional information required includes the child's year of birth and parent information. There is no minimum age limit to obtain a library card. Upon reaching the age of 18, the patron must update his/her information and have the library staff change his/her status to an adult. Parents are legally responsible for any fees incurred by children under the age of 18.

Bethel Public Library
Bethel, Connecticut

Juvenile cards: A Bethel resident age 5 through 13 who wishes to receive a library card must complete a borrower registration form provided by the Library. A child under the age of five may receive his/her own card provided he/she is able to print or write his/her own name. A parent or legal guardian will be asked to prove identity and residency and co-sign the registration form for his/her child under the age of 14. By co-signing, the parent or legal guardian accepts responsibility for settling fines, damages, losses, or other assessments against the library card of his/her child.

NOTE: An adult card will be issued to a child age 14 or older without parental permission. However, the child's parent or legal guardian remains responsible for all materials borrowed, as well as any and all associated fines and/or fees, on the child's card until the child reaches the legal age of 18.

15.13 Accessing Materials by Minors

Bethel Public Library
Bethel, Connecticut

The Library staff and trustees are charged with the responsibility of providing free and equal access to Library materials and services to all eligible people. Moreover, it is impossible for them to know or predict the opinions of parents and guardians regarding the specific borrowing selections made by minor children.

It is the policy of the Bethel Public Library that parents or guardians, not the Library staff or trustees, are responsible for monitoring and approving the selection of materials made by minor children. It is the parents or guardians – and only these – who may restrict their children – and only their children – from borrowing specific Library materials. Parents or guardians who wish their children not to have access to certain materials should accompany or otherwise advise their children. The Library staff and trustees cannot and do not act in loco parentis.

Lawrence Public Library
Lawrence, Kansas

Guarantees of Accessibility for Children and Youth

Children have access to all Library services, programming, and materials. Specialized children's reference, information and referral, reader's advisory services, and programming are provided.

Children are assured access to books and materials when issued a library card, and may check out any circulating item in the library. The only restriction for acquiring a library card is that a parent or legal guardian must sign a responsibility agreement for children under the age of 12 years.

Parents or legal guardians who so wish may instruct Library staff to restrict borrowing privileges for their child under the age of 12 years within the Library's circulation system to the check out of materials in the Youth Services Department.

15.14 Privacy Guidelines for Protecting Patron Confidentiality

Mill Valley Public Library
Mill Valley, California

Our Commitment to Children's Privacy

Protecting the privacy of children is especially important to us. We attempt to minimize exposure of children's personal information when possible by using children's first names only when promoting events on and off our website. We are also prudent in our use of children's email information; using it to promote specific children's programs, and being careful not to display email addresses in broadcast lists. Due to the ease with which children can divulge personal information on the Internet as well as the possibility of inadvertently bringing up inappropriate sites, we urge parents to supervise their children's use of the Internet. Information collected by the Mill Valley Public Library is not shared with any other agency or organization.

Omaha Public Library
Omaha, Nebraska

In the case of children in the eighth grade or lower, information may be released to any parent or guardian who is listed in the child's library account as the parent or guardian. The parent or guardian must present the request in person at a library agency and must provide current identification. Information will not be released to a parent or guardian whose name is not in the account or if his/her address is different than the child's.

15.15 Filtering Software

New York Public Library
New York, New York

Filtering

As required by the Children's Internet Protection Act ("CIPA"), in order to remain eligible for certain federal funding, the Library has implemented software filtering on all of its Internet-accessible computer terminals. The software installed on Internet-accessible computers at the Library protects against access to visual depictions of obscenity, child pornography, and, in the case of persons under the age of 17 years, materials that are "harmful to minors." Users should be aware, however, that all currently available filtering software results in a degree of both "underblocking" (i.e., permitting access to certain material that falls within the foregoing categories) and "overblocking" (i.e., denying access to certain constitutionally protected material that does not fall within the foregoing categories). The Library has attempted to select filtering software that best complies with CIPA while providing Library users with the broadest possible access to constitutionally protected speech and information. The Library cannot and does not guarantee that the filtering software will block all obscenity, child pornography, or materials that are harmful to minors. Nor can the Library guarantee that the filtering software will not restrict access to sites that may have legitimate research or other value. In order to help address the overblocking problem and to enhance users' access to constitutionally protected speech and information, the Library requests that all users, both adults and minors, contact the Library at filtering@nypl.org (or at such other contact point as the Library shall designate from time to time) to request unblocking of an incorrectly blocked site. In addition, any user who is 17 years of age or older may disable the filtering software in order to obtain unfiltered Internet access for bona fide research or other lawful purpose by following the instructions provided on the computer screen or such instructions as the Library shall otherwise provide from time to time.

Jefferson Madison Regional Library
Charlottesville, Virginia

All adults (17 years and older based on library card registration) seeking unfiltered Internet access for their own use may temporarily disable filtering for each session. Adults may not share unfiltered computers with minors (under 17 years old). Library staff will not disable filtering/blocking technology on computers located in children's or young adult areas of the library. The Library will consider formal requests to block or unblock specific websites with procedures similar to those for consideration or reconsideration of print materials. Computer logs maintained by the filtering software will be deleted when no longer administratively useful.

15.16 Access to Internet by Minors

New York Public Library
New York, New York

Access by Minors

Parents or legal guardians must assume responsibility for deciding which library resources are appropriate for their own children. Parents or legal guardians should guide their children in use of the Internet and inform them about materials they should not use. While the Library affirms and acknowledges the rights and responsibilities of parents and guardians to monitor and determine their children's access to Library materials and resources, including those available through the Internet, the Library has taken certain measures designed to assist in the safe and effective use of these resources by all minors.

To address the issue of access by minors to inappropriate material on the Internet, including material that is harmful to minors, the Library:

- Develops and maintains special web sites for children and teens;
- Develops and provides training programs on safe and effective Internet use;
- Encourages staff to guide minors away from materials that may be inappropriate;
- Distributes a publication entitled "A Safety Net for the Internet: A Parent's Guide"; and
- Has implemented filtering software as more fully described above.

To address the issue of the safety and security of minors when using electronic mail, chat rooms and other forms of direct electronic communications, as well as the unauthorized disclosure, use and dissemination of personal identification information regarding minors, the Library provides training programs and also urges minors to keep in mind the following safety guidelines:

- Never give out identifying information such as home address, school name, or telephone number.
- Let parents or guardians decide whether personal information such as age, marital status, or financial information should be revealed.
- Never arrange a face-to-face meeting with someone via the computer without parents' or guardians' approval.
- Never respond to messages that are suggestive, obscene, threatening, or make one uncomfortable.
- Have parents or guardians report an incident to the National Center for Missing and Exploited Children at 1-800-843-5678 if one becomes aware of the transmission of child pornography.
- Remember that people online may not be who they say they are.
- Remember that everything one reads may not be true.

To address the issue of unauthorized access, including so-called "hacking," and other unlawful activities by minors online, minors and all other Library users are hereby advised that use of the Library's computers for hacking or any other unlawful activity is strictly prohibited.

Jefferson Madison Regional Library
Charlottesville, Virginia

Library staff is not in a position to supervise juveniles' use of the Internet (see Policy Section 4.234). As with other library materials, restriction of a juvenile's access to the Internet is the responsibility of the parent or legal guardian. In compliance with the Children's Internet Protection Act (CIPA), Jefferson-Madison Regional Library provides Internet workstations equipped with filtering/blocking technology. However, the library recognizes that filtering/blocking technology is not a completely reliable means of protection from materials that may be offensive, controversial or illegal. To help Internet users find useful information while avoiding unwanted information, library staff will provide Internet instruction. The Jefferson-Madison Regional Library website will include links to other websites selected by library staff on the basis of their informational or educational value in compliance with the library's' Material Selection Policy.

Pierce County Library System
Tacoma, Washington

ACCESS BY MINORS:

In compliance with the Children's Internet Protection Act the Pierce County Library System will provide a filter on all Library computers available to minors. A child is defined as a minor if he or she is under the age of 17. The Library will offer tools to assist parents, guardians, and caregivers in their work with their own minor children. The tools include but are not limited to filters or technological means to structure access to the Internet, skilled staff, handouts, and recommended websites and search engines. Internet filtering or blocking software is an imperfect technology and can filter material that is not harmful to children and can fail to filter other material that may be harmful. Even with these limitations, it is a tool to assist library users in limiting access to the full spectrum of Internet interactions. PCLS has selected a filter which is intended to block access to the following:

Visual depictions that are obscene, contain child pornography and are harmful to minors.

Sites that have the potential to pose safety and security issues for minors, such as chat rooms, message/bulletin boards, free pages, and other forms of electronic communications. This does not include electronic mail.

Sites that instruct and encourage minors in performing unlawful activities, such as "how to hack." Use of Pierce County Library computers for hacking or other unlawful activity is prohibited.

Sites that encourage and/or allow unauthorized disclosure, use of, and dissemination of personal identification information with regard to minors.

The Library will maintain a description of filter criteria used and will provide the description upon request. Pierce County Library System will also continue to monitor and evaluate technological changes related to Internet blocking tools.

Sources

Alverno College, Milwaukee, Wisconsin. (May 30, 2005)
   Available: www.depts.alverno.edu/library/reserves.html.
   (September 2005) Available: www.depts.alverno.edu/library/illpolicy.html.

Ames Public Library. Ames, Iowa. (August 2005)
   Available: www.ames.lib.ia.us/policy/3-generalguidelines.htm.

Apache Junction Public Library, Apache Junction, Arizona. (May 2005)
   Available: www.ajpl.org/library/policies.htm.

Athens-Limestone Public Library, Athens, Texas. (September 2005).
   Available: www.athenslimetone.lib.al.us/interlibrary_loan.htm.

Athens Regional Library System, Athens, Georgia. (April 22, 2005)
   Available: www.clarke.public.lib.ga.us/policies/reference.htm.
   www.clarke.public.lib.ga.us/policies/ill.pdf.

Aurora Public Library. Aurora, Colorado. (September 2005) Available:
   www.aurora.lib.il.us/interlibrary_loan_policy.htm.

Austin College. Sherman, Texas. (September 2005) Available:
   http://abell.austincollege.edu/Abell/Srvpoco/coldev.html.

Austin Public Library. Austin, Texas. (June 15, 2005) Available:
   www.ci.austin.tx.us/library/refpolicy.htm.

Avalon Public Library, Pittsburgh, Pennsylvania. (September 6, 2005) Available:
   http://alphaclp.clpgh.org/ein/avalon/ll.html.

Ball State University, Muncie, Indiana. (September 2005) Available:
   www.bsu.edu/library/article/0,,23754--,00.html.

Benedictine University, Lisle, Illinois. (September 2005) Available:
   www.ben.edu/resources/librarytour/ReferencePolicy.pdf.

Bethel Public Library, Bethel, Connecticut. (August 2005) Available:
   www.bethellibrary.org/child/ch_policies.htm.

Boerne Public Library, Boerne, Texas. (August 2005) Available: www.boerne.lib.tx.us/faq/referencepolicy.pdf.

Boise Public Library, Boise, Idaho. (July 2005) Available: www.boisepubliclibrary.org/Ref/Jim/guidelines.htm.

Boston College, Boston, Massachusetts. (July 23, 2005) Available: www.bc.edu/libraries/resources/collections/s-journalpolicy/.

Boston Public Library, Boston, Massachusetts. (August 23, 2005) Available: www.bpl.org/general/policies/Reference%20Services%20Policy.pdf.

Brampton Public Library, Brampton, Ontario. (August 2005) Available: www.bramlib.on.ca/policies/info_services_policy.pdf.

Brandeis University Libraries, Waltham, Massachusetts. (July 2005) Available: http://http://library.brandeis.edu/collmgt/selection.html.

Braswell Memorial Library, Rocky Mount, North Carolina. (May 28, 2005) Available: www.braswell-library.org/refpol.htm.

Bridgewater Public Library, Bridgewater, Massachusetts. (May 2005) www.bridgewaterpubliclibrary.org/ref_policy.htm www.bridgewaterpubliclibrary.org/illpol.htm.

Brownwood Public Library, Brownwood, Texas. (November 2005) Available: www.bwdpublib.org/index.htm.

Bucknell University, Lewisburg, Pennsylvania. (August 2005) Available: www.bucknell.edu/Library_computing/Policies_and_Guidelines/Borrower_Privileges/Faculty_and_Staff.html www.isr.bucknell.edu/Collections_and_Borrowing/Reserves/Reserves_Request.html.

California State Polytechnic University–Pomona, Pomona, California. (July 2005) Available: www.csupomona.edu/~library/html/privacy_policy.html.

California State University Library, Los Angeles, Los Angeles, California. (September 2005) Available: www.calstatela.edu/library/subasklib.htm.

California State University–Northridge, Northridge, California. (September 2005) http://library.csun.edu/pubserv/illuse.html.

Carbondale Public Library, Carbondale, Illinois. (July 2005) Available: www.carbondale.lib.il.us/art_print_policies.htm www.carbondale.lib.il.us/materials_selection.htm www.carbondale.lib.il.us/borrower's_card.htm.

Carroll Public Library, Carroll, Nebraska. (August 2005) Available: www.neilsa.org/policy_manual/education.html.

Chelmsford Public Library, Chelmsford, Massachusetts. (June 2005) Available: www.chelmsfordlibrary.org/library_info/policies/reference_policy.html.

Clemson University, Clemson, South Carolina. (August 2005) Available: www.lib.clemson.edu/aboutlib/overview/missvissg.htm.

Colgate University, Hamilton, New York. (September 2005) Available: http://exlibris.colgate.edu/services/ill.html.

Colorado State University–Pueblo, Pueblo, Colorado. (September 2005) Available: http://library.colostate-pueblo.edu/ill/index.asp.

Columbia University. New York, New York. (August 2005) Available: www.columbia.edu/cu/lweb/services/reference/askusnowfaq.html.

Cornell University Library, Ithaca, New York. (November 2005) Available: http://commandepository.library.cornell.edu/cul-dp-framework.pdf.

Comsewogue Public Library, Port Jefferson Station, New York. (August 2005) Available: http://cpl.suffolk.lib.ny.us/taaf.html.

Culver-Union Township Public Library, Culver, Indiana. (September 2005) www.culver.lib.in.us/circulation_policies.htm.

Dartmouth College, Hanover, New Hampshire. (July 2005) Available: www.dartmouth.edu/~cmdc/cdp/electronic.html.

Denver Public Library, Denver, Colorado. (November 2005) Available: www.denver.lib.co.us/about/disabilities.html.

Dominican University of California, San Rafael, California. (September 2005) Available: www.Dominican.edu/Library/ill.cfm.

Dorchester County Public Library, Cambridge, Maryland. (June 2005) Available: www.dorchesterlibrary.org/library/refpolicy.html.

Eastern Washington University, Cheney, Washington. (September 2005) Available: www.ewu.edu/x5527.xml.

Emory University, Atlanta, Georgia. (June 2005) Available: http://web.library.emory.edu/services/ressvcs/emailpol.html.

Enoch Pratt Free Library, Baltimore, Maryland. (June 2005) Available: www.epfl.net/ask/epfl_guidelines.html.

Falmouth Public Library, Falmouth, Massachusetts. (June 2005) Available: www.falmouthpubliclibrary.org/refpolicy.htm www.falmouthpubliclibrary.org/interlib.htm.

Fitchburg State College, Fitchburg, Massachusetts. (May 2005) Available: www.fsc.edu/library/reference.html.

Florida International University, Miami, Florida. (September 2005) Available: www.fiu.edu/~library/services/illpolcy.html.

Fresno County Library, Fresno, California. (July 2005) Available: www.fresnolibrary.org/about/privacy.html.

Galway-Cavendish & Harvey Township Public Library, Toronto, Ontario. (June 2005) Available:
www.sols.org/links/clearhouse/accreditation/samplepolicies/galway/childrenservices.doc.

Gleason Public Library, Carlisle, Massachusetts. (June 2005) Available:
www.gleasonlibrary.org/index.php?ac=privacy.htm.

Glen Cove Public Library, Glen Cove, New York. (August 2005) Available:
www.nassaulibrary.org/glencove/mission.htm.

Glen Ellyn Public Library, Glen Ellyn, Illinois. (June 2005) Available:
www.gepl.org/adultservices/refpol.html.
www.gepl.org/youth/homeschool.html.

Glenview Public Library, Glenview, Illinois. (May 2005) Available:
www.glenview.lib.il.us/refpol.html.

Grinnell College, Grinnell, Iowa. (May 2005) Available:
www.lib.grinnell.edu/about/mission.html. (July 2005) Available:
www.lib.grinnell.edu/about/facltylns.html.
www.lib.grinnell.edu/places/reservpolicy2.pdf.

Hamilton College, Clinton, New York. (July 2005) Available:
www.hamilton.edu/library/departments/audiovisual_dept/copyright_intro.html.
www.hamilton.edu/library/copyright/copyrightonweb.pdf.

Hartford Public Library, Hartford, Connecticut (June 2005) Available:
http://198.134.159.33/emailguidelines.html.

Hershey Public Library, Hershey, Pennsylvania. (September 2005) Available:
www.hersheylibrary.org/illoan/illproc.html.

Horsham Township Library, Horsham, Pennsylvania. (September 2005) Available:
http://htl.mclinc.org/Policy%20manual.html#circulation.

Houston Public Librar, Houston, Texas. (August 2005) Available:
www.hpl.lib.tx.us/hpl/interactive/answers.html.
www.hpl.lib.tx.us/hpl/interactive/eref_form.html.

Humboldt State University, Arcata, California. (June 2005) Available:
http://library.humboldt.edu/.

Huntington Public Library, Huntington Station, New York. (November 2005) Available:
www.suffolk.lib.ny.us/libraries/hunt/libinfo.htm.

Huntsville Public Library, Huntsville, Ontario, Canada (July 2005) Available:
www.huntsvillelibrary.net/copyright_privacy_policy.shtml.
(September 2005) Available:
www.huntsvillelibrary.net/internet_use.shtml.

Indiana University Kokomo. Kokomo, Indiana.(August 2005) Available:
http://iuk.edu/~kolibry/about/MissionStatement.shtml.
www.lib.ipfw.edu/723.0.html.

Indiana University – Purdue University Fort Wayne, Fort Wayne, Indiana. Available:
(August 2005) www.lib.ipfw.edu/1557.0.html.

Jacksonville State University, Jacksonville, Alabama. (June 2005) Available: www.jsu.edu/depart/library/graphic/RefPolicy.pdf.

Jefferson-Madison Regional Library, Charlottesville, Virginia. (November 2005) Available: www.jmrl.org/li-internet.htm

Keene State College, Keene, New Hampshire. (August 2005) Available: www.keene.edu/library/policies/privacy.cfm.

Kennebunk Free Library, Kennebunk, Maine. (November 2005) Available: http://kennebunklibrary.org/homeschool.htm.

Kent State University, Kent, Ohio. (August 2005) Available: www.library.kent.edu/page/10965/. www.library.kent.edu/page/10724/.

Las Positas College, Livermore, California. (September 2005) Available: www.laspositascollege.edu/library/colldev.php.

Lawrence Public Library, Lawrence, Kansas. (August 2005) Available: www.lawrence.lib.ks.us/policies/circulation.html. www.lib.ks.us/policies/materials.html. www.lib.ks.us/policies/request_reconsideration.html

Lawrence University, Lawrence, Kansas. (May 2005) Available: www.lawrence.edu/library/circ/newrespol.shtml.

Lincoln Public Library, Lincoln, New Hampshire. (August 2005) Available: www.lincoln.lib.nh.us/policies.htm.

Logan Library, Logan, Utah. (June 2005) Available: www.logan.lib.ut.us/library/linfo2/policy.html#referencepolicy.

Long Beach City College, Long Beach, California. (June 2005). Available: http://lib.lbcc.edu/illpolicy2.html.

City of Louisville Public Library, Louisville, California. (May 2005) Available: www.ci.louisville.co.us/library/refpolicy.asp.

Louisiana State Universit,. Baton Rouge, Louisiana. (July 2005) Available: www.lib.lsu.edu/admin/policies/lpm7.html.

Manhattan Public Librar,. Manhattan, Kansas. (September 2005) Available: www.manhattan.lib.ks.us/policy/.

Mansfield Public Library, Mansfield, Connecticut. (June 2005) Available: www.biblio.org/mansfield/Policies/Reference.htm.

Memorial Hall Library, Andover, Massachusetts. (June 2005) Available: www.mhl.org/about/policies/reference.htm.

Merrimack College, North Andover, Massachusetts. (June 2005) Available: www.noblenet.org/merrimack/researchform.htm.

Mill Valley Public Library, Mill Valley, California. (July 2005) Available: http://millvalleylibrary.org/policypriv.html.

Milwaukee Public Library, Milwaukee, Wisconsin. (June 2005) Available: www.mpl.org/File/policies_web.htm.

Missoula Public Library, Missoula, Montana. (June 2005) Available: www.missoula.lib.mt.us/policies.html.

Mohawk Valley Community College, Utica, New York. (August 2005) Available: www.mvcc.edu/library/copyright.html. www.mvcc.edu/acdmcs/library/circulation_information.html.

Monona Public Library, Monona, Wisconsin. (November 2005) Available: www.scls.lib.wi.us/moo/parents.html.

Monroe County Library System, Rochester, New York. (June 2005) Available: www.libraryweb.org/ask.html.

Monroe Township Public Library, Monroe Township, New Jersey. (May 2005) Available: www.monroetwplibrary.org/additional%20pages/refpolicy.htm (July 2005) www.monroetwplibrary.org/additional%20pages/circulationpolicy.htm www.monroetwplibrary.org/additional%20pages/collectionsdevelopment.htm.

Morton Grove Public Library, Morton Grove, Illinois. (May 2005) Available: www.webrary.org/inside/polref.html#refmission.

Muskego Public Library, Muskego, Wisconsin. (September 2005) Available: www.ci.muskego.wi.us/library/libraryboardpolicy.htm.

Nashville Public Library, Nashville, Tennessee. (November 2005) Available: www.library.nashville.org/Library/Depts/Children.html.

New College of Florida, Sarasota, Florida. (September 2005) Available: www.ncf.edu/library/libvisitor.htm.

New Haven Free Public Library, New Haven, Connecticut. (June 2005) Available: www.cityofnewhaven.com/library/refquest.htm.

New York Public Library, New York, New York. (September 2005) Available: www.nypl.org/questions/about.html. www.nypl.org/pr/pubuse.cfm.

Newark Public Library. Newark, New Jersey. (May 28, 2005) Available: www.npl.org/Pages/AboutLibrary/reference_policy.html.

Norfolk Public Library, Norfolk, Virginia. (September 2005) Available: www.npl.lib.va.us/policies/pol_collection99_app3.html.

North Harris College, Houston, Texas. (June 2005) Available: http://nhclibrary.nhmccd.edu/library/guidelines/livechathours.html.

North Seattle Community College, Seattle, Washington. (August 2005) Available: http://northonline.sccd.ctc.edu/pwebpaz/LibraryPolicies.html.

North Smithfield Public Library, Seattle, Washington. (August 2005) Available: http://web.provlib.org/nsmlib/NSLPolicyServices.html.

Northeast Iowa Library Service Area, Waterloo, Iowa. (August 2005) Available:
www.neilsa.org/policy_manual/education.html.

Northern Michigan University, Marquette, Michigan. (August 2005). Available:
www.nmu.edu/olsonlibrary/collect_ref.htm.

Oakland University, Oakland, California. (September 2005) Available:
www.kl.oakland.edu/library_information/departments/circulation/services.htm.

Omaha Public Library, Omaha, Nebraska. (September 2005) Available:
www.omahapubliclibrary.org/aboutus/policies/confidentiality_of_records.html.

Palm Beach County Library System, Palm Beach, Florida. (June 2005) Available:
www.pbclibrary.org/legal-about.htm.

Palo Alto City Library, Palo Alto, California. (September 2005) Available:
www.city.palo-alto.ca.us/library/reference/purchase.html.

Pennsylvania State University, University Park, Pennsylvania. (July 2005) Available:
www.de2.psu.edu/faculty/saw4/vrs/about.html.

Peoria Public Library, Peoria, Illinois. (July 2005) Available:
www.peoria.lib.il.us/reference%20questions/ereference.htm.

Philadelphia University, Philadelphia, Pennsylvania. (August 2005) Available:
www.philau.edu/library/confidential.htm.

Pierce County Public Library, Tacoma, Washington. (November 2005) Available:
www.pcl.lib.wa.us.

Public Library of Enid and Garfield County, Enid, Oklahoma. (August 2005) Available:
www.enid.lib.ok.us/childpolicy.htm.

Queens Borough Public Librar,. Jamaica, New York. (August 2005) Available:
www.queens.lib.ny.us/infoline/chat.asp.

Reading Area Community College, Reading, Pennsylvania. (August 2005) Available:
www.racc.edu/Library/policy_ref.aspx.

Rice University, Houston, Texas. (July 2005) Available:
http://sparta.rice.edu/~keckker/policies/fulltext.html.

Richmond Public Library, Richmond, Virginia. (July 2005) Available:
www.richmondpubliclibrary.org/rpl/legal.htm.

Riverside Regional Public Library, Jackson, Missouri. (August 2005) Available:
www.showme.net/rrl/general/select.html.

Rockford Public Library, Rockford, Illinois. (May 2005) Available:
www.rockfordpubliclibrary.org/about/admin/ReferenceServices.asp.

Roselle Public Library, Roselle, Illinois. (August 2005) Available:
www.roselle.lib.il.us/forms/HomeworkAlert.htm.

Rutgers University, Newark, New Jersey. (June 2005) Available:
www.libraries.rutgers.edu/rul/about/pub_serv_policies/pspm_02.shtml.
www.libraries.rutgers.edu/rul/lib_servs/ill.shtml#fines.

Ryerson University, Ryerson, California. (July 2005) Available:
www.ryerson.ca/library/info/policies/refpolpublic.html#non-u.

St. Ambrose University Library, Davenport, Iowa. (November 2005) Available:
http://library.sau.edu/depts/97POLMAN.htm.

St. Joseph County Public Library, South Bend, Indiana. (June 2005) Available:
http://sjcpl.lib.in.us/aboutsjcpl/policies/publicpolicy/psmanual.html.

St. Charles Community College, (August 2005) Available:
www.stchas.edu/library/copyright.shtml.
www.stchas.edu/library/permissionletter.shtml.
www.stchas.edu/library/reserveform.shtml.

St. Paul Public Library, Saint Paul, Minnesota. (July 2005) Available:
www.stpaul.lib.mn.us/weblinks/website-criteria.html.

San Jose Public Library and San Jose State University, San Jose, California. (August 2005)
www.sjlibrary.org/legal/policies.htm.

San Jose State University Library, San Jose, California. (November 2005)
http://willoof.sjsu.edu/Institute/Miller/R.T.S./RefStandards3-22.pdf.

Santa Fe Community College, Lawrence W. Tyree Library, Gainesville, Florida. (May 2005)
Available: http://cisit.sfcc.edu/~library/ref_policy.htm.

Santa Monica Public Library, Santa Monica, California. (June 2005) Available:
www.smpl.org/depts/ref/index.htm.

Sarasota County Libraries, Sarasota, Florida. (May 2005) Available:
www.suncat.co.sarasota.fl.us/Services/Reference.aspx.
http://suncat.co.sarasota.fl.us/Services/Circulation.aspx.

Schiller Park Public Library, Schiller Park, Illinois. (July 2005) Available:
www.schillerparklibrary.org/policies/Reference%20Policy%20and%20Plan.htm.

Shiawassee District Library, Owosso, Michigan. (July 2005) Available:
www.sdl.lib.mi.us/policies.htm.

Sonoma State University, Rohnert Park, California. (August 2005) Available:
http://libweb.sonoma.edu/about/comborrower.html.

Southern Connecticut State University, New Haven, Connecticut. (May 2005) Available:
http://library.scsu.ctstateu.edu/refdep.html#Reference.

Southern Ontario Library Service, Toronto, Ontario. Trillium Public Library sample policy.
(August 2005) Available: www.olsw.ca/downloads/policy-planning/children.doc.

Spokane Public Library, Spokane, Washington. (September 2005) Available:
www.spokanelibrary.org/about/coll_dev_policy.pdf.

Stetson University, Deland, Florida. (August 2005) Available: http://stetson.edu/library/refmission.html. www.stetson.edu/library/refstandards.html.

Stillwater Public Library, Stillwater, Oklahoma. (July 2005) Available: www.stillwater.lib.ok.us/Policies/confidentiality.html. www.stillwater.lib.ok.us/Policies/research.html. (May 2005) www.stillwater.lib.ok.us/Policies/reference.html. (July 2005) www.stillwater.lib.ok.us/Policies/colldev.html#selection. www.stillwater.lib.ok.us/Policies/circulationpolicy.html.

Tazewell Public Library, Tazewell, Virginia. (July 2005) Available: www.tcplweb.org/interlibraryloanpolicy.html.

Tempe Public Library, Tempe, Arizona. (August 2005) Available: www.tempe.gov/library/admin/colldev.htm. www.tempe.gov/library/admin/illpolicy.htm.

Tulane University, New Orleans, Louisiana. (August 2005) Available: http://library.tulane.edu/about_the_library/library_policies/recalls_and_holds.php.

University of Alabama, Tuscaloosa, Alabama. (July 2005) Available: www.lib.ua.edu/policies/guideselejourn.htm.

University of Albany, State University of New York, Albany, New York. (July 2005) Available: http://library.albany.edu/ill/overview.html.

University of California Policy on the Rreproduction of Copyrighted Materials for Teaching and Research. (August 2005.) Available: www.ucop.edu/ucophome/coordrev/policy/4-29-86.html.

University of California–Bakersfield, Bakersfield, California. (September 2005) Available: www.lib.csub.edu/policies/E_ReserveRequestForm.pdf.

University of California at Berkeley. Berkeley, California. (June 2005) Available: www.lib.berkeley.edu/AboutLibrary/values.html. (July 2005) Available: www.lib.berkeley.edu/AboutLibrary/privacy/UCBLibrary_PersonalData_06252004.pdf.

University of California–Irvine, Irvine, California. (August 2005) Available: www.lib.uci.edu/services/cards/policies.html.

University of Central Florida, Orlando, Florida. (August 2005) Available: http://library.ucf.edu/Administration/Policies/Copyright/default.asp.

University College London, London, UK. (November 2005) Available: www.ucl.ac.uk/Library/preserve.shtml.

University of Illinois at Urbana-Champaign. (August 2005) Available: www.library.uiuc.edu/circ/services.htm.

University of Kentucky. (June 2005) Available: www.uky.edu/Libraries/illpolicy.html.

University of Louisville, Louisville, Kentucky. (July 2005) Available: http://library.louisville.edu/ill/policies.html.

University of Louisville, Kornhauser Health Science Library, Louisville, Kentucky. (October 2005) Available: http://library.louisville.edu/kornhauser/info/colldev.doc.

University of Louisiana Lafayette, Lafayette, Louisiana. (May 2005) Available: http://library.louisiana.edu/Resv/policy_resv.shtml. (September 2005) Available: http://library.louisiana.edu/Spec/policy_rarebooks.shtml.

University of Maine–Fort Kent, Fort Kent, Maine. (August 2005) Available: www.umfk.maine.edu/infoserv/library/about/policies/eref/.

University of Maryland, College Park, Maryland. (July 2005) Available: www.lib.umd.edu/CLMD/COLL.Policies/epubjournal.html#journal.

University of Michigan, Ann Arbor, Michigan. (July 2005) Available: www.lib.umich.edu/policies/privacy.html.

University of Minnesota, Duluth, Duluth, Minnesota. (July 2005) Available: www.d.umn.edu/lib/librarycopyright.html (August 2005) Available: http://www.d.umn.edu/lib/copyright/policy.html.

University of Montana, Missoula, Montana. (August 2005) Available: www.lib.umt.edu/about/policies/ilp.htm.

University of Nevada Reno, Reno, Nevada. (September 2005) Available: www.library.unr.edu/policy/borrow.html.

University of New England, Armidale, NSW, Australia. (August 2005) Available: www.une.edu.au/library/menu/reference_policy.htm.

University of Oregon, Eugene, Oregon. (July 2005) Available: http://libweb.uoregon.edu/colldev/cdpolicies/internet.html. http://libweb.uoregon.edu/colldev/cdpolicies/ejournals.html. http://libweb.uoregon.edu/colldev/cdpolicies/eresources.html.

University of Pittsburgh, Pittsburgh, Pennsylvania. (July 2005) Available: www.pitt.edu/HOME/PP/policies/10/10-04-01.html. www.library.pitt.edu/reference/.

University of Rhode Island, Kingston, Rhode Island. (July 2005) Available: www.uri.edu/library/reserves/ereserves.html.

University of Scranton, Scranton, Pennsylvania. (July 2005) Available: http://academic.scranton.edu/department/wml/ask_a_librarian.html.

University of South Carolina, Columbia, South Carolina. (July 2005) Available: http://ill2.tcl.sc.edu/policies_and_procedures.htm.

University of South Florida, Tampa, Florida. (August 2005) Available: http://usfweb2.usf.edu/usfgc/gc_pp/genadm/gc105. (September 2005) Available: http://lib.sar.usf.edu/tour.htm.

University of Tennessee–Knoxville, Knoxville, Tennessee. (August 2005) Available: www.lib.utk/edu/refs/askusnow/policy.html. http://www.lib.utk.edu/disibilities/.

University of Texas at Arlington, Arlington, Texas. (May 2005) Available:
http://library.uta.edu/Main/refServicePolicy.uta.
http://library.uta.edu/Main/privacyPolicy.uta.
http://library.uta.edu/Main/copyResPolicy.uta.
http://library.uta.edu/policies/interlibraryLoan/illPolicy.jsp.

University of Texas at Austin, Austin, Texas. (May 2005) Available:
www.lib.utexas.edu/admin/policies/policy_25.html.

University of Texas–El Paso, El Paso, Texas. (June 2005) Available:
http://libraryweb.utep.edu/policies/policies.cfm?page=reserves.

University of Texas Pan-American, Edinburg, Texas. (July 2005) Available:
www.lib.panam.edu/libserv/askalibglines.asp.

University of West Georgia, Carrolton, Georgia. (August 2005) Available:
www.westga.edu/~library/depts/ref/RefCollDevPolicy.shtml.

University of Wisconsin–Platteville, Platteville, Wisconsin. (July 2005) Available:
www.uwplatt.edu/library/deptnserv/reserves.html.

University of Wisconsin–River Falls, River Falls, Wisconsin. (August 2005) Available:
www.uwrf.edu/library/info/policies/refpol.pdf.

University of Wyoming. Laramie, Wyoming. (July 2005) Available:
www-lib.uwyo.edu/cdo/cp_internet.htm.

Washington County Public Library System, Abingdon, Virginia. (June 2005) Available:
www.wcpl.net/general/policies/reference.asp.

Washington Research Library Consortium, Upper Marlboro, Maryland. (July 2005) Available:
www.wrlc.org/virtualref/wrlcguidelines.html.

Washington State University, Pullman, Washington. (May 2005) Available:
www.wsulibs.wsu.edu/science/refman/inquiry1.htm.

Washington University in Saint Louis, St. Louis, Missouri. (July 2005) Available:
http://library/wustl.edu/about/privacy.html.

Weber State University, Ogdon, Utah (June 2005) Available:
http://library.weber.edu/libadmin/lppm/interlibrary_loan.cfm.

Western Kentucky University, Bowling Green, Kentucky. (May 2005) Available:
www.wku.edu/Library/forms/webrefpol.htm.

Western Massachusetts Regional Library System, South Deerfield, Massachusetts.
(August 2005) Available:
www.wmrls.org/policies/PDF/berkshireathenaeumreference.pdf.

Wheelock College, Boston, Massachusetts. (May 2005) Available:
www.wheelock.edu/library/liabout/licirculation.htm.
www.wheelock.edu/library/liservices/lilLL_article.htm.

Whistler Public Library, Whistler, British Columbia, Canada. (August 2005) Available: www.whistlerlibrary.ca/pdfs/Policy%20Manual%20PDFs/Policy%20700%20pdfs/ 702.2%20Code%20of%20Ethics.pdf.

Whitman County Library, Colfax, Washington. (June 2005) Available: www.whitco.lib.wa.us/policy/Appendix/Appendix%20I%20-%20Reference%20Policy.htm.

Wichita Falls Public Library, Wichita Falls, Texas. (June 2005)
Available: http://www.wfpl.net/assignmentalert.htm.
Available (July 2005)
www.wfpl.net/teachercollections.htm.
www.wfpl.net/policies-privacy.htm.
www.wfpl.net/purchaseform.htm.
Available: (August 2005)
http://www.wfpl.net/policies-collection.htm.

Wilmington Public Library District, Wilmington, Illinois. (May 2005) Available: www.wilmingtonlibrary.org/ref.html.

INDEX

ABOUT THE AUTHOR

Rebecca Brumley has worked as a librarian in both public and academic libraries. She worked for many years in the Humanities Division at Dallas Public Library, Dallas, Texas. She was the religion, philosophy, and paranormal selector for the Dallas Public Library. She is currently a librarian at Navarro College Library at the Waxahachie and Midlothian campuses in Texas.

Brumley has also worked as an information literacy workshop instructor for Dallas Independent School District teachers. She has served on the board of the Desoto Public Library in Texas and as a consultant to small libraries and communities interested in updating policy and procedure manuals.

Brumley received her master's in Information Science from the University of North Texas. Brumley is the author of two other books, *Public Library Managers Forms, Policies, and Procedures Handbook with CD-ROM* and *Neal-Schuman Directory of Public Library Job Descriptions with CD-ROM*. In her free time, she supports the efforts of Frisco Humane Society by fostering cats and kittens.